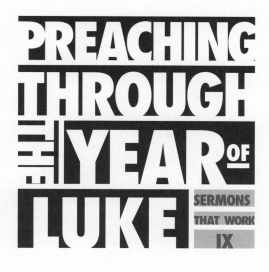

PREACHING THROUGH THE YEAR OF LUKE

SERMONS THAT WORK IX

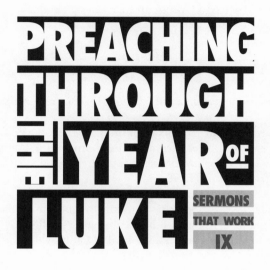

PREACHING THROUGH THE YEAR OF LUKE

SERMONS THAT WORK IX

Edited by
Roger Alling and David J. Schlafer

MOREHOUSE PUBLISHING

Harrisburg, Pennsylvania

Morehouse Publishing
P.O. Box 1321
Harrisburg, PA 17105

Morehouse Publishing is a division of The Morehouse Group.

Printed in the United States of America
00 01 02 03 04 05   10 9 8 7 6 5 4 3 2 1

Preaching through the year of Luke/edited by Roger Alling and David J. Schlafer.
    p. cm — (Sermons that work ; 9)
    Includes bibliographical references.
    ISBN 0-8192-1817-0
    1. Episcopal Church—Sermons. 2. Sermons, American.
    3. Church year sermons. 4. Episcopal preaching (Episcopal Church)
    I. Alling, Roger, 1933– II. Schlafer, David J., 1944– III. Series.
    BX5937.A1 A4   2000
    252'.6—dc21   00-009266

EDITORS

Roger Alling is president of The Episcopal Preaching Foundation, and director of the Foundation's widely acclaimed Preaching Excellence Program for students in Episcopal seminaries. He has edited each of the nine volumes in *Sermons That Work*, this sermon anthology series committed to the celebration and nurture of preaching in the Episcopal tradition. He has been a parish priest and diocesan stewardship officer. Currently he serves as priest associate at parishes in Central Pennsylvania and Southwest Florida.

David J. Schlafer is a former philosophy professor and seminary sub-dean, who has taught homiletics at four Episcopal seminaries and The College of Preachers. An adjunct instructor at Virginia Seminary and a faculty member of the D. Min. in Preaching Program at the Association of Chicago Theological Schools, he devotes primary energy to leading conferences on preaching across the United States, Canada, and England. He has written *Surviving the Sermon: A Guide to Preaching for Those Who Have to Listen, Your Way with God's Word: Discovering Your Distinctive Preaching Voice,* and *What Makes This Day Different?: Preaching Grace on Special Occasions.*

CONTENTS

3   *Preaching Through Easter*

4   *Preaching Through the Season After Pentecost*

5   *Preaching in Perspective: Biblical, Historical, Theological, and Spiritual Essays*

FOREWORD

MOST EPISCOPALIANS, clergy and laity alike, agree that preaching is an important, even vital part of the Church's ministry. Yet, the quality of sermons actually heard varies widely-from "insightful and outstanding" to "substantially below satisfactory." It is probably fair to say that excellence in preaching is an essential ingredient in the life of healthy parish communities. It is probably also the case that many of the Church's "alumni" have "graduated" to non-attendance status (except perhaps on Easter and Christmas) because of preaching that sounds uninteresting and seems to have no relevance to their lives.

The Episcopal Preaching Foundation is dedicated to raising the level of preaching with the aim of attracting back such "alumni" and winning new members, while enriching the spiritual lives of active Episcopalians.

As in the past, the Foundation solicited sermons from every parish priest in the country last fall. This book contains those that were selected and arranged by our skillful editors, the Reverend Roger Alling and the Reverend Dr. David J. Schlafer. In keeping with our recent practice, they all relate to liturgical year "C" that will commence late in calendar year 2000 with many of the gospel readings from Luke. As a result, these sermons should be relevant to both those in the pews and those in the pulpits as the next liturgical year progresses.

As in our previous eight sermon books, this one also contains the sermons and lectures delivered by the faculty and guests at our annual Preaching Excellence Program held in early June 1999 in Washington, D.C. As in the past, the program included more than fifty Episcopal seminarians who were selected by their seminary deans and preaching professors for their outstanding promise as preachers. They spend the usual intensive week on the art and practice of preaching, led by six homiletics professors and six skilled parish preachers.

Our Foundation is now in its thirteenth year of promoting excellent preaching. I hope that you personally are benefiting from our efforts, and not only by reading the sermons in this book, which are selected to recognize excellent preachers and broadcast their work to a wide audience. Most of the nearly six hundred graduates of our Preaching Excellence Conference are active parish preachers. Perhaps one of them is in your midst.

We thank those who have, over the years, made the programs of our Foundation possible, especially the Honorable John C. Whitehead, former Deputy Secretary of State who has generously underwritten our sermon books since their inception. We hope our efforts are also worthy of your tax-deductible contributions.

Dr. A. Gary Shilling
Chairman, The Episcopal Preaching Foundation, Inc.
500 Morris Avenue
Springfield, New Jersey 07081
973-467-0070
e-mail: shil@ix.netcom.com

INTRODUCTION

"If These Were Silenced, the Stones Themselves Would Shout!"

THE PROLOGUE in Luke's Gospel sounds prosaic, even pedestrian, when compared with the prologue to the Gospel of John. Instead of rich insights, carried by ringing cadences, about an Eternal Word Made Flesh, Luke's introduction sounds like the start of a sermon that would barely earn a grade of C. Rather than setting forth a spellbinding vision or plunging directly into the action, Luke commences by "telling us what he's going to tell us." More accurately, Luke makes us listen in from the sidelines while he summarizes for someone named Theophilus what he is going to hear—something that Theophilus himself has heard already!

"Many writers have undertaken to draw up an account of the events that have happened among us, following the traditions handed down to us by the original eyewitnesses and servants of the Gospel" (NEB). This does *not* much sound like the start of something interesting—or a preaching strategy worth emulating! All Luke intends to do, apparently, is to tell the Jesus story one more time, adding his voice to those who have said it before.

But more is going on in Luke's approach than it might sound like, on first hearing.

Luke is often described as the Gospel writer especially concerned with the marginalized. Women and persons of diverse ethnic backgrounds are given considerable space in the narrative he weaves. But in Luke's Gospel, these people are not just spoken *for*, or spoken *to*, by Jesus. They are *given distinctive voices, and a significant share, in the proclamation of the Gospel*.

With its low-key beginning, Luke's Gospel sets in motion a drama every bit as engaging as the Fourth Gospel's. Luke's telling, as he signals subtly in his short prologue, is going to be *a story of others' tellings*. These different voices will not conflict with the sounding forth of the grace that Jesus sings. Rather, they will contribute variation, counterpoint, resonance, and harmony. In the end, all "lovers of God" (*Theophilus*) will thereby be offered an "authentic knowledge about the matters of which [we] have been informed" (NEB). And, almost before we know it, we will find ourselves joining in, adding the experiences and characteristics of our own distinctive voices.

"In this and many other ways, he made his appeal to the people, and announced the Good News," Luke notes concerning John the Baptist. Luke adopts an analogous strategy. He often turns his characters loose to do their own talking. Elizabeth, Mary, Zechariah, and Simeon all have eloquent "says" in the first two chapters. (Think of *Magnificat, Benedictus,* and *Nunc Dimittis.*)

Later on, such unlikely spokespersons as Zacchaeus, a Roman centurion, and a crucified thief get significant lines as well. In three uniquely Lukan parables, characters make significant statements. A penitent tax collector utters a desperate prayer, a feisty widow gives a judge no peace. "Take care of him—I'll pay," says the Samaritan to an innkeeper, on behalf of a poor fellow mugged on a dangerous road.

Sometimes witnessing voices are not heard through dialogue, but in the contexts of their social interactions. Shepherds "spread the word" of what they have heard and seen. Ancient Anna tells her temple-visit story to all who will listen. A Samaritan returns to praise God when he discovers he has been healed of leprosy. A woman takes the risk of sharing her healing experience aloud; and Jesus proclaims that her faith has been integral to her healing.

Often the "voice" of the witness comes not in words, but in "body language." By the mite she puts in the temple treasury, a widow says a lot. More dramatic are the moves of another woman who breaks an alabaster jar to anoint Jesus and covers his feet with tears and kisses. Similar faith is manifested by pallet-bearers, depositing a crippled friend before Jesus through a hole they have cut in the roof. Resources from women make the ministry of Jesus possible. Levi announces his new vocation with a grand dinner party for a host of socially undesirables. John the Baptist is heard from before his birth with an *in utero* leap.

Some obvious voices (Jesus' mother and his brothers) are not automatically granted definitive speaking parts. Conversely, when a zealous disciple tries to squelch voices that do not come from the chosen few, Jesus stops him cold: "Whoever is not against you is for you."

In Luke's Gospel, Jesus commissions disciples twice, sending out not just "The Twelve," but seventy (or seventy-two). In one case there is a "field commissioning." A man released from demon possession asks leave to come along with Jesus. His request is denied, but he is charged: "Go back and tell what God has done for you." The man does exactly that. The "noncommissioned" turn up to speak as well. "News gets around" after Jesus raises the son of a widow. The word that goes out after several healings is not a report but a doxology. "Praise to God" is also offered by a soldier who has watched how Jesus dies. (As an evangelism strategy, *overheard praise* may be more effective than theological explanation or moral exhortation.)

Perhaps most interesting is the way in which Luke handles the accounts of the Resurrection. Mark's visitors to the empty tomb say nothing; they are terrified. In Matthew and John, the women get the word and pass it on. In Luke, however, the women's witness bearing is recounted in great detail. They receive the Good News, recognize that it resonates with what Jesus has told them previously, and share it—even though the men dismiss their words as nonsense. At last their voices are ringingly confirmed through the word of two other disciples who have been radically rerouted from a journey to Emmaus.

The Gospel's end is its beginning. Luke's prologue is a statement that he is only following the risen Christ's command, preaching "repentance and forgiveness of sins to all nations." And all of this is but a prelude to The Acts of the Apostles.

To preach through the year of Luke, therefore, is to be swept into awareness of what religious leaders discovered when they tried to silence "Hosanna!"

cries as Jesus rode into Jerusalem: *"If these were silenced, the stones themselves would cry out!"*

The sermons in this volume are an honoring, and an extension, of how Luke hears preaching: *many different voices bearing distinctive but coherent witness.* That many preachers are represented here is obvious from a glance at the table of contents. A second look will show that their sermon texts and topics are diverse, as well. Attention to the sermons themselves will reveal all sorts of other voices who conjoin to sing the story of the Gospel: bank tellers, physicists, a landscape architect, a tortured prisoner of war, a potbellied, red-necked, right-wing Samaritan, a *real nag*, Anthony Hopkins, Gandhi, and Edgar Allen Poe!

The hope—and belief—animating this anthology is that those who listen to this chorus of Gospel-proclaiming voices—be they "professional" preachers or those whose profession of faith takes place primarily in the liturgy of daily life—will find their own voices confirmed, clarified, strengthened, and imaginatively challenged.

A feature included for the first time this year is the giving of three hearings to each of two familiar biblical texts: the much-loved story beginning, "a certain man had two sons . . . ;" and the challenge issued every Second Sunday of Easter by "Doubting Thomas." The interplay of three preaching voices on each of these two texts will give, we think, fresh energy to the ears and lips of many, on both sides of the pulpit, who "have heard it all before."

This is the second year that sermons selected for this volume follow the rhythm of the liturgical year. A similar volume for "Year A," *Preaching Through the Year of Matthew*, will follow. An explanation for how these sermons are gathered and how they are intended appears in the "Year B" volume (*Preaching Through the Year of Mark*).

Those who have followed this series through its nine-year history will anticipate the final section of sermons, distinguished by their common presentation in the Episcopal Preaching Foundation's annual Preaching Excellence Conference for seminary students. The collection this year coincides particularly well with the centering theme described for this Year of Luke.

Worthy of special note is the section of reflective essays on the preaching art, two of which were first presented at a meeting of Episcopal homileticians, held prior to the Preaching Excellence Conference, and two of which were presented within that conference. Robert Kysar's essay, based on a lifetime of Johannine scholarship, sets an excellent context for professional consideration of the sermons in this volume that are shaped by the Fourth Gospel. Since Johannine texts make strategic entry throughout the three year lectionary cycle, Kysar's contribution complements the somewhat synoptic emphasis of a volume (and a series) focussed on preaching throughout a liturgical year. Essays by O. C. Edwards and Thomas Troeger explore theological implications for preaching in the present day. Edwards's article, based on a career of homiletical scholarship, addresses what we can learn from the history of preaching as a whole. In an age when there is strong pressure in the Christian community to enforce uniformity of content and to restrict the range of credible witnesses to the Gospel, Thomas Troeger's article offers a new appreciation for the generating genius of Anglican theology, Richard Hooker. A. Katherine Grieb places compellingly before us an uncompromising mirror, considering the life of the preacher as an essential and unavoidable "text" in any sermon.

Taken together, these four essays also speak distinctively of how *our* voices may be tuned—individually and in concert—to sing their Maker's praise in such a way that the sound of celebration may reach unto the ends of the earth.

SECOND SUNDAY OF ADVENT

Revelation at the Teller Windows

Luke 3:1–6
George M. Chapman

I WALKED through the front door of the bank one afternoon last week and breathed a sigh of relief. The line had only four people in front of me, and there were four tellers working. My relief soon faded, however, when I saw who was standing not only in the line but also up at the teller windows. At one window stood a woman who was clearly transacting a series of complex deposits and accountings, even though this was not a commercial bank. At the second window was an elderly person counting out piles of coins and small bills, asking a variety of questions, and not fully understanding the teller's responses on the first try. Facing the third teller was a relative newcomer to this country whose level of familiarity with both language and banking system did not make for speedy transactions. The fourth spot was occupied by a person with disabilities both of sight and intellect. Clearly I had arrived on a day when various types of assistance checks had appeared in people's mailboxes. Some of these people were in front of me dealing with their meager resources. I just knew that it was going to be a very long wait—and it was.

I stood there for nigh unto half an hour, watching the various folk conduct their various transactions (like depositing money in a child's passbook account without the passbook, or buying several money orders to pay rent and other expenses). I became increasingly impressed by the behavior of two groups of people.

The first group was the tellers themselves. None of them ever betrayed the slightest irritation as they explained the simplest of steps to their customers— often over and over. One teller, assisting the blind man, put himself close to sainthood. Not only did he deposit the man's check (dealing in the approved manner with signatures for those who cannot see), he also divided up various amounts of cash into a series of envelopes so that the man could pay for his rent, his food, and his personal needs, including Christmas shopping. The customer made his requests to the teller in a very loud voice, several times. The teller carefully explained each step, gently and pleasantly repeating himself as often as necessary. It took twenty minutes to complete a transaction that usually would have required less than five.

The second impressive group was my fellow customers. Only once did anyone comment on the interminable wait. The man who did so wryly observed to the person standing next to him: "I am being held hostage in a bank line." But the man smiled as he said it, and was careful not to be overheard either by the tellers or the people they were serving. I don't know if others shared my growing sense of appreciation for what was transpiring in front of us, but there was certainly an air of patience and acceptance among those who were waiting so long. I actually found myself wondering if I was witnessing a miracle. Later I conjectured that perhaps the seasonal glow of goodwill had come into play.

The more I thought upon the experience, the more I realized that this was not just a feel-good episode to use in a sermon. What could have been frustrating to those in line, unpleasant for the tellers, humiliating to customers disabled in one way or another, and what, in short, could have turned ugly might, indeed, have been a miracle—an experience wherein one can see the presence of God at work among us. It certainly was a revelation.

What was revealed, at least for me, was a new meaning of the words written thousands of years ago in the book of Isaiah the prophet and repeated (still thousands of years ago) by John the Baptist: "Prepare the way of the Lord, make his paths straight. Every valley shall be filled, and every mountain and hill shall be brought low, and the crooked shall be made straight, and the rough ways shall be made smooth; and all flesh shall see the salvation of God." What was also revealed for me was the answer to a question I had not really considered before.

Those who are blind, those of limited intellect or education, those with minimal understanding of the language of the country they are in, those who do not understand how the system works have rough going in life. People with multiple deficiencies or disabilities face many barriers so great that they can seem to be veritable mountains. To be occasionally demeaned, often ridiculed, constantly confused, and never quite able to take care of oneself can leave a person feeling low—right down in the valley of despair. None of this is surprising and all of it was very clear that afternoon in the bank.

The tellers, however, through their patience, their caring, and their ministry of service (for such it truly was), smoothed the way for those who were in danger of stumbling. They removed the mountainous barriers facing the most challenged of their clients. They lifted up those in danger of feeling incompetent and depressed. They gave real meaning and sense to the words of Isaiah, and turned what has always seemed to most of us a metaphorical passage about a massive engineering effort into a near-at-hand possibility for personal involvement in the process of salvation.

This shift in focus also answered another question (the one I hadn't asked): Who is going to do all of this hill and valley stuff? To the extent that I had thought about it at all, I suppose I had assumed that the Lord was going to do his own prep work: bring low the hills, straighten out the curves, and so forth. But that does not seem to be what either Isaiah or John had in mind. "Prepare the way of the Lord" is an exhortation to act, not an invitation to go watch a construction project. Those who heed the call to prepare are the ones who fill the valleys, lower the mountains, and smooth out the path of life for others as they live every day.

It was a long wait in the bank that afternoon, but God knows it was a revelation. Now I understand what Isaiah meant about hills and depressions and rough going; now I understand what John's cry in the wilderness was all about; now I understand how I can heed John's call to prepare, truly and meaningfully, the way of the Lord.

George M. Chapman is rector of St. Paul's Church,
Brookline, Massachusetts.

THIRD SUNDAY OF ADVENT

The Trouble with Turning Down the Volume
Luke 3:7–18
Beth Maynard

"John! Chill! This is supposed to be the Good News you're proclaiming? 'Brood of vipers'? Some tidings of comfort and joy that is!"

You know, this guy is unbelievable. All signs point to his being a madman. I mean, think about it. . . . He's got an ax! Not only that, but he's going to use it! Where? At "the root of the trees." This isn't trimming we are doing here; we are razing the forest!

"Don't plan on just lopping off a few dead branches. No, the whole tree has got to go!" According to John, God wants to plant an entirely different species on your plot of land.

"You can't hang a wreath on the door to spruce things up. Down with the house, bring in the wrecking ball!" According to John, God plans on rebuilding from the ground up.

If this sounds extreme to you, join the club. If you're thinking John just isn't in the holiday spirit, you are right. And he's not going to be getting in the holiday spirit any time soon. There will not come a point when John the Baptist settles down, gives us a polite smile, and passes the eggnog. He belongs to Advent, and he will not be rushing Christmas.

Isn't the tension in keeping Advent enormous? The pressure is on: give in and get the tree up! Play the Christmas music already! And of course, people just don't understand you when you try to explain why you aren't. Keeping Advent seems to get more and more difficult every year.

There was an article about this tension in the local paper a few weeks ago. A woman said she wasn't even able to find purple candles for her Advent Wreath, because the red and green candles had already taken over the store. I've seen, a hundred times, the reaction she described—the blank face of the clerk: *"Advent? What?"*

The rest of the world is decking the halls, and we're looking for purple candles. The rest of the world is at the mall, and we're being harangued by a first-century revivalist with a deadly weapon. It's "Tidings of Comfort and Joy," versus "Flee from the Wrath to Come."

John the Baptist turns up like this every year, you know—both the second and the third Sundays of Advent. Just when society is bubbling over with chestnuts and cheer, rumors of angels, heartwarming tales on the TV, and a different holiday choral concert every night. Just when they've started wishing you Merry Christmas at the Jiffy-Lube, you walk into church two weeks in a row and encounter the Brood of Vipers Guy.

But whatever the rest of the country is doing, John keeps on keeping Advent, telling us exactly what we don't want to hear, and doing it with a total, fixated conviction that means one of two things: either he's nuts, or he's got us pegged.

There's one sure sign that John the Baptist has gotten under someone's skin. We see it three times in today's Gospel. The crowds: "What, then, should we do?" The tax collectors: "Teacher, what should we do?" The soldiers: "And we, what should we do?" One after the other, people hear themselves blurting out that question. If this guy is for real, then something's got to change here. "What now, John? What happens next?"

And if you're like me, John the Baptist catches you by surprise every year. You get that terrified feeling in the pit of your stomach that maybe this time around you'll actually have to take him seriously and change your life. You feel welling up inside you that question people always ask when John the Baptist has gotten to them: "And *me* . . . what should *I* do?" That's one of the sure signs that God's tidings have gotten through to you unmuffled—you respond from the gut. It gets you where you live.

But then the L. L. Bean catalog comes, and flipping through it, just for laughs, you get caught up in picking out a polo shirt. Or you start to scan the rightly named *Self* magazine. "Hey, this month's issue is called *Your Spiritual Life*! How bad can it be? You really do have to get those hotel reservations made or finish the Christmas card list. And afterwards it's too late in the evening to do any serious thinking anyway. . .

And the ax is blunted, the wilderness voice muffled. But not without a price.

If we muffle God when he speaks to us in one way, his voice invariably gets muffled elsewhere in our lives as well. Knowing God isn't a pick-and-choose affair. Turn down the volume on one part of the Gospel, and the whole thing gets quieter, less compelling. If we never let ourselves be compelled by prophetic passion, the rest of the passionate Gospel of love will get turned down too.

With the volume down, when Zephaniah cries from the lectern, *"Sing out, rejoice and exult with all your hearts,"* or Isaiah shouts in the canticle, *"Cry aloud, O Zion, ring out your joy, for the great one in your midst is the Holy One of Israel,"* the words will sound remote, too muffled to make a difference. The reactions of those who hear it loud and clear will seem a tad extreme. We will do something reserved and decorous, instead of exulting with all our hearts or crying aloud in praise before the Lord.

If we lower the volume on God's Advent voice, it stays down when Christmas comes. And we miss the fact that eventually, sure enough, the tidings John proclaims do turn into the tidings of comfort and joy.

They have to. They are the harbingers of Christ, the Lord of Life become flesh for us. The God who created us comes to re-create us, to make bags of flesh and bone into partakers of the divine nature. The only real tidings of comfort and joy are the tidings of Jesus, the whole Jesus, the crucial and complex Savior to whom John points the way.

There aren't two Christs, one the sweet infant and the other the thresher and winnower of chaff. The cherubic creche child is the same as the baptizer with spirit and fire. We can't listen to the one we like and turn down the volume on the other. No, the Christ for whom we wait this season is one. His message is one. His love is one. And they're like John the Baptist in at least this way: with the volume up, they'll get you where you live.

Beth Maynard is priest-in-charge of The Church of the Good Shepherd, Fairhaven, and priest assistant at St. Gabriel's Church, Marion, Massachusetts.

LEARNING TO BE LITTLE

Fourth Sunday of Advent

Micah 5:2–4; Luke 1:26–38
Tobias Stanislas Haller, B.S.G.

THERE'S SOMETHING in us all that loves to see the underdog finally get ahead, to see the little guy bring down the big bully, and to share the joy of the little shopkeeper who wins the lottery or of the hard-working laundress who inherits a fortune. This is the stuff of folk tales: of Cinderella raised from the dust and ashes of the hearth to become a princess; of the Ugly Duckling turning out to be a swan; of the Little Engine That Could finally making it over that hill; or in keeping with the season, of Rudolph the Red-Nosed Reindeer, shunned at first for his odd and shiny nose, later turning out to be just the one Santa needed to accomplish his Christmas Eve mission.

Yes, this is the stuff of fantasy, but it is also the stuff of salvation. For once long ago (almost three thousand years ago) in a little suburb of Jerusalem— a little town belonging to the smallest clan in Judah, a little town called Bethlehem—an unlikely young man came to the forefront of everyone's attention: David, son of Jesse—a shepherd-boy who would knock down the towering Philistine giant Goliath with his slingshot and later go on to become the king of all Israel.

The prophet Micah, remembering this savior from his people's past—much the way we might remember Abraham Lincoln or George Washington—spoke to his people in their present turmoil to comfort them with the promise of another king who would rise from this little town of Bethlehem. From this little backwater, from little Bethlehem, one would come forth who would be great to the ends of the earth, who would "feed his flock in the strength of the LORD, in the majesty of the name of the LORD his God."

Such stories, such promises, give hope. It *is* wonderful when the tables are turned and the haughty, mighty ones are toppled, especially by poor, simple souls lifted up from where they've been downtrodden for so long. It is so wonderful that it's worth singing about. That's what Micah did, and that's what Mary of Nazareth did, too.

Little Mary, the carpenter's wife, housewife, and working-class mother-to-be, left her home in upstate Galilee to spend some time visiting her cousin Elizabeth, also soon to become a mother.

And as soon as Elizabeth heard Mary's greeting, she felt the child leap in her womb, the yet-unborn John the Baptist already sensing and wordlessly announcing the arrival of his Lord hidden in his own blessed mother's womb. And Elizabeth, too, was urged to prophetic utterance. She addressed Mary as "blessed," as "mother of the Lord," a Lord only just conceived, yet already announced by his unborn cousin.

And that's when Mary sang. The song she sang has been repeated since in every language on earth. It is sung to many melodies, throughout the world sung every day as part of the evening worship of the church. It is a reminder before bedtime that our God is a mighty One who does great things, lifts up the lowly, afflicts the comfortable and comforts the afflicted, fills the hungry with good things, but sends the rich away empty; and who, above all, is faithful to his promises.

Mary's song is the song of all the little people, of all the underdogs, of all the people who never got a fair shake finally winning their reward. In Mary's song is summed up all the history of God's chosen people, loved by their faithful God even when they were unfaithful; chosen, not because they were numerous or powerful, but just because they were little and insignificant.

There's an advantage, you see, to being little! Little people can fit into places big people can't. They notice things that the big people are too busy to see, or too caught up in their own importance to notice. As Saint Therese of Lisieux, the "Little Flower," once said, "We are too little to be able to rise above difficulties; so then let us quite simply pass beneath them!"

The humble and meek have this advantage over the rich and powerful: they pay attention, they listen, they keep their eyes open—they have to! For they know their lives depend on it. The rich, the powerful, who imagine themselves to be self-sufficient, fail to remember how dependent they are on others and on God. And so they lose their grip on what they have, and when the tables are turned they slide from their thrones. It was precisely when Israel got rich, comfortable, and big that the people lost sight of God, and slid into exile or captivity. Only when reduced to a point where they could acknowledge their failings would they turn to God, their deliverer, in meekness and repentance. The meek, unlike the proud, are receptive, open to God's arrival. As Phillips Brooks's hymn says, "where meek souls will receive him, still the dear Christ enters in."

What is it that Christ enters into? We find the answer in the collect for today: "Purify our conscience, Almighty God, by your daily visitation, that your Son Jesus Christ, at his coming, may find in us a mansion prepared for himself." Or, as Brooks put it in the same hymn: "O Holy Child of Bethlehem descend to us we pray; cast out our sin and enter in, be born in us today." When we become little, when we become meek, God dwells among us, with us, and in us—truly Emmanuel, God-with-us.

God chose Mary to bear his Son as he chose Israel to be his people. It wasn't because Mary was great, but because Mary was simple, humble, meek, and lowly that God chose her. It was God who *made* her great. It was God who lifted up the lowly handmaiden and made her the mother of his Son. That same meekness, that same humility is available to us. We can be like Mary. We can open our hearts to God and to each other, to receive the Christ who is always willing to enter into a humble heart.

If God, even God, could become so little, an infant lying in a manger, cannot we, too, shrink ourselves? Pare down our egos and our angers? Engage in a fast of righteousness, and shed the pounds of pride and past resentment, freeing ourselves to run like happy, naked children through the sprinklers of God's abundant grace?

It is a challenge. It's hard to become little when you've gotten used to living large. Israel had to learn that lesson, over and over again. And we stumble and fall, too. We're so often told to act like grown-ups; that big is better; that maturity is judged by power instead of wisdom. But in God's world, it is better, far better, to be like a child, like one of the blessed little ones who behold God's face in everything they see.

So, brothers and sisters, let's be little together. Let us sing Mary's song now, and as we move toward Christmas, and thereafter. When we feel ourselves getting big, we can remember little Mary's song. We can join in the chorus of praise, the chorus of souls who magnify the Lord, echoing down the corridors of time and space. We can watch with charity, and with faith hold open the door of grace. Our hands can help lift up the lowly, as we are lifted up ourselves. Our hands can feed the hungry, as we are fed at the hands of God. We can open one-room hearts that, by the grace of God, will become mansions prepared for his Son at his coming. "O come to us, abide with us, our Lord, Emmanuel!"

Tobias Stanislas Haller, B.S.G., is pastor of St. Paul's Church, Yonkers, New York.

FIRST SUNDAY AFTER CHRISTMAS

What *Is* This Light?
John 1:1–14
Nancy L. J. Cox

The light shines in the darkness, and the darkness did not overcome it.

Recently, I called a friend of mine who is a physicist and also a Christian. "What does it mean to you, as a physicist," I asked him, "that Jesus Christ is the light of the world?" "Well," he replied, "I usually take those words as poetry."

I suppose his answer was to be expected. The enlightenment world view has taught us that the two worlds of religion and science do not meet, though they may uneasily coexist. But this world view is now beginning to crumble, as scientists and others have come face to face with our inability to describe all of what goes on about us in exclusively concrete and linear terms.

And so, my friend, because he was my friend, was not going to escape so easily. "What does it mean," I insisted, "to you, a physicist and Christian, that Jesus Christ is the light of the world?" "Could you give me a few days?" he pleaded. "Tonight is the last of Monday night football for a year."

After Christmas, I called again. This time he was ready for me. "I've been thinking," he said. "There is wisdom and truth in this poetry. Without light, there is no life. The speed of light is a great constant of physics; but light itself is manifested in many forms, most of which we do not see. We tend to focus on the visible, the light that illuminates the surface, forgetting that there is more, forgetting that light penetrates beneath the surface. Light is not just the happy rainbow; it is a transmitter and carrier of information. It is energy, and its awesome power can tear apart atoms, the very building blocks of creation. And even in the most remote regions of empty space, there is light."

The light shines in the darkness, and the darkness did not overcome it.

Light is a fundamental image for Christians, particularly at this time of year. I think it does us some good to "push" the image around. To fill it out. To release it from too-easy domestication. To reclaim it from Hallmark.

I used to teach chemistry. Across the side of the classroom, just above the periodic table, ran a graphic display of the electromagnetic spectrum. Light in all its forms. The chart was over ten feet long; yet, visible light, the light we can see, covered less than six inches of the spectrum. The light we can see is only a tiny part of the light there is.

Jesus is the light that gives life. Constant, but present in many forms, most of which we do not see. Penetrating beyond the surface to reveal our deepest selves. Shining into the darkness and filling the universe.

The light shines in the darkness, and the darkness did not overcome it.

For communities north of the Arctic Circle, winter is the dark time. Even midday offers only a dim twilight, since the sun does not rise beyond the horizon. Insomnia and depression run rampant during this time of darkness. But not everyone has that experience. Some welcome this time as a time to see lights they normally do not see: the moon, planets, stars, the aurora borealis or northern lights. Where some see only darkness, others see light.

Darkness *is* a reality of human life, however. This darkness is not merely a lack of knowledge, but rebellion, conflict, hostility, rejection. The world does not recognize—indeed, it outright rejects—the light by which it was created; and yet. . .

The light shines in the darkness, and the darkness does not overcome it.

Jesus is the child of Christmas, the Lord of creation, the light who shines in the darkness. Jesus accepted not only the birthing into life, but the dying that comes along with it. The angels at Christmas call us to Bethlehem to find a baby wrapped in swaddling clothes and lying in a manger. We come and kneel, we give glory and thanks to God.

"What child is this?" asks the English carol. What child is this? On this first Sunday after Christmas, we gather to celebrate the Incarnation and to begin making sense of it for ourselves. The question I asked of my friend is submitted to all of us: What does it mean that Jesus Christ is the light of the world? This is the question we must answer for ourselves.

The writer of John's Gospel tells us that this child is God. In this great hymn (known as the Prologue), in some of the most sublime poetry in Scripture, comes the foundation for our theology of the Incarnation. Believing that the world is rational, early Greek philosophers used the term *Logos*, or Word, to denote the principle of reason by which the universe is sustained. The writer of John's Gospel picks up that term, and identifies the *Logos* as Jesus Christ. Here is stated explicitly what is alluded to in the rest of the Gospels, that Jesus is the emissary of God, who is Light and who calls people out of darkness into his marvelous light; that Jesus is, himself, the Incarnate Word of God.

Week by week, with Christians of many generations, we confess Jesus is "God from God, Light from Light, very God of very God, through whom all things were made." God has not remained a dark mystery. God is made known in Jesus, the True Light that enlightens everyone. What Moses requested and was denied—a vision of the face of God—has been made visible in Jesus Christ.

We have the witness of Scripture and tradition; but that will be nothing more than words on paper without our own answer to the fundamental question: What does it mean that Jesus is the light of the world?

Without our own answer, Jesus remains for us no more than a figure in history, a piece of information, a footnote to Religion 101. We have to decide for ourselves whether we will live in darkness, or whether Jesus will be the light, the one who makes all the difference, the one who provides the ground of deepest meaning in our lives.

As followers of the light of the world, we, too, are called to let the light shine forth into the darkness through us. We let that light shine into the darkness each time we forgive a grievance, ask forgiveness, seek reconciliation. We transmit the light each time we offer a gift of gentle grace, an unexpected phone call, a word of reassurance, comfort, or thanks. We also show forth the light when we use the power we have been given to penetrate beyond the superficial, to cut through bonds of injustice, or maybe just layers of red tape.

The light shines in the darkness, and the darkness does not overcome it.

On Christmas Eve, all was quiet and still as I was driving to church. On my way, I passed many churches at worship. And I realized something I had not thought about before: that stained glass windows work both ways. The light we usually see only from the inside, also shines out. Light does not avoid the darkness, but shines into it—in many colors, through many faces, across the world, and for all time.

The light shines in the darkness, and the darkness does not overcome it.

Nancy L. J. Cox is associate rector of Trinity Church,
Southport Connecticut.

SECOND SUNDAY AFTER THE EPIPHANY

Evermore

Isaiah 62:1–5; John 2:1–11
Richard I. H. Belser

*Once, upon a midnight dreary, while I pondered weak and weary
over many a quaint and curious volume of forgotten lore . . .*

Even if it's been a while since English literature class, many of us recognize, and some can quote the opening lines of Edgar Allan Poe's poem, "The Raven." With somber cadences, ominous images of a dark December night, dying embers, rustling curtains, mysterious tappings, and a haunting black bird, the poet conjures a mood of oppressive sadness. He is grieving for his lost love, the sainted maiden named Lenore. She has died and left his life in perpetual darkness. The raven bids entrance to Poe's chamber by gently tapping. With the window opened, it brazenly enters and takes a perch just above the door. In a croaking voice, it reveals its name: "Nevermore!" That word becomes a curse for Poe, an omen that grief will never heal, sadness will always burden, and joy will never again be his—"Nevermore!"

I think many of us have a hint of what the poet feels. Some of us know with painful certainty. Poe's life-crushing loss is the death of one he deeply loved. Some of us have been there. In place of Lenore, softly say the name of your lost loved one, and listen for the gentle tapping. Incurable grief is waiting to come in. But other things can be a window for the raven. Something lost by random accident, by someone else's cruelty, by our own choice—something we can't take back again.

Perhaps we made immature choices about sexual intimacy at an age when we thought we knew everything. Ever since, there's been a sense of loss. We wonder how things might have turned out if we had done them differently. But a voice says, "Nevermore!" Once we fell in love with somebody who seemed to satisfy our longings. We ignored disturbing hints that were obvious to those who cared about us. We married, and discovered the truth about our spouse, and about ourselves. Now we remember others we dated; we imagine the flawless suitor who might have turned up a week after our engagement. We wonder if we've thrown away all hope for happiness. A mocking voice croaks, "Nevermore!" We grow too tired to struggle anymore, and end up divorced. After the relief of finished conflict, we face the reality of being alone. We realize that even if we marry again, we'll never, ever, celebrate a fiftieth anniversary. There's a rustle of black wings and an echoed reminder, "Nevermore!"

Unchangeable loss can enter our lives in so many ways! Failed relationships, overheated ambitions and ruined careers, careless habits that do irreversible damage to our bodies. We might have loved that person better. Nevermore! We might have chosen differently and retired in comfort. Nevermore! We might have quit smoking and retained the stamina to travel with friends. Nevermore!

Now and then I talk with people who tell me, "I feel as though I'm living somebody else's life! These things I'm dealing with—they're not supposed to be part of my experience. It's like I got sidetracked somewhere. I can see over to where I ought to be, but I can't get there—'Nevermore!'" We suffer loss; we hurt for a while. If we're wise, we let others comfort us. We try to learn from the experience and get on with our lives. "No use worrying over what might have been. Just make the best of it!"

But picking up the pieces and looking for new directions, we often hear that gentle tapping. "Nevermore!" comes back at predictable times: when we're tired, fearful of a new venture, or sorry for ourselves. But sometimes it loudly taps when life is great—reminding us that, good as things are, they might have been better, and such chances will not be ours. "Nevermore!" If we ignore the tapping, if we block the memories of failure and feelings of loss, we can avoid that gloomy presence taking a permanent perch in our consciousness. But keeping that window closed is hard work!

We all cope differently with the nagging reminders. Some of us give less than our full energies to the choices that remain. A young man who couldn't get motivated in graduate school quits to take what looks like a good job. But though he seldom thinks about the opportunities he gave up, the young man is miserable in his work. It's not really what he wanted. He doesn't try very hard. Every Monday he scans the employment section in the newspaper. When "Nevermore" haunts us, it's hard to enjoy here and now.

Some of us welcome distractions to deal with inner ambivalence. Poe found himself up at midnight reading quaint and curious volumes of forgotten lore. These days, the bizarre contents of late-night TV can distract us from the lingering wound. Do you know the feeling? Disappointed over today, unexcited about tomorrow, mindlessly absorbed in the most trivial trash, just to avoid nagging reminders of how things might have been? TV is one kind of anesthesia. So are alcohol and easily gotten medication. When we don't like where we've been and aren't happy about where we're going, we can escape into the esoteric or the illegal.

Now and then we try to camouflage distress by charging full speed ahead. Do you know people who stay so incredibly busy that you marvel at their motivation and stamina? Maybe they really like what they do, but maybe it's their only way to still a nagging voice—by endless efforts at everything. Work is their tranquilizer. Their own noise drowns out the haunting voice of the raven: "Nevermore!"

Beloved, all of us live with the painful reality of things that will never be. But there is a better way to silence that ominous tapping at our chamber door! And if we've already let in the doomsayer, there's a better way to make him fly!

Long ago Jesus went with his mother and his friends to a wedding in the Galilean town of Cana. They soon discovered a disaster in progress.

Apparently there was a larger crowd than the bridegroom had anticipated, and well before the celebration was to end the host ran out of wine. It was the kind of thing we've all been through—we've made our best plans and taken all reasonable precautions to make sure everything will turn out as we hoped, and something goes wrong. We study all night for an exam on chapters six through twelve, and discover when the test is handed out that it covers chapters twelve through eighteen! We buy the most expensive corsage for our prom date. We go to pin it on, and she shrieks that she's allergic to roses! We pick a contractor to redo the kitchen. We check his references before signing the contract. The work begins, the plumbing is unhooked—and he's indicted for tax evasion!

We get only one chance to do things right the first time. That poor groom in Cana was on the verge of starting married life with an embarrassing blunder that could easily dull the brightness in his sweetheart's eyes, and make his furious father-in-law say, "I told you so!" It was the kind of thing that never goes away, no matter how well things turn out afterward. "Well, it was only a party, after all," we might shrug. But it wasn't our party! A little empathy reveals a raven: "Nevermore!"

Mary knew what was at stake, and she said something to Jesus. His response suggests he hadn't planned to begin his public ministry just yet, but his actions make it clear that he wasn't about to let this marriage be haunted forever by an embarrassing start.

Now, here we need to make an important observation. Jesus Christ can help us deal more effectively with our sense of lingering loss, but only if he's invited into our lives! Imagine that bridegroom saying, "Jesus, the carpenter over in Nazareth? Yeah, I know him, but not that well. Don't send him an invitation!"

Some of us know Jesus by reputation. We know the familiar stories about him. But we've never invited him into our lives. I mean deliberately, personally. It's not enough to grow up knowing about him, being a church member all our lives. For Jesus to make a difference, we need to invite him, "Come, Lord Jesus, be a permanent part of my everyday life!"

This groom invited Jesus, and when the party was in jeopardy, the solution was there! Mary told the servants, "Do whatever he tells you!" The story doesn't tell us if the servants went to the bridegroom to see if it was okay to take orders from a guest. What happens depends only on the fact that somebody in the situation is willing to do what Jesus says.

And this is the key to dealing with our old wounds and our failures. Instead of shrugging and sighing, "Well, it's done! Too late! Might as well just resign myself," we can pray, "Lord, what do you want me to do?" Instead of redoubling our efforts to fix what our blunder has ruined or compensate for our loss, we can say, "Lord, I'm way out ahead of you, and I'm in trouble. I'm sorry! How should I handle it from here on?"

What the Lord brings to our mind in situations of pending disaster almost always comes as a surprise! Jesus didn't tell the servants to get money from the host and run to buy more wine. Instead he told them to fill six large jars with water. Can you imagine their faces? "Water? This is a wedding, not a baptism! What good is 120 gallons of water?" That's how we're likely to look at what the Lord brings before us when we turn to him in time of need. "Jesus, give me back the life I expected to live. Restore my marriage, my child, my job, my health, as it was before." And he says quietly, "Let it go. I have something better for you. Offer me what you have left, and I will transform it beyond your expectations."

When we've been inappropriately intimate with someone, or too many some-ones, and there's no way to retrieve our innocence, Jesus says, "Give me your body as a Temple for my Spirit. Because you've too easily said yes, begin to say no—even to one who claims to love you—until the time is right. And I will bless you with the joy of a virgin bride or husband."

When we've been all our life alone, or alone for years since divorce, and des-perately lonely, Jesus says, "Give me your singleness. Let me make you whole as my Father made me—unmarried—a whole person. Let me fill you with such love that, married or single, you will be a blessing to all who know you."

When we've torpedoed our career with bad choices or half-hearted effort and are years behind our contemporaries, Jesus says, "Give me all your talents and experiences. I will find a place for you to make a difference for me. Will you get rich? Ask that question five years after you follow my lead. The answer will surprise you!"

Jesus asked those servants to give him water. When they took a glassful to the headwaiter, it had become wine. Not just ordinary, screw-top, bag-in-a-box, refrigerator wine, but the best anybody had tasted! Instead of a disastrous begin-ning to that marriage, Jesus provided an unforgettable blessing. "Nevermore!" had become "More and more!"

It's what Isaiah had promised God's people centuries before. When their short-sighted, self-directed plans had exploded in their faces and left them cap-tives in a hostile land, God wasn't willing to leave them hanging their heads, endlessly rehearsing their failures, hearing that mocking voice say, "Nevermore!" He saw they were ready to obey him, willing to give up self-centered ways, and he revealed his plan to bless them beyond their fondest hopes. "The nations shall see your vindication, and all the kings your glory; and you shall be called by a new name that the mouth of the Lord will give. You shall be a crown of beauty in the hand of the Lord, and a royal diadem in the hand of your God. You shall no more be termed Forsaken, and your land shall no more be termed desolate; but you shall be called My Delight Is in Her, . . . as the bridegroom rejoices over the bride, so shall your God rejoice over you."

Beloved, this was not divine reward for the people's faithfulness to his orig-inal plan, or for good moral management of their own lives. The celebration God promised was a gift to people who had lost everything important; people who had failure perched permanently in consciousness. "Will I ever again be happy?" "Nevermore!" sneered the enemy of truth. And God said, "Begone! Fly away, you discourager of my people. They have let you in and listened too long to your depressing refrain. You call them 'Hopeless' and they have believed you. I call them by a new name, and invite their new surrender."

Don't listen to that voice of discouragement! Yes, we've all suffered. We've wasted so many chances and covered our pain with so many new mistakes. But there's nothing lost to us that God can't restore in abundance—to our great surprise!

We offer him loneliness and grief. He changes them into sensitivity and friendship. We offer him disappointment; he offers us unexpected opportunities. We offer him the hateful things people call us and the cruel labels we have for ourselves. He offers us new names, filled with promise. We offer him water; he gives us wine—if we will trust him and follow his lead.

Are you haunted by an accusing raven of your own? With apologies to Poe, let me borrow his meter and offer these lines to flush "Nevermore" from your life.

Is thy heart by sadness shattered? Are thy prosperous plans now scattered?
And thy cup of celebration spilled with tears upon the floor?
Scorn the raven's somber warning; set thy mind upon the morning,
And yield thy wounded will like water to the Savior saints adore,
Jesus will transform thy offering, joy like wine not known before,
Savored now and evermore.

Richard I. H. Belser is rector of St. Michael's Church,
Charleston, South Carolina.

FIFTH SUNDAY AFTER THE EPIPHANY

Fishers and Failed Poets

1 Corinthians 15:1–11; Luke 5:1–11
Dayle Casey

SEVERAL years ago, Rabbi Joseph Telushkin wrote a little book called *Jewish Humor: What the Best Jewish Jokes Say about the Jews*.[1] In it he tells this story: A man takes some very fine material to a tailor and asks the tailor to make him a pair of pants. He goes back a week later, but the pants are not ready. Two weeks go by, and still the pants are not ready. Finally, after six weeks, the pants are ready. The man tries them on, and they fit perfectly. But when it comes time to pay for them, he says to the tailor, "It took God only six days to make the world. And it took you six weeks to make just one pair of pants." "Yes," says the tailor, "but look at the pair of pants, and look at the world!"

The world spins wondrously on its axis, but as the evening news reminds us every day, it rotates still unfinished and unperfected. Despite being made by God himself, creation still shows some ragged hemlines—and more than just a few—because God did not make dresses and pants, but people; and people have a way of not fitting perfectly. People have a way of going their own ways and not the way God made them.

And it's into this imperfect world, into the world of people, into the world of sin and poverty and blindness and oppression, into this world of bad news, that Jesus comes to announce good news to the poor, release for the captive, and sight for the blind.

What meaning would Jesus have in a world that was perfect? Bringing good news to the poor would make no sense if "bad news" had not preceded it. To proclaim release for the captive, sight for the blind, and freedom for the oppressed would be meaningless in a world that was not afflicted by such suffering. It's only in light of creation's ragged and revealing hemline, only in light of creation's fallenness, that the good news proclaimed by Jesus has full meaning. It is only in the light of the "bondage of our sins" that it makes sense to pray, as we do on this day, that God will "set us free and give us the liberty of that abundant life which you have made know to us in our Savior Jesus Christ." As Jesus says, it's only the sick who need a physician.

So, it's as God deals with an imperfect world that the world's need for redemption becomes clear. It's as Jesus heals the sick and casts out unclean spirits, as he undertakes the healing of the fallen creation, that he shows the fishermen, Peter and James and John, how to make a huge catch of fish. Then he tells them that from now on he will show them how to catch people, how to be "fishers of men," how to share the good news of redemption and life with a world in danger of dying.

What does it mean to be a "fisher of men," a "catcher of people"? What does it mean to be an evangelist, a sharer of good news in a world of bad news?

I remember going fishing with my grandfather once when I was a boy. The only thing I really recall clearly about that day was my grandfather's saying to me at one point, "Dayle, if you talk too much, you'll scare away the fish."

William Faulkner wrote millions of words to produce dozens of novels, for which he won the Nobel Prize for Literature. Yet he described himself as "a failed poet" because he had used so many words to convey his meaning, while the genius of poetry is to pack as much meaning into as few words as possible. *Poet* comes from the Greek word, *poiein*, "to create." God the Creator is God the Poet. Jesus, the One who creates good news—on the Cross—is Jesus the Poet.

St. Francis offered an evangelistic version of this same truth: "Proclaim the Gospel at all times. If necessary, use words."

Preachers, like Faulkner, are failed poets. To be a "fisher of men," a "catcher of people," means telling it simply. It means telling it the way it was with Jesus, using words, if necessary, but as few as possible. It means passing on the good news about Christ that Paul tells us about this morning, the tradition that he, and we, have received: that Christ died for our sins. That, even with its hemline such as it was, Christ loved the world and persisted in sharing with it the tremendous loving mercy of God—even to the point of dying for us to drive the truth home. That he was buried, and then raised by a loving Father on the third day. That even though Paul was (and we are) unworthy of this love, Christ nonetheless took Paul (and takes us) for what we are, shares God's love with us, and sends us to share it with the world. Using words, if necessary.

Surely, evangelism, the sharing of the good news of Christ, is not the kind of theological or ecclesiastical imperialism we've come to see a lot of in our day, an insistence that others must cross every *t* in a creed the way we cross them. It would be more bad news, not good news, to proclaim a God who requires that people subscribe to "truths" they have not personally experienced. The good news, rather, is that Christ loves even those who persecute him (like St. Paul once did). The good news is that when, somehow, by the grace of God, we experience this love and truth in our own lives, our lives can be redeemed, remade, refashioned into all they were created by God to be!

Jesus made "fishers of men" out of Peter, James, John, and Paul not through propositions, but through personal example; not by promotion of agendas or creeds, but by attraction of personality. "Catching people," for Jesus, was not a matter of throwing out a net to corral, control, or manipulate them. People were "caught" by the way he lived in the Spirit of God, in the Spirit of the original creation. By the way he walked, the way of the cross, when he could have taken another way. By the way he brought health to those who were sick, hope to those in despair, fellowship and love to those who had been fed the bad news that they did not count. Jesus made disciples by the way he lived and died.

So what does this mean for us? How are we to be "fishers of men," "catchers of people"? In exactly the same way. By being "caught" ourselves in the creative Spirit of God in which Jesus lived. By seeking to live, as Jesus did, lives of reconciliation and peace that attract others to that Spirit. By being poets, creators of good news, not just talkers about it.

I want to offer four examples of how the saving good news has been shared by others, four stories of real and effective evangelism, of people who were not failed poets, but creators of good news.

Gandhi was a Hindu who rejected Christianity in his youth because of how he saw it practiced in South Africa. Gandhi preached and walked the way of peace in India during the days of India's struggle for independence. Late in Gandhi's life, as independence from Britain was achieved, bitter civil war broke out between Hindus and Muslims. Distressed by the continuing fighting of his brothers and sisters, Gandhi went on a fast, determined not to eat until the fighting among fellow Indians stopped.

The movie *Gandhi* portrays an encounter that occurred in the midst of this fast. Gandhi was so weak he could hardly lift himself from his pallet. A fellow Hindu burst into his room, afraid the great man would die. In tears the man begged Gandhi to give up his fast. During their conversation, the man confessed to Gandhi that he was in torment and hell. In his own anger with Muslim neighbors who had killed a Hindu in the civil war, he had grabbed a little Muslim boy and in retaliation killed him by smashing his head against a wall. Gandhi listened, and thought for a moment. Lifting himself slightly from his pallet, he whispered, "I know a way out of hell. Find an orphan, a young boy whose parents have been killed in the fighting. Take him into your home as your own. Only, be sure to raise him as a Muslim."

Proclaim the Gospel at all times. If necessary, use words.

Robert McCahill is a priest, the only Roman Catholic in Kishorganj, Bangladesh. He lives by himself in a hut on the edge of town. The law in this Muslim town forbids any proselytizing, any preaching or public proclamation of the Gospel. Father McCahill cannot even offer a mass. He is allowed only to live in Kishorganj.

So he does, by spending his days serving his Muslim friends and neighbors. He provides the sick with medicines. When they need it, he helps them get to a hospital. He gives food to the destitute. He is a familiar figure in Kishorganj, going to the homes of those too sick to come to him.

Father McCahill is also a regular at a small restaurant in town. The owners are used to seeing him invite beggars from the street outside to come in and share a meal at his table. What they can't figure out is why this Christian priest and foreigner, who cannot offer a mass or talk about Jesus, pours tea for these beggars as if he were their hired servant.

Father McCahill cannot talk about Jesus. When someone asks, he responds with a few words only. He tells the seeker what St. James wrote in his epistle, that "in the eyes of God, true religion is helping those in need." That makes sense to his Muslim friends, who have heard the same thing in the Koran. Maybe that is why, as he walks the streets of Kishorganj, Father McCahill is greeted as bhai Bob, brother Bob.

Preach the good news at all times. If necessary, use words.

Golda was a young Jewish girl living in Germany during World War II. Golda's father, mother, brother, and sister all died in the Nazis' gas chamber at Maidenak. Golda, too, was on her way to the ovens, but because she was the last one in line that day, the guards could not squeeze her in. So they pulled her out and slammed the door shut. She was the only survivor.

When Maidenak was liberated, all Golda wanted was some way to avenge the death of her family. "But it struck me," she said, "that I would then be no better than Hitler himself." So Golda went to work in a hospital for children in the town of Maidenak. She deliberately chose to nurse German children, most of them victims of the war like herself, to purge her bitterness toward the German people. And she decided she would remain in Maidenak until she had completely forgiven Hitler. "When I do that," she said, "then I am allowed to leave."

Proclaim the Gospel at all times. If necessary, use words.

Finally, a story about a missionary, shipwrecked at sea, who washed up at the edge of a remote village. Half dead from injury and exposure, he was taken in by the villagers and nursed back to health. And for the next twenty years, he lived in the village. During that time, he preached no sermons, he sang no hymns. He neither read the Bible nor taught it to anyone. He made no personal claim of faith. But when the villagers became sick, he attended them as they had attended him, sometimes long into the night. When people were hungry, he shared his own food with them. When they were lonely, he was available to talk and listen. A well-educated man, he spent much time tutoring the uneducated. And he always took the side of those who were wronged.

After twenty years had passed, other missionaries came from the sea to the village and began talking to the villagers about a man named Jesus. And the villagers said, "Oh, we know him. He has been living here for twenty years, We'll take you to meet him."

Preach the Gospel at all times. But why would it ever be necessary to use words?

Because, like Peter and Paul, we are failed poets incapable of articulating such love. But, by the grace of God, we, too, can learn to live better poetry. We can learn how to create good news, how to fish instead of talk.

> *Dayle Casey is chaplain of The Chapel of Our Savior,*
> *Colorado Springs, Colorado.*

---

1. Joseph Telushkin, *Jewish Humor: What the Best Jewish Jokes Say about the Jews* (New York: William Morrow and Company, 1992).

LAST SUNDAY AFTER THE EPIPHANY— FEAST OF THE TRANSFIGURATION

A Tale Too Big to Get Your Arms Around

Luke 9:28–36
J. Scott Barker

BEFORE I'D had any organized and systematic education about the church inflicted on me, I used to think a lot about what it might be like to be a priest. I used to think about how I'd make the whole "church experience" better if I were in charge.

One of my favorite schemes was a plan to celebrate Christmas—in the church—in the middle of the summer. I was always so impressed, you see, with how rich people's spiritual lives became during the Christmas season. I was so impressed with the extent of people's generosity, kindness, prayerfulness, and joy during the season of our annual celebration of Christ's Incarnation. I was always disappointed that the whole year can't be like this.

So my plan was that, when I got to be a priest, one sweltering summer day each year—say, some time during the first week in August—I would surprise my congregation with Christmas. I wouldn't tell them it was coming. They would just walk into church one day. (Maybe I would even keep them all out in the narthex until exactly 10:30!) The doors to the nave would swing open, and the organ would blast out the opening strains of "Joy to the World!" There would be the holiday hangings on the pulpit and altar, evergreen garlands everywhere, tons of candles, red ribbons, and a creche. At coffee hour there would be turkey, eggnog, and presents. Nothing would be left out. Christmas in the summertime!

It was going to be such a wonderful surprise. And people were going to be transported totally to that magic time of year—and way of being—when we all seem to try so much harder at loving Christ and each other. And we all seem to take such joy in it!

Well, then I went to seminary, and I learned all about the cycle of the church year. I learned about fixed feasts and moveable feasts, holy times and ordinary time. And I learned about how it all fits together in this special way that maybe we shouldn't mess with because if we had Christmas in August, then maybe something else would get left out. This week I have had Christmas on the brain. And the reason I suspect, is that today's feast, The Feast of the Transfiguration, is so much the same.

Both the Feast of the Incarnation and the Transfiguration are built upon very unusual stories: major miracles, miracles around which the biblical narrative is shaped, miracles upon which our understanding of the person of Jesus is built. Both stories are, frankly, pretty far-fetched. They are the kind of stories with which the skeptics among us have so much trouble. After all, it's one thing to believe that Jesus existed, that he taught wisely, that he healed effectively, and that finally he sacrificed his life for those he loved. But it is something else again to believe that Jesus was born of a woman who had never made love to a man (with angels directing traffic in the background!). Or that one day he hiked up a mountain and talked to Moses and Elijah, and that the voice of God rang out from the skies! I don't know about your brain, but mine's a little small to wrap around stuff like this. A virgin birth! An encounter with two long-dead prophets and their God! What astounding stories!

But maybe that's the point. Maybe it's the audacity of these stories that makes Christmas and this Feast of the Transfiguration so special. Suddenly, on days like this, God through the church invites us to stretch our faith. God asks us to put our hearts and souls, and yes, even our minds, firmly behind a proposition that is difficult to understand and impossible to prove. It is a challenging and uncomfortable place to be, isn't it? Why should I assent to the truth of these stories? I hate being pushed like this!

But look what happens if we believe! Look what happens around December 25 every year when we get behind the idea that the same almighty God who created time, space, and life was born as a human being. Suddenly life changes, doesn't it? Human beings become much more important and valuable to us because God is one of us. We become kinder, gentler, and more loving people, because suddenly, loving human beings means loving God. It's amazing! It really works. Accepting the authenticity of the incarnation changes lives. It changes the world.

I don't know about this vision of the Transfiguration. I can't really understand this story, any more than I can really understand the God of creation lying in a manger and depending upon his mother to be fed. But if I had to take a stab at explaining it, I'd say the Transfiguration is the flip side of the Incarnation coin. If Christmas is the celebration of God becoming human, then The Feast of the Transfiguration is the celebration of that same human's becoming God. The Transfiguration is a timely reminder for us that this "man" Jesus whom we have come to know and love so well, this same Jesus of flesh and blood and real, live thoughts, feelings, and emotions, just like us, is real divinity. God incarnate. Flesh and the Word in one. If Christmas draws us closer to humanity because *in Christ God is human*, then this Feast of the Transfiguration draws us closer to divinity because *in Christ a human is God*.

The Feast of the Transfiguration is an opportunity for us to draw closer to God. It is an opportunity to let *our* lives be transfigured, by the radical proposition that Jesus is Lord.

"Listen to him!" the voice in the vision proclaims. He is more than our "buddy," this Jesus. He is more than a teacher. More than a healer. More than human. Jesus is one with God. He is one with that power that creates and destroys at will. He is one with that power that breathes life and brings death into creation. He is one with that One who will sit in judgment over all things. "Listen to him!" the voice in the vision proclaims. If you do, your lives will be changed.

It's all here this morning, you know. The festival hangings. Beautiful hymns of joy that are stories about this special day. Friends. Family. A Gospel tale that's way too big to get your arms all the way around. And Christ in the center of it all. Take some time right now, here today, to engage this wonderful good news of the Transfiguration. Let it challenge you. Let it move you. Let it push your buttons if it will. And be not afraid. Close your eyes and drink it in with your hearts. The Incarnation is closer than you think. You can almost smell the evergreen and hear the angels sing.

J. Scott Barker is vicar of The Church of the Resurrection,
Omaha, Nebraska.

FIRST SUNDAY OF LENT

Remembering What We Have Forgotten

Deuteronomy 26:1–11; Luke 4:1–13
James E. Flowers, Jr.

I AM SOMEWHAT absent-minded, and sometimes I tend to forget stuff. I forget where I put my keys, my glasses, my wallet, or my checkbook. It is pretty common for me to have to make several trips back into the house after I've kissed Madelyn goodbye. It's really rather comical, and a little embarrassing. I come huffing and puffing back through the door. "Forgot my coffee," I say. "Well, goodbye." Two minutes later, back I come. "Forgot my communion set. Okay, see you later!" Then maybe five minutes later, because this time I've made it to the city limits, I come back through the door. "Have you seen my umbrella? No? Well maybe it's in the trunk. Okay, I'm gone!"

I guess we're all a bit forgetful from time to time. But sometimes forgetfulness is not nearly so humorous. Because sometimes I forget myself. Sometimes I forget who I am. And when I forget who I am, I am capable of doing and saying terrible things. You see, God created me and died for me. Mom gave birth to me. She and Dad raised me. The bishop laid his hands upon my head and proclaimed that I was a priest. Madelyn loved me and pledged herself to me. These are among the facts by which I define myself, among the gifts out of which I live a life of gratitude. But when I forget about them, even for a moment, I am no longer grateful, and I can become a different person altogether.

That person is capable of all manner of pettiness, of slander and gossip, of cruelty and base behavior. That person doesn't know gratitude from a ham sandwich. That person will rant and rave and carry on. That person is righteously indignant, astoundingly grandiose, shamefully self-centered, relentlessly irritable, and with an arrogance that knows no bounds.

You see, when I forget myself, when I forget who I am—when I forget that I am a child of God, the son of Jim and Dee Flowers, a priest of the church, the grateful husband of Madelyn—when I forget these things, I am no longer constrained by them. I am no longer guided by them. I am no longer defined by them. At those times, I am quite simply a loose cannon, my only identity shaped by whatever momentary outrage happens to cross my path.

Memory is perhaps the most important of notions for Jewish folks. Today's Old Testament reading contains a passage that is thought by many to be the most momentous in all the Jewish Scriptures. "A wandering Aramean was my ancestor; he went down into Egypt and lived there. . . ." So it begins. And it goes on to tell the story with which we are all so familiar, the story of the Exodus, of Moses and Aaron, and the Ten Commandments. I can still hear Professor Murray Newman recite it in Hebrew. It is this story by which all faithful Jewish people define themselves. It is the memory of these events that makes them who they are.

I believe that Lent is a time for remembering. It is that time specially set aside to give you and me the space to remember who we are, to remember how we came to be here, and what we have been called to do. To remember that "God so loved the world that he gave his only Son, so that everyone who believes in him may not perish but may have eternal life." So that you and I can be children of God, and heirs of God's Kingdom. As Christians, our defining moment, our defining event is the passion and death of Jesus Christ. We forget it at our peril. For when we forget it, we forget ourselves as well. Giving stuff up or taking on some particular Lenten discipline will do us little good if we don't remember why we do what we do.

Actually, we Episcopalians take this notion of remembering pretty seriously. That is why we have Communion so often. Jesus said, "Do this in remembrance of me." And we do. The body and blood of Christ remind us of the cross, of his death and passion. They remind us also that upon that cross was wrought our salvation. In the Ash Wednesday liturgy, the priest says, "Remember that you are dust, and to dust you shall return." In other words, remember who you are. Remember your place in the cosmos. Remember your mortality, and so your need for God.

In truth, of course, we often forget ourselves. We often forget that we are but dust. We often forget that God loved us and that Christ died for us. When we do, we lose the best part of ourselves. It is at this point when we are in the most danger, the gravest of peril. For when we forget, we are reduced to the lowest human common denominator. We are without the grace of God, and it is not a pretty picture.

If you've ever said or heard someone say, "I don't know you anymore," then perhaps you understand. If you've ever looked in the mirror and beheld a stranger staring back at you, then you know. You know the pain and the despair that comes with forgetting—with forgetting, but also with betrayal; betrayal of God and betrayal of self.

Lent is a time for remembering and for discovery. Jesus went into the wilderness to remember who he was and to discover who he was; to remember what he was called to do and to discover what he was called to do. When he emerged, he knew who he was. He knew what he would do.

The forty days of Lent provide us with an opportunity to remember and to discover. And when we emerge, we will have a better idea of who we are and what we have been called to do. But Lent is no magic bullet. To observe a Holy

Lent we must be willing to set aside some time each day to remember: to remember who we are, to remember who God is, and what God was willing to do to secure our salvation. I have said it often enough in the past, but it bears repeating. When we *know* who we are, then we can *be* who we are. Then we can be true to ourselves and true to God.

Forgetting where I put my keys is one thing. Forgetting myself is quite another. Lent is a time to remember. I invite you to a Holy Lent.

James E. Flowers, Jr., is rector of Christ Memorial Episcopal Church, Mansfield, Louisiana.

SECOND SUNDAY OF LENT

Black Holes

Genesis 15:1–12, 17–18
Patricia Bird

"A DEEP and terrifying darkness fell on Abram." Many of us have been around long enough to have had some experiences that allow us to understand intuitively what Abram's deep and terrifying darkness might have been like.

I am deeply interested in astronomy, and I have recently been reading and watching documentaries on "black holes" in space. A black hole is created by a dying star that has collapsed in upon itself. The resulting tightly packed mass produces a gravity so intense that even light, the fastest thing in the universe, cannot escape its pull. The force draws everything in its vicinity into itself with irresistible power. Once something enters a black hole, the force of gravity causes it to disintegrate completely. Inside a black hole, matter ceases to exist. Space and time have no meaning.

At least, this is what scientists and cosmologists believe about black holes. Obviously, no human being has actually entered a black hole. If anyone did, it's highly unlikely that he or she would come back to tell us what the experience was like. Regardless of the answer, it wouldn't surprise me to hear that some of us have experienced our own black holes, right here on earth—those deep and often terrifying darknesses where matter, space, and time become irrelevant. I certainly have.

This past week I have been deeply involved with a dear friend and his family who are in such a place. They must make the heartrending decision of whether or not to remove life support systems from a loved one who has been in a coma for almost two weeks. The tests indicate that even if he wakes up, his brain is so damaged that the chances are very small that he would have any meaning-ful life. Throughout the week I have heard various ones say, "What day is it?" "What time is it?" "Is it raining?" "Is the sun shining?" Matter, space, and time have almost ceased to exist for them as the gravity of this overwhelming event pulls them into itself.

Abram, who would later be called Abraham, was in a deep, terrifying dark-ness, right in the midst of a process in which God was making a forever type of covenant with him. Abram had probably never been closer to God than he was at this time, and yet here he was in a black hole. Is this what happens when one gets that close to God?

The biblical evidence seems to point to the fact that the journey into God often leads through a black hole: Abram in his deep and terrifying darkness; Jonah inside the whale; Jeremiah in prison; Paul—who at the time was called Saul—being knocked down and blinded; and, of course, the one chief exam-ple on which this season of Lent focuses: Christ's crucifixion and sojourn in the tomb. In our Apostles' Creed we even say he descended into hell.

Genesis says that the very creation of this universe in all its mystery was pre-ceded by utter darkness. Scientists and cosmologists, who now believe that there is little doubt that the universe began with the "Big Bang," also say that it was preceded by complete darkness.

Why would God choose to work with us in the dark? Why are we pulled into black holes where all that is familiar is altered, sometimes beyond recog-nition? I am drawn back to my friend who is in a coma right now. Imagine the darkness he is in. Yet we are told by the doctor that he can hear everything. Whatever else may have ceased to exist for him, we are told he can hear. In that belief, several friends who play musical instruments have gone into his room in the intensive care unit. They stand by his side, playing their music for him, hoping that the love they feel, which he may not now be able to com-prehend, will at least be transmitted through the music.

Perhaps God forces us into black holes of our own and removes all that is familiar so that we may be led to hear whatever it is God would like to tell us. Perhaps the love God has for us (which, in the coma-like lives we often lead, we cannot comprehend) can only be comprehended in a darkness so complete that the only faculty left to us is to listen to what God is playing for us in the dark.

There's no denying that it's frightening to be in the dark. The first part of the message that God gave Abram in his deep and terrifying darkness was not all good news. God said that Abram's descendants, who had just been promised to him, would start out as slaves in a foreign land. But then, God said, they would afterward come out of that land with great possessions.

One thing that intrigues scientists—and me—is what is on the other side of a black hole. If one entered a black hole and reemerged on the other side in some other form than we now know, where would one be? Some have won-dered if we might find ourselves in another, parallel universe. Perhaps the uni-verse we know may not be the only one there is. With matter, space, and time becoming meaningless inside a black hole, would one enter another place where matter, space, and time are of no importance?

Though we lack the knowledge right now of what lies on the other side of the black holes in space, one astronomer said that the entrance to black holes— and what lies in their mysterious depths—is where, for him, science, theology, and faith meet. My faith experiences, including my own personal journeys into black holes, have shown me that they are what Clarissa Estes, author of *Women Who Run with the Wolves* calls "the night between two days."[1] The life-death-resurrection theme we celebrate during Lent and Eastertide tells us over and over again that new life follows darkness, always.

Some of God's greatest acts have taken place in the dark: the creation of the universe, a birth in a stable, and resurrection from within a closed tomb.

Patricia Bird is priest in residence, St. John's Church, Lower Merion Township, Pennsylvania.

---

1. Clarissa Pinkola Estes, author of *Women Who Run with the Wolves: Myths and Stories of the Wild Woman Archetype* (New York: Random House, 1997).

FOURTH SUNDAY OF LENT

Searching for Squandered Treasure

Luke 15:11–32
Jane Patterson

THE WEEK before last when I took some time off to get things settled in a little better at my house, I got some new bookcases. Finally, I had a place to put out some of the things that really matter to me, besides just books. I dusted off a photograph that I treasure of my grandmother at sixteen. Another of my mother at sixteen. One of me at sixteen, and one of my daughter Emily at sixteen that was actually taken right out here in our courtyard. As is true for a lot of Southern families, I think, continuity is very important in my family, especially the imaginary thread that stretches through the line of women in my family. I have been entrusted with the care of things that my mother and grandmothers and great-grandmothers and aunts cared for before me. I polish their silver. I iron their tablecloths. I scrub their embroidered bed linens to keep them white. I mend the christening gown, sewn all by hand with minuscule stitches. I have recently hung up a silk and velvet wedding quilt made by my great-grandmother and all her friends for my great-uncle Charlie (only he never got married, so it came down to me). I have literally miles of tatting done by my grandmother and her sisters. It makes me chuckle to think of the hours and hours of scandalous gossip exchanged over all that industry.

I am also the keeper of the family jewelry. I have four little boxes of my grandmother's and mother's most treasured rings. And also the string of pearls that my father gave my mother on their wedding day, which I wore in November at my wedding. One of my favorite series of pictures from the wedding is of Emily closing the clasp on the pearls around my neck and then trying to get them to lie straight on the front of my dress. I love these pictures, because one day I know that we will take another series just like them, only I will be putting the pearls around Emily's neck. I am even the keeper of jewelry that isn't mine, like the ring that is to be for my brother's bride, should he ever marry.

I have been hiding this jewelry in various clever places since I was sixteen. When Heloise announces a new hint about where to hide valuable things, or how to disguise them (say by freezing them into ice cubes), I always pay attention. Are my things safe enough? I check them again to be sure.

The thing about getting married in late November is that then you're left with all the details of packing and moving at the same time that you are trying to prepare for Christmas. I packed things and then had to unpack them again when we decided to have Christmas at our old house instead of our new house. Then I repacked everything just before New Year's, with the help of friends, as we began the flow of goods from one house to the other, station-wagon load by station-wagon load.

Over the course of several weeks, I became aware that I hadn't seen those four boxes of jewelry in a long time. I felt quite certain that I had brought them over earlier in the first loads, but they weren't in any of the kinds of places I was fairly sure I would have put them. I looked in my underwear drawer. I felt in my tall boots. I pulled out all the contents of my sewing box. They weren't there. Finally, I told my husband that I was worried about them. No, he hadn't seen them. Had I left them out on my dresser the day the movers came for the big furniture? I wasn't sure anymore. For twenty-seven years, I had known where each box was at all times, and now, suddenly, I had no recollection at all of what I had done with them.

I was heartsick. I rarely have occasion to wear a single piece of that jewelry, but I am the person responsible for it in our family. What would I do if my brother suddenly, out of the blue, chose to propose to some woman? How could I explain to my mother that her trust in me had been unfounded? I felt a weight in the pit of my stomach that would not go away. I confessed all of this to Jean, my spiritual director, and she gave me an interesting charge. "Don't look obsessively," she said, "but when you do look, let your searching be a prayer. Remember Jesus' parable about the woman who turned her house upside down, looking for her lost coin. That's not only you, looking for your jewelry; that's God, looking for you. Let your looking be a reminder of that relentless seeking that God does." The story of the woman who looks for her coin comes just before the story of the Prodigal Son. Luke has put together a whole series of stories that Jesus told about precious things lost and found.

Throughout January, February, and into March, I looked for those jewelry boxes, and every time, thanks to Jean, I called to my mind God's search for us. I feel as though I have spent the last three months living with the father in the story of the Prodigal Son, during all that long time that the son was missing. Our living room was loaded, almost floor to ceiling, with boxes full of the contents of my former house. I prowled through those boxes, time after time, just sure that I would come across the jewelry. I went through the laundry hamper multiple times. That would have been the kind of place I would have hidden it—only, I hadn't. I went through the boxes so often that I knew their contents by heart. At night I could rehearse the contents of each, while lying sleepless, searching even by memory for my family's treasure.

This must have been the life of that father, rehearsing all the places his son might be. In this city? With these people? At a table like this? Is he laughing with his friends? Is he hurt? Is he hungry? Is he still alive? As time passed, the father must have become aware that the only logical conclusion was that his son had died. But then, as I did, his mind would return to the familiar track. Is he here? Or maybe here? Is he married? Does he maybe have children of his own now? Is he safe?

Week before last, with my time off, I was determined to get the last of the boxes emptied. I had pretty much come to the conclusion that I had so cleverly disguised the jewelry, whether as dog food, or trash, or Tupperware, or something, that it had gotten thrown out. Friday, when I was really getting to the last of the boxes, an unexpected and powerful feeling of sadness came over me. Maybe it was that Emily's eighteenth birthday had been the day before and I was very aware that she will be leaving us soon to go to college. I kept coming across old pictures of the children when they were little. Where had all that time gone? Had I really been awake enough to it?

I looked at Jacob's first grade picture that was taken on the day that the "Good Citizen" of the month was chosen for his class. His construction-paper medal—GOOD CITIZEN—winks back at me from the picture, and his dear, bright little face. Did I really love these children enough? These human treasures entrusted to me—had I always treated them as though they were as precious as they really are? I recognized these thoughts again as the thoughts of the father, whose son was missing. I mourned the loss of my children's childhoods, the loss of the time to hold them close again, the loss of bedtime stories, and field trips, and make-believe games. I mourned my failed marriage, even as I was doing all the physical things to move into this new marriage, this amazing and gracious gift from God.

I mourned in all these ways that father must have mourned and felt that if only he had done something differently, his son would not have left. "I have squandered my treasure," I thought, "and I have wandered far in a land that is waste. I have sinned against God and against my family."

I walked into the living room to straighten up the last few things. There was a box of Christmas ornaments that would need to be sorted through, and a box of letters. And on a ledge by the dining table was a wooden box of makeshift dog toys—old socks and shoes and things that Scout likes to chew on. I was about to pitch the whole thing straight into the trash, when I noticed that there were some knee pads in it that might still fit someone. To get to the knee pads, I picked up a plastic grocery bag that was on top of them, and almost absentmindedly opened it to look inside. There were the four boxes of jewelry.

I was stunned. I took the bag into the bedroom and sat on a bench at the foot of the bed so I could take out each box and look at its contents. I laid everything out on the coverlet, piece by piece, and then I wept in thanksgiving. But what I thought as I wept was not, "Finally, I have found you!" Jean had led me to look, always mindful of God as the woman who searches. And maybe because I had been inside that story all those three months, I found myself crying to God: "My God, *you* have found *me*!" In the midst of my inadequacy as mother and caretaker, I ceased to be the finder, and God found me.

In my months-long search and unexpected finding, I learned how it was that the father in Jesus' parable—whose eyes were trained to scan the horizon for his son's silhouette—how it was that he, almost without thinking, lifted his eyes at the moment his son appeared in the distance. I know how he must have gazed at his son when they were finally within touching range; how he must have felt his son's hair for its familiar texture; how he must have delighted to recognize just this tilt of the head, just this shape of the ear, just this characteristic gesture with the hands.

For a few months, I became the faithful seeker that God is all the time. I got to know a little of the intensity of God's search for us. Every person in this room is someone for whom God has searched, someone for whom God has been awake, someone whom God has remembered in the night watches. The shape of each one's hand—incomparably precious; the quirks of each one's personality—indescribably dear to this God who searches without ceasing.

The glory of the season of Lent—the season each year when we look to see how far we have wandered, and turn our faces once again toward home—the strange glory of the season of Lent is this: The moment when we let go of our defenses enough to see our own inadequacies, that moment becomes, somehow, the moment when we know ourselves found again by God. In a few minutes, we will all join in a circle around the altar for a celebratory meal together, the feast of those who have been found by God. "Let us eat and celebrate, for we, God's sons and daughters, were lost and are found!"

Jane Patterson is assistant rector at the Church of Reconciliation,
San Antonio, Texas.

FOURTH SUNDAY OF LENT

How Much Is Enough?

Luke 15:11–32
Wesley W. Hinton

AFTER WE clergy graduate from seminary, we seldom have the time to do the kind of scholarly research we did in school, even when we have the inclination. From my own perspective, then, this preaching series on the Seven Deadly Sins has been an inspiring and spiritual challenge intellectually. But more importantly the series has been a challenge to my heart, because in spite of stereotypes, clergy aren't really in any bigger hurry than you are to think too much about either their sins or their sinful nature.

So it's been a long time since I poked around in the works of the blessed St. Thomas of Aquinas. It was in the thirteenth century that Thomas gave us our current lineup of the Seven Deadlys. Basing his work on that of earlier theologians, Thomas breathed new life into our understanding of them. And he's still the first authority. Searching through Thomas's *Summa Theologica* was a lot easier this time than when I was in seminary. Now, thanks to the Dominican Brothers and the Knights of Columbus, I can sit at home and point and click my way through this great work on the Internet. I wonder how St. Thomas would feel about that!

Nonetheless, my first discovery was that we had missed the mark, ever so slightly. It seems that the classical Deadly Sin for this morning's sermon is *not* Greed, as advertised, but Avarice. We don't use the word *Avarice* very much. And although we may think of Greed as an equivalent, to the scholars Greed is actually one of the children of Avarice.

What is Avarice? Avarice is excessive and unbridled desire—excessive and unbridled desire for things, things of monetary value, money. Avarice is the hoarding of things we have, but do not need. And Greed? Greed is simply the desire for more and more. Greed is the desire to add to that stockpile of stuff we don't really need.

When Lee and I were living in Virginia, we built a house. Any of you who have ever done this know that it takes a while for a house to truly become a home: the right curtains in this room, the right wallpaper in that one, the right bushes and flowers in the yard. And we could not do it all ourselves. So on three or four occasions during the first couple of years, we got some help with the heavier landscaping from a delightful *Christian* man. Now, I don't normally make that designation of someone in general conversation. But I make it now, because it was very clearly important to him and because it offers some explanation of what I am about to tell you.

This man had a college degree in agriculture. As many of you know, that's nothing to sneeze at. Farmers all have computers now. They keep track of

weather trends, the performance of different hybrids. They can fertilize different parts of a field with pinpoint accuracy, employing equipment that utilizes
military positioning satellites. The days when you plowed a furrow, dropped
in a seed, and stood around waiting to see if anything happened are long gone.
He had worked for the state agricultural department for a while, but decided
he wanted more time with his family. So he started a landscaping and yard care
business. His wife did the scheduling and kept the books. He would work on
site with a few carefully chosen helpers.

And he was good! Word spread. He had a full load of regular customers for
general yard and garden care. People like me, who just wanted to get him once
in a while had to wait awhile. So one day, when he was out at our house to
give us a price on some work, I asked him why he didn't expand his business,
hire some more people, *make some more money.*

He said to me, "I considered that. I could do that. But part of the reason I
went into this was to have more time with my family. And God has blessed me
with that. I also wanted more time to do things with my church. And God has
blessed me with that. If my business gets bigger, and I spend more time in a
supervisory capacity, I'll lose that. I know, because I tried it once, because I
didn't want to say no to people. It felt good being in demand."

And then he said, "It was also at that time that we considered whether we
really needed more income. I know that there are some things we can't do
now that we could do if we had more money. But my wife and I talked about
it, thought about it, prayed about it. And we came to realize, perhaps in a
more concrete way than we ever had before, that we have enough." *We have
enough.*

Do you think that's a sappy story? Tell the truth, at least to yourself. Does
this guy just not get it? Are you thinking that maybe he's just lazy, doesn't want
to work that hard? Don't you think this guy could have his cake and eat it too?
And why is it important to you and me to be able to discount his motive?
Because we all like our stuff. And we all want more of it.

Or try this one on. Can you remember the last time you had *this* conversation with God? "Lord, I want to thank you for all the blessings you have given
me. I really appreciate them. But you know, Lord, I just realized yesterday that
I have enough blessings now. So you don't need to give me any more. I'm sure
there's someone else out there who could use them."

Or better yet, how about this conversation with God? "Lord, do you remember how sometime last October I thanked you for all of the blessings you'd given
me? And I told you that you could quit because I really have enough? Well,
I'm not sure if you heard me, because you're still blessing me.

"But that's okay, because this morning I woke up with a really great idea,
an idea that will make us both look good. What I'm going to do is take all of
those extra blessings that are more than I need, and I'm going to give them to
people who really do need them. And I'm going tell everyone that they're from
you because—well, because they really are. Then maybe some other folks will
come to love and appreciate you as much as I do!"

Are you uncomfortable yet? I am. I like my stuff. Some of my stuff I like a lot! And I struggle with how much stuff is enough. I say to myself, "Well, *enough* isn't all that much more than I have right now." When I say it that way, you see, it doesn't sound greedy. I don't have to feel too bad about myself. I mean, God wants me to have some stuff, right? Or he wouldn't keep blessing me with it.

Anyway, isn't a little Avarice a good thing? Isn't it the American way? Don't we elect politicians who promise more stuff, and keep politicians with a track record of delivering more stuff? Besides, it's so hard to distinguish when one has passed through that gray area, moving from an ethical profit motive to outright greed. Some things are just too hard to think about, so why try?

The late Reverend Urban T. Holmes was the dean of my seminary in 1980. I remember that he would often speak to us about the warm sins and the cold sins. In terms of the Seven Deadlys, the warm sins would be Lust, Gluttony, and Anger. These are the sins of misdirected passion, sins of the heart. They are the *dis*respectable sins, the ones we love to catch other people doing. These are the sins that adorn the reading rack in the supermarket checkout line.

But not the cold sins. Because the cold sins are also the *respectable* sins. We have turned Pride into a virtuous antidote for low self-esteem. Sloth has become little more than a well-earned vacation for those who work hard. Envy *in moderation* helps to prod us up the secular ladder of success. (How bad can that be?) And Avarice—Avarice makes the American dream come true. It's so respectable! And it's so *ugly*!

All you have to do is listen to the words of the older son in the parable of the Prodigal Son. "Listen! For all these years I have been working like a slave for you. Yet you have never given me even a young goat so that I might celebrate with my friends!" Or even better, look at the cold, resentful expression on the older son's face in Rembrandt's painting, *The Return of the Prodigal Son.* Anger like ice, judgment without mercy. Probably wondering what else the old man is going to give his no-good, lusting, gluttonous wretch of a brother after he has already blown his half of the estate.

Avarice, you see, has no heart. Avarice is self-love in one of its most perverted forms. Avarice is about protecting ourselves and hoarding what we have. We even imagine that we're creating and hoarding our own happiness. If having this much will make me this happy, then having ten times this much will make me ten times as happy. But it never does.

Because Avarice is like holding a penny so close to my eye that it blocks out the sun, blocks out the light of love and concern for others. If there is any joy in things that cannot be shared, it is fleeting at best. You really can't share stinginess. And misers don't smile.

I can no longer tell you, at this point in my life, how many Decembers I have watched old Mr. Scrooge move from a private, joyless, unholy hell of his own making to a joyful redemption that, perhaps, astounds him more than anyone else. And every time it's the same. Tears still fill my eyes. And when the lights come up, I look around at others and discover that I have lots of company.

Why? For whom do we weep? A make-believe character on stage, a gross exaggeration of the worst we could be? Certainly we do not see ourselves as being anything like him! Then why would we weep tears of joy time after time? Because that man lives within each and every one of us. Because he lurks in the darker corners of our hearts. Every day, the side of us that would be generous and open, and giving of our material blessings, must do battle with him.

You and I don't much like this part of ourselves. That's why we prefer to see him as an exaggerated caricature up on a stage. It makes it harder to recognize ourselves. Yet in our heart of hearts, we know that he is our darker reflection. So you see, it is not the character on the stage for whom we weep. It is for ourselves. We weep in sadness for the true nature of our being. And we weep for joy over the hope that we too might escape that nature and experience some of that heaven we see on the stage before our eyes.

Avarice cuts us off from others. It also cuts us off from God. And our model for that today, more than we may realize at first glance, is the younger son. Looking through the lens of twentieth-century Western culture and law (partial gifting of estates before death and that sort of thing), we don't fully comprehend what has happened here. But this is an Eastern story.

Author Kenneth Bailey, concerning this parable, wrote, "For over fifteen years I have been asking people of all walks of life from Morocco to India and from Turkey to the Sudan about the implications of a son's request for his inheritance while the father is still living. The answer has always been emphatically the same. The conversation runs as follows. Has anyone ever made such a request in your village? Never! Could anyone ever make such a request? Impossible! If anyone ever did, what would happen? His father would beat him, of course! Why? (Because) The request means—he wants his father to die."[1]

St. Thomas Aquinas refers to Avarice as "a special kind of sin." And this is why. You and I cannot trust in, place our faith in Pride, Envy, Anger, Sloth, Lust, or Gluttony. But we do trust our stuff. We trust and love our material wealth to make us secure and to bring us happiness. And inasmuch as we do, it seems perfectly reasonable to believe that the more we have, the more secure and happy we will be.

And we imagine that we have full control over that. We pile up our stuff higher and higher around us. And it becomes harder and harder to see over the top, harder and harder to know that God was ever there. But, with our houses and cars and stocks and bonds, we don't feel much need for him anyway. He might as well be dead, because he's certainly dead to us.

So do you see why Thomas called Avarice "special"? When we engage in the other sins, we turn our backs on our Lord. But with Avarice, for all practical purposes, we contemplate murder.

You do understand, don't you, that it was the younger brother, the one who left home with his share, who was the lucky one—because he lost everything. Because the walls of his stuff came tumbling down, because he hit rock bottom, he was able to see clearly again. He was able to find his way home. I do not grieve for him.

No, it's the older brother I grieve for. The one who stayed home, the one who tried to have it both ways—one eye on his father and the other eye on his stuff! I grieve for him, because he's too much like me.

Wesley W. Hinton is rector of St. Thomas' Church, Terrace Park, Ohio.

1. Henri Nouwen, *The Return of the Prodigal Son* (New York: Doubleday, 1992), 32; primary source: Bailey, Kenneth, *Poet and Peasant and Through Peasant Eyes: A Literary-Cultural Approach to the Parables* (Grand Rapids, MI: William B. Eerdmans, 1983), 161–2.

FOURTH SUNDAY OF LENT

Conjugating the Verb "To Be"

Luke 15:11–32
Robert T. Brooks

"THERE WAS a man who had two sons." So begins one of the most memorable and famous stories in all the New Testament, a story commonly called The Parable of the Prodigal Son, or The Parable of the Prodigal and His Brother. Both of these popular titles for this story focus our attention on the two sons portrayed in the parable, the younger son who demanded his inheritance but then squandered it, and the older brother who stayed home, only to be disappointed and embittered when his younger brother returned home into the arms of his loving father.

But it's just as important for us to focus on the father in the story. After all, isn't this what Jesus invites us to do when he opens the story as he does: "There was a man who had two sons"? Or at the very least shouldn't we consider the entire family? This parable, which appears only in Luke's Gospel account, draws its power and attraction from the fact that it so accurately displays the way families are. I'm not a psychologist, but I do know that there's a huge body of evidence to suggest that family dynamics such as those portrayed here are the very essence of how families work, or don't work, depending on the lens through which one examines this extraordinary tale.

We all have parents. Most of us have siblings, and those who don't at least have indirect experience, through the stories told by friends, of situations like the one Jesus describes here. This story strikes a resonant chord for anyone at all in touch with the human condition. The dysfunctionality portrayed here has provided many a health care professional with hours of counseling opportunities.

When I was growing up, one of my best friends was an attractive, multi-talented young man, the quarterback of our high school football team, and one of the most brilliant people I've ever met. My friend took the inheritance given him by his father, with whom he did not get along, and squandered it on race cars and fast living. (*Squander*, by the way, is the meaning of the word *prodigal*.) He took great satisfaction in this, because it was a way to show his disrespect for his dad, with whom he was never reconciled. Being myself the youngest of three children, I know how it appeared at times that our parents treated each of us differently. I received at times more favored treatment than did my older siblings.

All this to say, it's no wonder we relate to one or the other of the sons in this story, and perhaps to both of them at certain times in certain situations. There is much to learn about ourselves in them. The younger son puts us in touch with our self-centeredness. His return home is a brilliant portrayal of what it means to repent for bad behavior. The older son reminds us, when we smugly see ourselves as righteous, of how dangerous it is to assume that our sense of duty can assure us a place of favor in God's eyes.

When we lived in Philadelphia, a neighbor of ours, a man who was a member of our parish, was arrested by the federal government for trafficking in child pornography. He served time in prison. When he returned, our rector invited him to take part in our liturgy as a lay reader. The reaction of some members of the parish to his return, and to the invitation, was horror and disgust. The trespasses of the younger son in the parable we heard today were just as horrific as those of our neighbor in Philadelphia.

It's easy for us to be like the older brother, isn't it? But we're a lot like the younger brother as well. His insistence on having it all now, his bull-headed exercise of his own independence, his disregard for the family that gave him so much—all these unflattering yet common attributes are traits we all carry.

Suppose this story were just about the two brothers. What a depressing tale it would be! This is the reason we need to consider the father as Jesus portrays him. And for those of you wondering about the mother who isn't mentioned in the story, think about this: the actions and attitudes of the father would hardly be possible were it not for his wife. She stands in the shadows of the story, but her influence is evident, I think, in the way the father treats both his sons.

Evelyn Underhill wrote a book called *The Spiritual Life*. In the first section she says: "We mostly spend [our] lives conjugating three verbs: to Want, to Have, and to Do. Craving, clutching, and fussing, on the material, political, social, emotional, intellectual, even on the religious plane, we are kept in perpetual unrest: forgetting that none of these verbs have any ultimate significance, except so far as they are transcended by and included in the fundamental verb, to Be: and that being, not wanting, having, and doing, is the essence of the spiritual life."[1]

The parable presents both sons as conjugators of the verbs to Want, to Have, and to Do. The younger son Wants his inheritance now. He must Have it, so that he can Do his own thing. The older son Wants his father's approval. He must Have it, so that what he Does with his life will be appreciated. I want, I have, I do; you want, you have, you do; he or she wants, has, and does. Thus we conjugate these three verbs in our lives.

But the father in the story, and by extension, the mother, just is. His life is a conjugation of the verb to Be. Underhill's comments remind me of the year I began my foreign language studies in the eighth grade. I was enrolled in Latin One. A man named "Spud" Parker, so nicknamed because of the shape and appearance of his head, was my teacher. I remember two things about Spud's class. First, he threw an eraser at me and hit me on the head one day when my behavior became particularly egregious. Second, and more to the point, I remember the verb we used to learn conjugations in Latin. Perhaps you remember this verb as well: *amo, amas, amat, amamus, amatis, amant—I love, you love, he or she loves, we love, you love, they love.*

The conjugation of the verb "to be" that we see in the person of the father in this story, "There was a man who had two sons," is really the conjugation of the verb "to love." That's what saves this story. Were it not for the father, loving both his sons, regardless of their birth order, their actions, or their attitudes, this story would be just another tragedy of a dysfunctional family wracked and ripped asunder by internecine squabbling. But the father's loves for his children paves the way for reconciliation, not only between father and son, but between brother and brother. And reconciliation is God's gift to us. As St. Paul said: "All this is from God, who reconciled us to himself through Christ, and has given us the ministry of reconciliation" (2 Corinthians 5:18).

We used this parable for our intergenerational Bible study recently. Part of each study is an opportunity for everyone to reflect on the story using his or her artistic talents. As I looked over the art work done that night, it struck me how many of you picked up on the father's words. Replying to the older son's objection about welcoming the prodigal home, the father says: "We had to celebrate and rejoice, because this brother of yours was dead and has come to life; he was lost and has been found."

The Parable of the Prodigal Son is a resurrection story, a parable about the possibilities and realities that are ours because we are people of the Resurrection: he was dead and has come to life, he was lost and has been found. It is God's love for the lost one that makes this possible, the God whose I AM, whose conjugation of the verb to be, is I LOVE YOU.

Robert T. Brooks is rector of Christ Episcopal Church, Kent, Ohio.

---

1. Evelyn Underhill, *The Spiritual Life* (London: Hodder and Stoughton, 1937), 20; reprinted by Morehouse, 1995).

GOOD FRIDAY

The Interval of Freedom

John 18:1–19:37
Susan M. Smith

"WHOM ARE you looking for?" Jesus asked. "Jesus of Nazareth!" came the blustery answer from the troop of armed soldiers, under flickering torchlight in the darkness. "I am he." At that, they stepped back and fell to the ground— a cohort of armed soldiers, schooled in the art of intimidation, masters in causing people to submit to their will.

What was it in Jesus' response that led them to fall back, as though the wind had been knocked out of them? The ones who came to intimidate were themselves intimidated. And all Jesus said was, "I am he." Was such a simple statement of truth, made by a man free enough to speak it, sufficient to reverse the flow of intimidation?

This part of the passion story amazes me, because intimidation often *does* work on me. I find myself wanting to fudge the truth sometimes in hopes of mitigating a negative reaction. I mean, Jesus could have said, "Which Jesus of Nazareth did you want?" I can really identify with Peter. When the consequences of speaking straight truth seemed too terrible, he dodged it. But Jesus stayed with the truth, unintimidated. What enabled him to stand up, humbly and freely presenting himself, with no defensiveness, unreactive to their bluster?

I imagine *a certain space, a moment's interval,* between the soldiers' demands and Jesus' response: a certain space from which there arose grounded freedom, the freedom that abides in truth. He did not fudge a bit. "Jesus of Nazareth!" they shouted. There was a pause, *an interval,* where I imagine the Holy Spirit to have filled Jesus' lungs and veins and mind. Then, truthfully, vulnerably, and with great power: "I am he."

No bluster for Jesus; no fudge. And the freedom to speak truthfully, vulnerably, throws people who themselves don't have it.

Every once in a while, I hear accounts of other Christians who have followed Jesus into this interval where free response is born, where a response that is true, without fear, in the face of what is clearly danger and threat, stops people cold. Laurens vanderPost tells the story of the grueling time in a POW camp during World War II in Indonesia. He and colleagues had started classes for other prisoners to make meaning out of the torturous and empty years. A new prison officer became enraged for some reason and ordered all the Allied military officers to be lined up and caned. It was horrible, vanderPost says. The guard yelled and beat them while the others looked on. VanderPost's mind and spirit leaned into the question, How can this be stopped? This must be stopped! How can I stop this?

His turn came. The guard yelled terrible derision at him; beat him on the head, the gut, and the upper body; and then yelled at him to move away. Laurens vanderPost began limping away, but something in him deeper than thought led him to turn back. He took the place of the next one in line, and presented himself again for a second caning. The guard lifted up a chair to break on the next prisoner. But somehow, in his delirium, the guard recognized that this man had been here before. The bleeding was proof. It threw the guard completely off. The power he invoked through anger and fear-making was not working. Mouthing invective, he threw the chair against the wall and stomped out of the room. The caning was finished.[1]

Freedom throws people who don't have it. And Jesus means freedom, as Ernst Kasemann has written.[2]

Yet how do we imagine ourselves "in Christ" on this day? How do we dare to connect with Jesus at this moment, with this demand to reveal oneself at the bleakest place of fear, intimidation, and impending death?

We have come to the turning point of the year, to the hinge. If life's drama were a tragedy, this would be its climax. Yet, with relief and gratitude, we Christians know that glory and life are imminent, that the story doesn't end with the guards and their deadly conclusion, that the climax is yet to come.

But there's something quite subtle in here that I want to invite us not to miss. Amidst all the *events* in the Triduum—the Last Supper, the footwashing, the betrayal, the denial, the Crucifixion, the Resurrection—there is that which is a *non-event*. In fact, it looks like empty space. It is the space between now and tomorrow night when the first Easter service occurs.

Not only in Holy Week, but throughout our lives, we have these spaces, these temporal intervals. Sometimes the in-between times and spaces in life are low periods, times of rest—like after the degree is finished but before we have a job, or after the children have left home but before we've rearranged our lives without them as the center.

Sometimes these in-between spaces are times of tension. It can be minor or unconscious tension—like after we realize we have a body ache but before we take a pain pill, or after we realize we're hungry but before we go to the refrigerator. But sometimes these in-between spaces are times of *great* tension—like after we realize we've done something hurtful or shameful but before we've acknowledged it and made amends. We feel edgy, irritated. Or after we sense a rift in a relationship at work or at home but before it's resolved. We feel anxious, vulnerable.

Whether in minor tension or great tension, my inclination is to shorten this interval down to zero if I can. I don't like the tension. My solution is to try to make it go away. I don't want to have to feel or think about what's in that space.

But that space, if we trust the liturgical terminology applied to Saturday, is HOLY. What if the space itself were not the *lack* of something, a non-event, but a *positive* something? What would happen if instead of resolving the tension right away, we lived into it? If we became conscious of it, and dare I say it:

savored it? If we actually felt the hunger, noticed it, welcomed it as a guest, and entertained it for a while? Maybe then we would go to the refrigerator—or maybe not. What if we allowed ourselves to experience the tension in a relationship or situation? To ask ourselves: How does this feel? I invite you to practice leaning into tensions where, at first, the stakes are not too high. I believe Laurens vanderPost practiced this earlier in his life, first in small things.

This experience is critical to our experience of Jesus' death on the cross, the cross where intimidation is reversed, where tension is inverted. Jesus turned around the liminal space "between," not just for tonight, but for all of our lives. We speak of Jesus' self-sacrifice on the cross as changing sacrifice forever. Tonight we live into the space created by the Crucifixion, like the intake of breath—held. And when the exhale occurred, sacrifice was transformed forever—from taking to giving, from death to life, from oppression to freedom.

Usually a sacrifice *relieves* tension. Isn't this why the Hebrew people, and many other cultures as well, sacrificed animals (and in the bad old days, even people)? Because they experienced a broken covenant, a tension in their relationship with the gods, a terrible guilt they couldn't get free of on their own accord?

Killing something relieved the tension.

It relieved tension even in the tragedy in Jonesboro, Arkansas, when, with rifles, in their school yard, an eleven-year-old and a thirteen-year-old killed four children and a teacher and injured ten more. Matthew, the thirteen-year-old, felt tension. His parents were divorced. He was in a new school, and he didn't fit in. He liked a girl and she wouldn't go out with him. He was tense, angry, unhappy. All was not well in his life. Out of that painful angst came the shooting, which probably alleviated that tension. (Until the next day in jail, of course, wherein a whole Medusa of new and much worse tensions arose.)

But the death of Jesus did not alleviate tension for the guards. In a reversal, it *created* tension for them. They tried to take his life. But because of his freedom, he *gave* his life, so it could not be taken. Judas' tension was so great that he did go and kill to relieve it—taking his own life.

Jesus' preemptive, redemptive gift creates a new rhythm in our lives. The whole character of the spaces is changed. And we are invited into a new relationship with tension, with space. Today Jesus' example invites us who would follow him, into a new rhythm that is ironic and uncomfortable: to *live into* this tension. *Not* to dissipate it, but to notice it, feel it, to choose to make friends with it.

Jesus created tension by accepting what was given to him and, in freedom, choosing it. And in the passion of giving his life this night, he turned the world. Today is the hinge of human freedom. Jesus redeemed tension and made it a space where fear is turned into love, violence into freedom, something wrested into something given: the blood of death into the blood of life.

Like Jesus, we do not ask for the "guards" in our lives, for the tensive and intimidating situations that happen to us. They can seem overwhelming. But if we jump from "tension is uncomfortable" to a quick fix, dissociation, or denial, then the creativity and salvation in it is lost to us. Jesus' response to the guards makes instead a creative tension, a salvific tension.

If Eastern religions have taught us one thing, it is that tension is not "bad." Taoists understand it to be half of a rhythm: tension/resolution; resolution/tension. The full becomes empty; the empty becomes full. We Westerners want to stay full. Christ gives his life and plunges us into emptiness. What shall we do with this?

We are privileged on this side of the Pascha, because we know that at Easter the emptiness will become overwhelming abundant fullness. But *let us not rush to be full.* It is still Friday. Remember it's called Good Friday. And tomorrow is the space where there is room for the presence of God. The French liturgical theologian Jean Corbon puts it this way: "The entire drama of history is located in the tension between this gift and this acceptance: God's passion for human beings, and the nostalgia of human beings for God."[3]

The gift has been given. But it is too great and too terrifying. We will not be able to accept it until another gift is given: the Resurrection. Here and now, however, we are planted right at the heart of the drama of human history. In a moment, we will be invited to an act of devotion around the cross. As you come forward to touch the cross, allow Christ to touch you, to be with you in the space of your authentic feelings of grief and sadness, in all the betrayals of your life, in all the denials and truth fudging, in blustery defensiveness, and in loss. Trust him to carry you as you sink into the space where fear is transformed into love, where freedom is born.

And then as we leave here, let us take home with us the heaviness in our hearts and allow ourselves this night to *feel* it. Tomorrow let us stop every couple of hours. To notice, to experience the emptiness, to identify with the disciples in their loss and uncertainty so that we may carry with us for the rest of the year this space between the cross of death and alienation, and the koinonia of life and community. It is the interval of freedom.

Susan M. Smith is a doctoral student in Liturgical Studies at the Graduate Theological Union, Berkeley, California.

---

1. Taken from a videotape "Hasten Slowly: The Journey of Sir Laurens VanderPost," produced by Mickey Lemle Pictures, Inc., New York.

2. Ernst Kasemann, *Jesus Means Freedom*, trans. Frank Clarke (from the German, *Ruf der Freiheit*) (London: SCM Press, 1969).

3. Jean Corbon, *The Wellspring of Worship* (New York: Paulist Press, 1988), 18.

The Great Vigil of Easter

Faith like a River

Propers for the Liturgy
Jeffrey A. Packard

WHEN I first came to Coudersport, someone pointed to the little stream that flows through town. "That's the Allegheny River," they said. "It is?" I responded, in all but disbelief. "That can't be the Allegheny! The Allegheny is a huge river that joins the Monongahela in Pittsburgh to form the Ohio River. The Ohio flows into the Mississippi and eventually into the Gulf of Mexico." But, of course, it is true. Here we are, living near the headwaters of a mighty river. One with a profound influence on the landscape, culture, industry, agriculture, wildlife, and conscience of our nation.

Rivers are wonderful creatures—always flowing, never static, always changing. The water we look upon as we gaze at a river is never the same, even here near the headwaters where the river is so small. A river is a dynamic system, a living thing. The biblical term *living water*, in fact, derives from such water— water that is flowing, water that is fresh, not stagnant. Living water is the best water for supporting life. And the Allegheny certainly does support life! I don't need to say that to the fisher folk in our congregation. But the river supports far more than fish; it supports all the surrounding wildlife. An entire ecosystem, from microorganisms to birds and large mammals, makes its living from the river. Why do people build cities along rivers? It is not only animals who make their living from them.

A river is always changing, never the same. Even its path changes. The river bed erodes; the river finds a new way. It meanders; it floods; it changes the topography of the land through which it flows. And yet something about a river never changes. There is something dependable, familiar, comforting about a river. A century ago Mark Twain wrote about life along the Mississippi. Society has changed tremendously since then, but what he wrote still speaks to us. The waters of the river Twain knew are the waters we still see. We who live near the headwaters can feel some kinship with those on the delta in Louisiana. It's the same river.

If you navigate a river, you can get to know its character: where the treacherous waters are, where the river runs smooth, where there is a good place to put in or get out. And yet you will never have the same ride twice. Your trip depends on the season, the weather—all sorts of conditions. You can maintain some measure of control over your course, but it is the river itself that is ultimately in control. Successful navigation depends on your openness to listen to the river and to go where it takes you.

A river is both a source of security and a challenge to self-assurance. A river connects us to a people and to a past.

The faith of the Church flows down to us through time. It connects us instantly with saints of old, yet it flows as fresh for us as it did at its source. God is a God of history. God is, to some extent, revealed in the cycles of the seasons, in the stars that shine from the heavens. But God is best revealed in how God deals with human beings in history. God is a God of history. God is a God of stories. It is in stories about God's acts in history that God reveals most fully who God really is.

God's nature is constant; it never changes. Yet with each new revelation we understand God anew. The stories of God's mighty acts are the same as when we first heard them as children in Sunday school. Yet each time we hear them, they offer fresh insight into eternal Truth. The stories tell us about ancient peoples with limited understandings of the universe, and strange, culturally conditioned expressions of faith. Yet their experience of the divine is strangely familiar and surprisingly relevant.

On this night we plunge headlong into the river of faith. In this ancient liturgy we hear the stories of salvation history: how God has been working from the beginning to bring order out of chaos, salvation to the doomed, redemption to the enslaved, and life to the dead. Tonight we are touched again by the waters of our own baptism: waters connecting us to the saints, martyrs, and apostles of ages past, to prophets and priests in ancient Israel, to Moses, to patriarchs and matriarchs, to Noah and his family, and to the common ancestors of all humanity.

Through the waters of our baptism we gain entry into this ever-flowing stream of divine experience, for these are the same waters over which the Holy Spirit moved in the beginning. They are the same waters that God separated in creation, the same waters with which God cleansed the earth in the flood and preserved a remnant of faithful people, the very same waters that God separated in the Red Sea, delivering the children of Israel from slavery in Egypt, and creating thereby a new nation. These are the same waters that poured forth from a rock in the wilderness to preserve God's people until they entered the Promised Land.

It is the same God who has created us and all that we see and don't see. It is the same God who has intruded on human history time and again to reveal himself in new, unexpected, and glorious ways. We celebrate our participation in the ongoing, living tradition of faith in this most awesome God. As we navigate this river of faith, we often find out afresh that it is not we who are in charge. The tradition *is*, as we have received it, even when we don't agree with it, even when we have trouble believing it. The stories speak to us and shape us, as we struggle to discover how these stories and our own stories work together to reveal and glorify the living God. The power of these stories carries us on. That power can buoy us up, even when we feel completely helpless. No two faith journeys are exactly alike, but if we learn to listen to the tradition, through Scripture, the history of the Church, and each other's histories as well, we will finally be led to where we need to go.

When I was a child and didn't yet know how to swim, I was afraid of the water. I remember my father standing in water that was over my head and coaxing me to jump. "I'll catch you," he assured me. It was not that I didn't trust my father, that I didn't believe he would catch me, or that he wasn't strong enough to hold me up. But he looked awful far away, and that water looked awful deep. But finally I found the courage to leap. First there was a feeling of falling, of being totally out of control. I hit the water and my head went under. Panic. Mouth full of water, and gasping for breath. Then, my father's arms were around me, and I was safe.

As we come to the water's edge of the great river of faith, those waters may appear very frightening. There is the cross of Christ. And it is our cross as well. Identification with him is a participation in his death. All we can think of is what we will lose. Somehow we find the courage to take the plunge. We hit the water. Our head goes under; we are in darkness. The tomb of Christ is ours as well. Then, we feel a power, see a light. We are raised with Christ to new life.

This night we celebrate our new life in Christ. We praise the God who continually reveals himself—merciful, loving, gracious, and strong to save. We follow in faith, navigating a course that is familiar, known to us from the stories we have received and pass on. But it is also a course that is as unique as our individual experience, and unpredictable as well.

Continue to work in human history, O God! Continue to remind us of what we know. Continue to surprise and challenge us with what we would never expect. Continue to send forth your living waters, that our witness, our stories, may be enfolded into the sacred story, that we may become instruments of your salvation!

Jeffrey A. Packard is rector of Christ Church, Coudersport,
and vicar of All Saints' Church, Brookland, Pennsylvania.

A Reason for Wounds in a Risen Body

John 20:19–31
Patricia Templeton

FATHER LEO, a crotchety old Catholic priest on the now-defunct TV show *Nothing Sacred*, has a serious problem. He is having doubts about one of the core doctrines of the Christian faith, Jesus' resurrection from the dead.

For a long time Father Leo's doubts keep him out of the pulpit. But finally, he stands before the congregation and shares with them his struggle. "I just can't understand why, if God were going to raise his son from the dead, he left those five gaping wounds," Leo says. "If God were going to make Jesus alive again, why not heal him? If he were my son, I would heal him."

Leo's question has a certain plausibility. Why would God overcome *death*, but leave the scars that caused this death so plainly visible? Why must Jesus enter everlasting life eternally bearing the wounds of life on earth—the nail marks in his hands and feet, the scar from the spear that pierced his side—plainly visible to all?

Today, we hear the story of another man who has doubts about the Resurrection. Thomas is not there on Easter night when Jesus suddenly appears in the locked room where the rest of the disciples huddle in fear, wondering if the authorities who killed Jesus are now after them.

Thomas hears his friends' fantastic story that Jesus has risen from the dead, hears them claim that they have seen him with their own eyes. But Thomas is not buying it. "Unless I see the mark of the nails in his hands, and put my finger in the mark of the nails and my hand in his side, I will not believe," Thomas says.

Within a week Thomas gets his chance. The disciples, including Thomas, are once again together in the house when Jesus suddenly appears among them. "Peace be with you," he says.

And then Jesus looks directly at Thomas. "Put your finger here and see my hands," he tells his friend. "Reach out your hand and put it in my side. Do not doubt but believe."

It is not until Thomas puts his hands in the wounds that he knows that Jesus is truly alive. It is not until he sees and touches the scars that he can proclaim, "My Lord and my God!" The wounds prove to Thomas that the risen Jesus is real.

That is why God does not heal Jesus' wounds, why the scars of this life follow him into eternal life. The wounded Christ comes to us saying, "Peace be with you," and invites us to feel his wounds, to touch his scars. And in doing so, Christ also touches the wounded places of our lives.

Not one of us goes through life unscarred. Even if we do not have physical scars on our bodies, we all have emotional and spiritual scars—wounds of loneliness and loss, wounds of rejection and despair, wounds of failure and fear. But we are reluctant to show our wounds. Unlike the risen Christ who openly invites us to touch his scarred and wounded body, we hide our imperfections, pretending that we are whole even if we are slowly bleeding to death.

The wounded Christ shows us that we must not deny our own wounds. The wounded Christ comes to us and shows us the Savior does not wait until we are perfect to meet us. The wounded Christ meets us at the places of our own wounds. It is through them that we enter each other's lives.

In the movie *Regarding Henry*, Harrison Ford plays a successful lawyer whose life takes a tragic turn when he is shot in the head during a robbery. Henry physically recovers from his brush with death, but his emotional and mental recoveries are much slower. Henry remembers little about his past life. His young daughter, Rachel, has to reintroduce herself to him. The father and daughter who were once close are now like strangers, hesitant and unsure of how to act around each other.

One day Rachel is showing her father family pictures, explaining to him the people and events of his own past. Suddenly she is silent, staring at her father's forehead and the jagged scar that rages across it. Henry meets her gaze. Then wordlessly he takes his daughter's hand and guides it to his forehead. Silently, slowly, softly she caresses his wound. Then Rachel wordlessly takes her father's hand and guides it to her ankle. A ragged scar, the result of a bicycle accident her father no longer remembers, twists its way around her leg. Silently, slowly, softly he caresses it. And in that moment father and daughter are no longer strangers. In touching each other's wounds they have entered each other's lives. Their wounds tell who they are, prove to each other that they are truly alive.

It is not only individuals who are wounded. Communities also carry scars. "You are the body of Christ," Paul tells the church in Corinth. The wounds that are borne in Christ's body are also borne in the body of the Church.

The wounds of the Episcopal Church have been very public in recent years. Wounds of division and alienation, wounds of accusations of heresy and unfaithfulness, wounds caused by fights over who should be allowed in the body and who should be kept out.

But in recent days I have experienced a different kind of wound in the body of Christ. St. Ann's Episcopal Church in Nashville, my home parish, was deeply wounded by a tornado that struck Nashville. The one-hundred-sixteen-year-old church, proud of its Tiffany stained-glass windows and place on the National Historical Register, is now reduced to rubble, a gaping hole in its side.

Yesterday my husband and I joined the steady stream of parishioners and friends who went to see the wounds with our own eyes, to put our own hands in the pierced side of the body of Christ. I stood in the rain and looked with tears and disbelief. The back pew, the one into which I slipped one Sunday morning thirteen years ago, not really sure why I was coming back to church after more than a decade away—the pew was gone. The pulpit from which I preached my first sermon—gone. The spot where I knelt to be ordained a deacon—gone.

Of course, I had known all of that from watching the news. I knew that the physical body of St. Ann's, that physical body that I love so much, was dead. But in touching those wounds, putting my hands in the gaping side, I, along with others who were drawn to the site, knew that this Body of Christ is still alive—the Body of Christ that welcomed me into its fold. That experience challenged me to grow in faith, that called me forth into leadership. The Body that gave me the truest glimpses I've ever seen of the Kingdom of God, that sent me to seminary and nurtured and sustained me while I was there. The Body of Christ is still alive.

And today the members of that Body gather together in the rubble to worship. They come together in the ruins to hear the risen Christ say, "Peace be with *you*." They come to hear the wounded Christ say to *them*, "Put your finger here and see my hands. Reach out your hand and put it in my side. Do not doubt, but believe."

And I have no doubt that the people gathered in the rubble this morning will believe. I have no doubt that when they proclaim, "Alleluia! Christ is risen! The Lord is risen indeed. Alleluia!" they will shout it out.

"The devastation is amazing," says St. Ann's rector, Lisa Hunt. "But the good news is that we are still the people of God. We will continue on."

I have no doubt that this wounded Body of Christ will live and continue to bring healing to a broken, wounded world.

Patricia Templeton is associate rector of St. Timothy's Church,
Signal Mountain, Tennessee.

Second Sunday of Easter

Encountering a Singularity

John 20:19–31
Franklin E. Vilas

SEVERAL WEEKS ago, sixty of our parishioners had the privilege of listening to a lecture by the Reverend Dr. Keith Ward, Regis Professor of Divinity at Oxford University, who addressed our adult forum. Dr. Ward gave a powerful presentation on the history of the interface between religion and science. In his lecture, he described that moment wherein, according to current scientific theory, the total matter of the universe, encompassed in a tiny, dense mass, exploded in the event from which our universe originated—an event popularly known as the "Big Bang."

In his vivid account of this event, Dr. Ward called it "the Mother of All Singularities." What existed before this event can never be known from the perspective of human beings (living, as we do, *within* the universe). To the best of our knowledge, in the story of this universe, at least, the Big Bang was, indeed, a singularity—something utterly unique.

For Christians, the event we know as the Resurrection is another such singularity: an explosion into history of forces beyond our comprehension, an event in the realm of human experience with consequences as real to our future as those of the expanding universe. Easter is not just another pretty story, but the expansion of matter into spirit, of time into eternity.

For those of you who, like me, have a smattering of scientific knowledge developed at the end of the Newtonian age, both the Big Bang and the Resurrection are hard to comprehend. As a natural skeptic, I find a friend in the apostle Thomas, who just could not take in what was for him "the Mother of All Singularities." He was the disciple with our age's concern for scientific certainty. He was the kind of person who does not rush to conclusions based on emotional reactions, without first weighing and considering all of the available evidence. Thomas was a realist. He was also a brave and faithful friend of Jesus.

It is Thomas who, as Jesus leads his disciples toward Jerusalem, understands the danger into which they are walking. He is not blinded by the acclaim of the crowds. He is cognizant of the peril that faces them all. Yet Thomas is the one, aware of the danger that lies ahead, who says to his friends, "Come, let us go too, that we may die with him."

Good, brave, courageous, realistic Thomas—whose willingness to follow Jesus to Jerusalem is the more impressive *because* of his realism! At the meal in the upper room, Jesus speaks in symbols—a language hard for Thomas to comprehend. His mind is fixed on the door to the room, a door liable to be broken down at any moment by the angry officials of Jerusalem!

Thomas is listening partially to Jesus and partially to the sounds in the street outside. If anyone is on watch this night, it is Thomas. With growing agitation he hears Jesus speak of heavenly mansions. He is sure that this Master whom he has followed through the dusty roads of Palestine is facing death. Small wonder that his anxiety cannot be contained and that he interrupts Jesus' discourse to voice his doubt: "Lord, we don't know where you are going; how can we know the way?"

It is unlikely that Thomas finds much comfort in Jesus' answer—"I am the Way, the Truth, and the Life." For Thomas, this would be just another riddle, inappropriate in a time of mortal danger. I am sure he is like many men in our culture, their thinking function far better developed than their feeling function. More head than heart. Slow to express deep emotions. Better at business than human relations.

With his particular character, I suspect that Thomas does not have much use for the more emotional and volatile of the apostles. He has probably watched in disgust over the years during the outbursts of Peter and the others watched their willingness to believe everything without question, their failure to understand the political implications of what Jesus has been doing.

And now, at last, there has been this tale of Mary and the other women at the grave. And this claim by the men that Jesus has appeared to them in the upper room. Thomas probably has been out, walking the streets with his own silent grief, while the rumored appearance is taking place. And this story is too much to take. He wants to believe, God knows! He envies the other apostles their simple faith. But he is just not made that way. And so he lays down his terms. "Unless I see the mark of the nails in his hands, and put my finger in the mark of the nails, and my hand in his side, I will not believe!"

I wonder what the next week is like for Thomas. Overwhelming confusion and pain! He has been asked to do something that has been impossible for him in the past. He is being asked to put his brain into neutral and his heart in full gear. He has heard his friends talking about their experiences of the past week, and he has probably grilled them over and over, trying to find holes in their stories.

Thomas has been on the road with Jesus, seen apparent miracles of healing, sat and listened with rapt attention to the powerful teachings. His loyalty has been won, and he has followed this strange rabbi into the teeth of danger. But now he faces what Keith Ward has called a "singularity," a unique experience in the natural order. He is asked to make a leap of faith that goes totally against his grain.

Then, a week later, the disciples meet again in the same place. The doors are shut again, locked against enemies, real or imagined. Suddenly, Jesus is there. And this time, so is Thomas. The risen Lord says to his skeptical apostle, "Put your finger here and see my hands. Reach out your hand and put it in my side. Do not doubt, but believe."

Can you imagine the rush of emotion that sweeps over Thomas as, in the face of all reason, Jesus stands before him? Suddenly the floodgates open. It is not that his thinking function is obliterated, but it gives way to a deeper understanding of a deeper reality. Dimensions of life he has never dreamed of appear before him. He falls to his knees with an explosive declaration of faith: "My Lord and my God!"

In this Gospel story, Jesus meets the needs and demands of his skeptical apostle—and in meeting them he utters the words that rush through the years to meet us, a generation of skeptics. "Have you believed because you have seen me? Blessed are those who have not seen and yet have come to believe."

Through the centuries, particularly in this last century, as science has pushed back boundaries that had been shrouded in mystery, claims about the resurrection of Jesus have seemed increasingly at odds with the world as we know it. Yet now, as Keith Ward has told us, the fields of quantum theory and astronomy have opened up worlds beyond the solid certainty of Newtonian physics. That we should have originated in "the Mother of All Singularities," the Big Bang, opens the way for our consideration of other singularities, for a breaking of energies and powers beyond our present understanding into what we know as "time."

It is the Christian claim and the promise of Easter that such a singularity occurred in the Resurrection, that the One described in the Revelation to John as "the Alpha and Omega, the beginning and the end," has moved in a singular way, breaking the bonds of death and introducing into history that energy, and that grace, which we know as eternal life.

Even with our skeptical modern minds at Easter we, too, may find the presence of the risen Christ a living reality. We also may open our hearts of faith, fall before the One who stretches out the arms of victorious love, and proclaim the explosive affirmation of joyful recognition: "My Lord and my God!"

Franklin E. Vilas is rector of St. Paul's Church, Chatham, New Jersey.

SECOND SUNDAY OF EASTER

Faith at Our Fingertips
John 20:19–31
Margaret Bullitt-Jonas

CHRIST IS risen. He is out of the box, out of the tomb. He's out and about. John's Gospel shows Christ breaking into a room even though the doors are locked. The reading from Acts shows how an angel of God opened the prison doors, setting the apostles free to speak the words they had been given to speak. The risen Christ is breaking in, breaking out. And yet, there are some folks who have their doubts.

I want to say a word about *two kinds* of doubt. Let's begin with so-called Doubting Thomas. He's the guy who wasn't there when the risen Christ appeared to the other disciples. When they report having seen Jesus, Thomas won't take their word for it. "Unless I see the mark of the nails in his hands, and put my finger in the mark of the nails and my hand in his side, I will not believe."

What do you think about that statement? Do you think less of him because he's not willing to believe the news of the Resurrection unless he can see the evidence with his own eyes, touch it with his hands? To me, Thomas sounds like the sort of guy who isn't willing to settle for secondhand truth. He's not going to believe something just because his father or his mother told him that it's true, or because his teacher says he should swallow it whole, no questions asked, or because anyone else in authority says it's so. "Because I said so, that's why" is not the sort of argument that will wash with Thomas. No, he wants to know about the Resurrection for himself. He wants to see the risen Christ with his own two eyes, touch him with his own two hands.

And when indeed the risen Christ appears to Thomas, what does Christ say to him? "Put your finger here and see my hands. Reach out your hand and put it in my side. Do not doubt but believe." Jesus welcomes Thomas and all his doubt. Jesus knows that doubt like the doubt of Thomas is energizing. When we want to know the truth for ourselves in our own experience, we set out on a spiritual quest, a search for our own authentic faith. Doubt is like wind in the sails of faith: it pushes us forward; it dares us to reach out, to risk, to learn. It is doubt and the desire to question, to test, to probe that has set many a spiritual pilgrim to try out the experiment of starting a practice of regular prayer or engaging in reflection or spiritual reading. Doubt may be uncomfortable; it may make us restless, but it will keep us awake and honest with ourselves, and it may blow us to explore uncharted seas.

What about the other kind of doubt? I am thinking now about the beginning of the story, when the disciples are huddled together in a locked-up room, as the text says, "for fear of the Jews." What does this mean? Are they afraid that the Jewish authorities will come after them because they are accomplices of an executed criminal? Are they afraid that the Jewish leaders will accuse them of conspiring to steal away Jesus' body from the tomb? Or could it be that it is Jesus himself they are afraid of? Jesus, another Jew, a Jew whom they abandoned at the end, whom one of them denied three times? Are they huddled in fear because they've heard rumors of the Resurrection and are full of guilt and anxiety?

Have you ever wronged someone and then been ashamed to look them in the eye? Have you ever found yourself avoiding someone because you know you treated that person badly? I wonder if it was something like that with the disciples. Imagine their reaction, then, when Jesus appears before them and his first words are "Peace be with you." It is peace he brings them. Forgiveness. Acceptance. However much they've abandoned and denied him, he loves them still.

"Here," he says to them. "See my wounded hands and side. It is I. And I love you. I will never leave you."

And it is not only peace that he gives them. He gives them a commission, a task. "As the Father has sent me, so I send you." Christ not only loves us and forgives us, Christ needs us. We have been sent here on a mission. We have a job to do. When I look at this story of Jesus and the disciples, I see Jesus confronting the kind of doubt that walls itself up in a locked room and says, "I've done wrong. I'm not good enough to show my face. In my heart of hearts I don't think it's true that God loves me or desires me or needs me. I don't believe it."

If that conversation is going on somewhere inside you, today Jesus comes to say, "Peace be with you. I've forgiven what you have done wrong, and I will give you the strength to amend your life. All that stuff you keep telling yourself about not being good enough, about not measuring up, about being inadequate—all that focus on your own sinfulness—that is one big red herring, a self-absorbed preoccupation that prevents you from seeing how much I love you, how much I desire you."

Is it possible that what you and I call our "doubts" about God—our doubts, say, about the goodness of God or the existence of God—are sometimes a way of protecting ourselves from the intimacy that God longs to offer us? For that is what God so desires: to be intimate with us, to draw close. The whole of Scripture can be read as a love story in which God constantly woos, seeks, and appeals to creation, trying to draw us close, longing for our loving response. Will we say yes to God's love?

To Thomas, who refuses to believe unless he can see Jesus with his own eyes and touch him with his hands, Jesus says, "Draw close. Gaze at me. Stretch out your hands and touch me. I am as close as your fingertips." To the disciples who hide out in a locked room, awash in fear and guilt, Jesus comes and says, "Peace. I forgive you. I love you. Today I send you out, as the Father sent me. Let me blow my breath into you so that, with every breath, you breathe in my Spirit. I am with you. You are mine. I will be with you to the end."

Some of us today will stretch out our hands to receive the body and blood of Christ, just as Thomas longed to stretch out his hands to touch Christ's wounded hands and side. We too long to know that the risen Christ is real, alive, here with us, and we will meet him today in the bread and wine of the Eucharist. Some of us will meet the risen Christ in the hands that touch our heads as we come forward for his healing. Whatever our doubts today, whatever our misgivings, wherever we're holding back, Jesus invites us to step forward, to step out, to accept the gift of his intimacy.

Margaret Bullitt-Jonas is associate rector of All Saints' Church,
Brookline, Massachusetts.

SIXTH SUNDAY OF EASTER

Comforter—Counselor—Advocate

John 14:23–29
John P. Streit, Jr.

ON OUR BED at home is a wonderfully thick, puffy, down comforter. In the winter it seems womb-like in its warmth and in the sense of security it provides. It makes you feel happy to crawl into bed, especially when it is really, really cold outside. It breathes, as they say, and so we keep it on the bed year round. Somehow its fluffy bulk allows air to circulate so it doesn't feel too hot, even in the summer. We sleep under it, except on the most oppressive and stifling nights. It is well named, our comforter. It comforts us, helps us feel secure, safe, comfortable in our bed. It helps us sleep. I'm very glad we have it.

At the Last Supper, Jesus is telling his disciples that he will not be physically with them much longer, that he is going to his Father's to prepare a place for them. He tells them that he will not leave them desolate, nor will God. He tells them that God will send to them the Holy Spirit, who will teach them and help them remember all the things that Jesus has taught and showed them. Jesus uses a name for the Holy Spirit. In Greek, the language in which the Gospels were written, that word is *paraclete*. The word has been translated a number of ways. In the King James version, the much beloved English translation that was the standard for three centuries, the Greek word *paraclete* is translated as *comforter*.

It sounds immediately reassuring. Jesus is leaving. He understands that this separation will make the disciples anxious. His physical absence from them changes everything. Now they will be the bearers of the Gospel in the world. This will be strange and hard for them, so Jesus tells them that God will send a Comforter to help them, to reassure them, to make them feel more secure and safe—much as they have felt in his presence before.

The trouble is, Christianity is not about being comfortable or safe. Even the most superficial look at Jesus' life and message leads one to conclude that any follower of this man is in for a wild ride.

"Follow me," says Jesus, as he crashes headlong into the established religious rules and the powers-that-be. "Follow me," says Jesus, as his words and actions so alarm one of this own disciples that he turns Jesus over to the authorities, who then trump up charges, so that his growing popularity among the people can be nipped in the bud. "Follow me," says Jesus, as the occupying political force plays out its role by executing him, with some pretense at reluctance. (Leaders who try to maintain power by force and oppression are always alert to potential unrest and are never really reluctant to remove anyone who provides even a hint of trouble.) "Take up *your* cross and follow me," says Jesus. This is not exactly a safe or comfortable invitation.

For almost three centuries English-speaking people read that Jesus told his disciples that God would send them the Holy Spirit, the Comforter; but that isn't quite right. When the King James translation was revised, the Revised Version translated *paraclete* as *counselor*. Not comforter, but counselor. And most recently, in the New Revised Standard Version, the one we use, the word *paraclete* is translated as *advocate*.

Comforter, Counselor, Advocate. It makes an interesting lesson in translation. It is a gentle reminder for people who believe that every word in the Bible is literally true because it is the Word of God. Even if this were true, we need to remember that we are not reading the words of God, but the translations of the original words. (Most biblical literalists don't read the text in the original Hebrew or Greek.) And so, if we are aiming for literal truth, which one of the names for the Holy Spirit is literally true: Comforter? Counselor? Advocate?

This is where it is important to move from linguistics to life, from strict academics to our own experience. The question isn't ultimately about Greek but about God. How does God's Holy Spirit move in your life? How *do* we experience the Holy Spirit?

Of course there is no single answer, particularly when we keep in mind Jesus' description (earlier in the Gospel of John) that the spirit is like the wind. It blows where it wills, and we cannot predict from whence it will come or whither it will go. How does the Holy Spirit move in your life?

Let me give a couple of examples of how it works for me. I woke up recently on a Monday, my day off, and thought about what I might do. Out of the blue I remembered a friend whom I hadn't seen for well over a month, a friend who is very, very sick. I called his home to see if I could come out and visit that morning. His wife answered the phone. She sounded startled and told me that she had just finished writing a letter to me. Her husband was not doing well. He had fallen a couple of weeks before and broken his leg, and he was very weak. I asked if I could come to see him. She assured me that a visit would be welcome. And so I went.

Why did I think of him that morning? What caused me to remember him when I got up? Nothing happened that overtly called him to mind. He just popped into my head, all of a sudden, absolutely unbidden. I would say that somehow, in some way, the Holy Spirit brought him to mind. And I was free to respond or not. I felt no compulsion to call and arrange a visit, but somehow it seemed important. I wanted to, and so I did.

The visit wasn't comfortable, at least in the way I would normally describe "comfortable." He is dying, and so there is sadness. But there is not just sadness. Visiting him, I am reminded of the richness of his life, my many memories of all the kindness he and his wife have shown our family. When our son, Josh, was little, we would drop him off at their home for them to baby sit. I was glad I went to see my friend.

I felt nudged by the Holy Spirit, encouraged to be my best self. I would not say the Holy Spirit comforted me so much as prodded me, invited me to do something that was very important. Of course, I can't prove to you, or to anyone, that this was God's spirit working in my life. I didn't hear God's voice commanding me to go see Tom. There was no angelic presence, no heavenly visitor. It was pretty ordinary, and not very spectacular. And I couldn't even swear that it wasn't just my own thoughts, my own feelings, that somehow called him to mind. But my experience was different from the usual, in that I wasn't thinking about him at all, when out of nowhere I remembered Tom, and it seemed important for me to go see him.

A couple of years ago I had been visiting a young boy in the hospital who was also very sick, essentially in a coma. At the end of the workday, I would go down to the hospital to check in with him and his parents, usually his mother, to see how she was doing and how her son was. I would pray with her, spend a little time, and then go on home.

One day, in the middle of the day, someone canceled an appointment with me, giving me a free hour before my next meeting. I was getting ready to return some phone calls, when suddenly it occurred to me that I could go to the hospital, have a short visit, and still be back in time for my next meeting. Somehow that felt right, and so I did.

I missed my next meeting, because when I got to the hospital the boy was dying. I stayed with him and his family as he died. It was profound, and holy. It wasn't comfortable. If I had known what I was going to face, I would probably have been anxious, if not terrified. But it was so sacred, and so important, and I was so glad to have been able to be there.

Why did I go? I hadn't really been thinking about him, and God knows there were plenty of tasks that I needed to do. But somehow it popped into my head to go right then. Once I thought of it I was free not to go. I could have attended to some of the work that always piles up on my desk. But I didn't, and I'm glad. Again, it felt as though the Holy Spirit was moving in my life, helping me do something that mattered, that would have been too late to do if I had waited until the end of the day.

What is the best name for this mysterious presence of God in our lives? Is it comforting? Not entirely, not solely. Is God's Spirit like a counselor? In a way, but often it is more than that. Is the Holy Spirit like an advocate? At times, if an advocate is one who helps us by reminding us what we are capable of being or doing, who nudges us into new places, or at least nudges us into being our best selves, or perhaps better selves.

This advocacy may be quiet, almost unnoticeable as God's Spirit, or it may be more forceful, more unmistakable. Martin Luther King, Jr., often talked about an experience he had, late one night, sitting alone at his kitchen table. It was early in his ministry, as the civil rights struggle was just beginning. King was feeling the enormity of the task ahead. He was feeling the animosity and hatred of many and the indifference of many more. As he began to feel more and more overwhelmed, he had a sudden feeling of the presence of God, not in a vague, "spiritual" way, but as a concrete presence, as someone who was really there with him. Dr. King got a strong, clear sense that God was with him, not just at that moment in his kitchen, but God would be with him in all he faced. He would not be alone.

King never forgot that experience. It was always real for him, and it changed everything for him. That experience of God's presence allowed him to continue moving forward into seemingly impossible situations. It helped him to keep focused and centered in the midst of all the hatred and opposition the civil rights movement faced from without, and all the confusion and conflicting ideas that arose from within the civil rights movement.

Jesus promised that God would send the Holy Spirit, the paraclete, a comforter, a counselor, an advocate. The reality of that promise is more important than the accuracy or precision of the language by which we understand it.

Pay attention. Listen. Be alert to the ways God moves in your own life. Have the courage to follow where the Spirit beckons you. It will change everything.

John P. Streit, Jr., is dean of the Cathedral Church of Saint Paul, Boston, Massachusetts.

THE DAY OF PENTECOST

Accomplishments and Meetings

Acts 2:1–11
J. Barrington Bates

HAVE YOU seen those posters and billboards and announcements all over town? I encounter them when driving, when riding on the municipal railway. I even see them pasted on street-corner kiosks. This particular ad is published by the company known as "3M." It isn't very glitzy. On a plain white background are printed only two words. The first, written three times: *Meetings, Meetings, Meetings.* Each is crossed out with a rough red stroke of what appears to be a gigantic crayon. The other word? Also written three times: *Accomplish, Accomplish, Accomplish.*

The people at 3M are reacting to a common phenomenon among professional people who spend so much time in meetings that there's no time to get anything done. I understand this, believe me. I've been here just a few weeks, and already I'm spending the bulk of my time meeting with people, in conversations short and long, on the telephone, via e-mail, in person, in groups large and small, and in many one-to-one discussions.

We can easily get frustrated by all this. Not that we don't enjoy the conversations. Not that it isn't good for us to engage in them. Not that we could do our work without such meetings. But I ask myself, "When am I going to get this sermon written, prepare that lesson plan, or write this letter?"

We know the phenomenon: "How can I get the report done on time if I have to spend half my week attending these inane meetings?" "I spend so much time driving my kids around to ballet, soccer, Scouts, school, and tutoring, that I have no time for anything else." It's no better for kids: "After I go to ballet, soccer, Scouts, school, tutoring, and a party or two, there's no time to do my homework." Or, how about this: "I volunteer in the church office, serve on two committees, and play bridge every week. There's just no time to cook supper anymore. I'm so busy meeting people, I can't get anything done."

3M thinks it has the answer to the problem: skip the meetings, just cross them off your calendar. Now, they also want us to invest in their products, of course, but they want us to buy their stuff and ditch all the meetings, so that we can accomplish, accomplish, accomplish.

If we didn't have meetings, we could find the time to read a book or even *write* a book. We could finally get around to cleaning out the garage, finding a better job, making long-put-off plans. If we didn't have meetings, we could just work, work, work like busy bees. We'd save energy. We'd save money. We'd get things done. Not meetings, meetings, meetings, but just accomplish, accomplish, accomplish.

3M's advertisement may be helpful in the world of sticky tape and not-so-sticky note pads; but to me it seems dangerous for those who call themselves Christians. On this day of Pentecost, I declare to you that 3M has got it backwards.

"When the day of Pentecost had come, they were all together in one place," says today's appointed reading from the Acts of the Apostles. *Together.* That's a meeting, isn't it? The Christian life is *about* meetings. About gathering together to meet and worship God. About coming together in one place to celebrate. These are meetings we can't give up, because they define, exemplify, and proclaim who we are.

But how can we get anything done? How can we accomplish, accomplish, accomplish? And that's the best part: *we* don't have to. Christian people don't have to *do* anything. The most important things about our life, our world, our very existence—those are already taken care of by the God who created us, redeemed us, and loves us more than we can imagine.

Accomplished is the amazing fact of our creation. Where we came from is a mystery so profound that it leads some to write stories of how this could have happened. It leads others to probing scientific investigation. But the fact remains, we're here. We didn't evolve ourselves, or create ourselves, or order ourselves out of a catalogue. God accomplished our existence, whether through a Big Bang or seven days of speeches. And it doesn't matter because, either way, it's a done deal.

Accomplished is the most amazing feat of all: the incarnation of God. Jesus, born of a woman and yet God, born in a barn and yet still King of all creation.

God did not visit us, the way gods of ancient Greece and Rome did. God became fully human, to see us more clearly and love us more dearly. God meets us *as one of us*, knows our joy, and shares our pain.

Accomplished is the ministry and witness of Jesus Christ, the miracles, the healings, the preaching, the stories. Pay attention to the theme here: throughout his ministry, Jesus is seldom alone. He is almost always meeting with someone. Oh, sure, he spent forty days in the wilderness, but even there he was tempted by the Devil and ministered to by the angels. The times when Jesus was alone are few and far between, and the day of Pentecost is *not* one of them. "Peace be with you," Jesus says today. And he, like us, needs to say it to someone.

Accomplished is the betrayal, the agony and suffering, the outrageous and shameful death. Something else that can be accomplished only when two or three are gathered together: God, hanging on the cross, dying. Even here, the meeting is really what we remember: Jesus, in his agony, speaks those "seven last words." He's meeting the people around him, saying, among other things, "It is finished," or, in another translation—"It is *accomplished*." And he's not talking about the death of the body, either. For . . .

Accomplished is the mighty resurrection and glorious ascension. So amazing, so bizarre, so unbelievable. The one who was nailed to the cross and buried in the tomb is not only alive, but thriving. That first Easter Day, Jesus walked and talked and ate and drank. After many convincing proofs of his resurrection, the Scripture tells us, Jesus was lifted up into the clouds to sit at God's right hand. That's done.

Accomplished today is the coming of the Holy Spirit like a violent wind, filling everyone and resting upon us. Jesus commissions his apostles, as he commissions us, breathing the prayer, "As the Father has sent me, so I send you." We don't need to accomplish anything, or prepare ourselves, or even wait around for this rapturous event; it has already happened.

And through all this amazing mystery, *accomplished*, too, is our salvation. A place for each and every one of us is reserved at the heavenly table. Not a place at the head of the table if we're *good*, a place *serving* at that table if we're *not* so good, or *no* place at *any* table if we're *bad*. Jesus, who knows us too well, is saving a place for each of us.

If ever someone asks, "When were you saved?" you can answer with confidence, "On Good Friday." We don't need to do anything, for all we can imagine and hope is already accomplished. Our names are written in the book, and we are marked as Christ's own forever.

Accomplish, accomplish, accomplish? God already has. What's left for us as a Christian people—our ministry and mission as individuals—what's left is the very thing 3M thinks we should avoid: meetings, meetings, meetings.

Imagine a world like that, one in which we listen attentively to the one who stutters, not interrupting so we can get to the matter more quickly. Imagine a world in which we go out of our way to discover people unknown to us, and seek out new experiences, instead of sticking only to our same friends and our familiar ways. A world in which we stand amidst every group we encounter and say, "Peace be with you" instead of "Let's get down to business."

Well, look around you, and behold that world. It is accomplished—all of it. And our vocation and ministry as Christian people is simply to come to the meetings, meetings, meetings—to meet the Spirit who flows through the world like a rushing wind, to meet the Christ in everyone we encounter, to meet the God who come to us in bread and wine.

J. Barrington Bates is assistant to the rector at St. Francis' Episcopal Church, San Francisco, California, and chaplain at San Francisco State University.

4

PROPER TEN

The Kingdom's Unexpected Friends

Luke 10:25–37
Susan W. Klein

HAVE YOU EVER owned a car that was a lemon? I've owned two or three. One of them, as soon as the one-year warranty ran out, proceeded to require the help of a mechanic at least once a month. No matter what the *solution* was, the *problem* was that the car would just stop. After owning it for two years, I decided that the only hope for the thing was an exorcism, but nobody knew how to perform one on cars.

One evening, quite late at night returning home, I had to pull over suddenly onto the shoulder of the road because once again the car had simply died. Those were the days before car phones and emergency assistance phones. I got out, put the hood up, and decided I'd just have to wait until some friendly police officer drove by.

Moments later, a rusty, dented pick-up truck pulled off the highway and parked in front of me. The truck was plastered with stickers advertising extremist political causes to the right of center. An honest-to-God shotgun was attached to the gun rack. Out of the driver's side came a very tall white man, large-bellied, wearing blue jeans and a cowboy hat. As he got closer, I could smell beer. My anxiety level exploded. The man asked if I needed help. I told him the problem. He looked at the engine and told me he thought he could fix it. Sure, I thought, that's probably what the Boston Strangler said.

I don't remember what he said the problem was, but I'll never forget what he did next. He took a large wad of chewing gum out of his mouth, put it on something in the engine, and told me to try to start the car. Skeptical, I turned the key. The car started. "Take it to a garage when you get home," he said, and roared off in his truck.

I was vulnerable that night. The story could have turned out differently than it did. How thankful I was that the man had a compassionate heart. He was not the Boston Strangler. For me, he was the Good Samaritan

The parable of the Good Samaritan: what a beautiful and powerful story Jesus tells in Luke's Gospel. A man, attacked by thieves and left on the road to die, is cared for, ministered to, saved. He is shown compassion. He is loved where he is, for no apparent reason other than that he is suffering. A stranger takes the risk of helping the man. The stranger takes money from his purse, time from his life. He cares so much that he takes the man to an inn for rest and recovery.

There is probably no one in this room who has not been helped by a Good Samaritan. Thank God for all of them. Without Good Samaritans there would be no soul, no heart, no love in the world, no reason for the world to exist.

Compassion means to "suffer with." It is the feeling of being touched by the pain of another, and it often leads us to help another. Compassion is the way we fulfill the Great Commandment to love our neighbors as ourselves. It is the way we become fully human. In one of John LeCarre's books, a character says, "You have to think like a hero to behave like a decent human being." Compassion, I believe, is the content and the energy of the kingdom of God.

Compassion is the child, touched by the bird with a broken wing, bringing it home in a shoebox to heal. Compassion is the adult deciding to be a mentor for the gang member. It is the research doctor trying to find a cure for cancer, the teacher trying to teach English to the immigrant. It is you and I at our best, being good neighbors to those in need.

Jesus tells this story to enlighten the lawyer who has asked him about how to gain eternal life. The lawyer knows what he should do: love the Lord and his neighbor as himself. And he probably has a good idea of who his neighbor is: the children next door, the neighbors across the street, the family, friends and coworkers with whom he relates. The lawyer is trying to justify himself, to make sure he has it right, to guarantee that he will be fulfilling the full requirements of the law—and to tangle Jesus up in the legal technicalities in the process.

But eternal life is not a law. It is a way, a process, a journey. "Our neighbor" is anyone in need. And compassion is being touched by their need and acting on their behalf. Jesus says that when that happens, there eternal life is found. When that happens, God is there. "Go and do likewise," Jesus says.

That is a main point in Jesus' story. But, as with so many of his parables, there is more when you dig into it. Jesus is also confronting the demons of tribalism. For Jesus' listeners, this Samaritan would not have been seen as anyone with the potential to become a hero, let alone as someone whose actions would illustrate the kingdom of God.

Any Jew, attacked by thieves and left to die, would be utterly astonished to wake up in an inn and find out that his rescuer had been none other than a Samaritan. If he were a typical Judean, he would have been brainwashed from an early age about Samaritans. On his parents' laps, he would have been told something like this: *"Samaritans think that they are like us, but they really aren't. They think they are really worshiping God and serving him, but they aren't. They are not 'real' Jews like we are. They worship in a funny way in a funny place. God does not hear their prayers. A long time ago, they intermarried with our enemies the Assyrians. Who knows what they do when they get together, but you can be sure it's bad. Don't even think of being friends with one of them. Remember that girl down the street who ran away and married one, breaking her family's heart? I heard she's dying of some disease that she caught from them. Just stay away from them, whatever you do."*

How ironic that one of "them" ministered to the man that fell among thieves! In the middle of such interesting, ironical stuff, Jesus says, you find the Kingdom of God. Be careful who you hate. That very one may turn out to be the one who saves your life.

How do we tend to avoid, stigmatize, even hurt people who come from different cultures, races, and religions? Within our communities and families, how do we create monsters of people who are merely different from us or who simply have the audacity to disagree with us? Racism is a form of tribalism. Gang violence is a kind of tribalism. Many economic and political issues are rooted in tribalism. Fear of the other, fear of what is different, fear of change—fears tempt us to see as threats people who are different.

But however we may see the world and its people, by this parable Jesus suggests that is not how God sees them. Jesus was constantly antagonizing members of his own tribe by inhabiting a place outside all tribes, or in between them, and by constantly challenging his own people to be inclusive, hospitable, compassionate. Jesus was regarded by many of his own people as a traitor for bearing witness to the vision that, in God's family, there are no outsiders. Jesus paid for that vision with his life.

In this parable the outsider, the Samaritan, is inside at the center, worshiping God and fulfilling the ethical demands of loving one's neighbor as oneself. The priest and Levite, both honored for their service as temple leaders, did not have the compassion and decency of the one who was regarded as an idolater, a pagan, an untouchable. More irony. Those who are out are really in, and those who are in are really out.

Imagine how this parable would have angered Jesus' own people. The ones who appear to be holy are shamed. The ones who appear to be shameful are holy. What is lowest in the world's esteem may be highest in God's Kingdom. In a world of hierarchy, classes, races, and tribes, Jesus encourages us to question what the world holds in highest esteem; to look toward what the world regards as lowest, even the most shameful, in order to find the Kingdom of God.

This is challenging stuff. The parable of the Good Samaritan suggests a different and difficult path: a way of feeling that opens up our hearts to the infinity of the world's sorrows and doesn't tell us how far we have to go before we can close up again. The parable suggests a way of acting that could deplete even the bank account of a Bill Gates. It is a parable that frustrates even as it enlightens. "Jesus," we yearn to ask, "how much is enough?"

And as soon as we ask the question, we realize we have come full circle back to the lawyer's question, trying like he did to justify ourselves, trying to keep life safe and manageable. Jesus has no formulas. He has no laws. But he does have a story. You and I, how will we make the story end?

You see, there once was a man, beaten, robbed, stripped, left for dead. . .

Susan W. Klein is rector of St. Aidan's Church, Malibu, California.

"There Is Need of Only One Thing"

Luke 10:38–42
Martha B. Anderson

"LORD, DO you not care that my sister has left me to do all the work by myself? Tell her then to help me." And Jesus said, "Martha, Martha, you are worried and distracted by many things."

And *I* said, "Yes, sir! I am worried and distracted by *many* things. I am worried and distracted by environmental destruction, by war and drought and poverty and disease and racism. I am worried about an eighty-eight-year-old woman from my last parish whose heart is failing. I am worried about my daughter who works too hard and is always tired. I am worried about all the folks who are listening to me today, coping with all they have been through in the last year and a half. I am worried about finding enough money to pay the mortgage each month, about whether the car is parked legally, about how to find time to get my hair cut.

"And today," I said to Jesus, "I am especially worried and distracted by this story of you and me and my sister in Bethany. It worries me, because I know what you are going on to say: that Mary, sitting at your feet and listening while I slave away in the kitchen, has the 'better part.'

"And this story will be used over centuries, even millennia, as a way of typing and stereotyping women. Used as a way of dividing women, setting up conflict and competition among them. This story will be used to draw lines between introverts and extroverts, contemplatives and activists. Between quiet, modest, restrained women, and outspoken, self-assured, assertive women. Between women who decided to stay home to care for house and family, and women whose work is in offices, factories, schools, law courts, the Church.

"Because of this story, for a long time I, Martha, will take second place to my sister, Mary. I will be relegated to cooking and housekeeping. I will become the patron saint of housewives and cooks. It will be written in *Who's Who in the Bible* that my name still (at the beginning of the twenty-first century!) 'epitomizes the practical and efficient but over-busy and intolerant housekeeper.'

"Martin Luther will say to me, 'Martha, your work must be punished and counted as nought. I will have no work but the work of Mary.' There will be a women's movement in England that is *opposed* to the emancipation of women, and it will be called the 'Martha Movement.'

"Oh, there will be a few who will prefer me to Mary. They will feel sorry for me, perhaps, or will see something of themselves in my story. They will point to the story in the Gospel of John, the one of me and Mary and our brother Lazarus, in which I challenge Jesus to act and recognize him as the Messiah. In the year 1300 Meister Eckhart will preach on our story. He will praise the 'mature Martha' and criticize Mary for not being 'ready.' He will postulate that Mary sat by Jesus more out of pleasure than out of a desire to advance in spirituality. In me he will see a picture of the woman who acts responsibly, who is concerned for the world and her duties.

"In other places, at other times, legends will arise about me. In various art works I will be shown as: 'Guardian Madonna,' 'The Mature, Older Woman,' 'The Wise Virgin' (contrasted with Mary, the foolish one).

"One Martha legend will report I led an ascetic life—a vegetarian in charge of a convent. In this legend I preach, heal the sick, and even raise a dead person (a young man who wanted so desperately to hear me preach that he tried to swim across a river and drowned).

"And there is more. To me will be ascribed a traditional masculine role— victory over evil in the form of a terrible dragon! In her wonderful book, *The Women Around Jesus*, Elisabeth Moltmann-Wendel will write, 'The inhabitants of the countryside between Arles and Avignon asked for [Martha's] help. A man-eating dragon called Tarascus, half animal and half fish, fatter than an ox and longer than a horse, with teeth like swords and pointed like horns, lay submerged in the Rhone and killed anyone who tried to cross, sinking their ships. Martha went out against the dragon because the people asked her to. She found him in the forest, eating a man. Immediately she sprinkled holy water on him and set a cross before him. Thereupon he was conquered and stood like a tame lamb. Martha bound him with her girdle. After that the people came and killed him with stones and spears.'[1]

"From harried housewife to undaunted dragon-slayer—flattering perhaps, but still divisive. In these versions where I come out looking better, Mary always gets criticized and put down. However you look at the two of us, it seems, one always will have to be superior, the other inferior. When one looks good, the other looks bad. And we will become representatives of whole groups of women, Christian and other. There will be a 'Martha type,' practical, competent, down-to-earth, and a 'Mary type,' quiet, restrained, a good listener, always receptive to others. Depending on which 'type' is considered appropriate in which situation, some women will always have to scramble and go through all sorts of contortions to fit the other mold.

"So you see," I said to Jesus, "this story, and how it will be used over the years worries and distracts me greatly."

And he heard me. He said it had never been his intention to divide us. He said he thought others had done that. Beginning with Luke, the Gospel writer, then the early Church Fathers, then priests and all kinds of lay and ordained ministers and Bible commentators over the years.

He said, "You know I love you both, and I value your connection with each other, your unity and your diversity, your hospitality that both feeds me and attends to my words."

And then he said again, "Martha, Martha, you are worried and distracted by many things. There is need of only one thing."

What is that *One Thing*? Perhaps I need to find and focus upon that, so that I can stop worrying about all the rest.

Martha B. Anderson is interim priest at St. John's Church, Brooklyn, New York, and a pediatric health care professional.

---

1. Elisabeth Moltmann-Wendel, *The Women Around Jesus*, trans. John Bowden (New York: Crossroad, 1982), 43–44.

PROPER TWELVE

Innocent by Association

Genesis 18:20–33
Raewynne J. Whiteley

SODOM AND GOMORRAH.

The very words bring a shiver. They have become a byword for all that is evil, all that is depraved, and for a vengeful God who takes swift and brutal action against those who oppose him.

With a story like this one, it is no wonder that many Christians struggle with the Old Testament. We read it Sunday after Sunday (largely because the lectionary tells us to), although we often skip it, ostensibly to speed up the service. Really, I suspect, we want to avoid confronting ideas we would rather not deal with. We tend to focus on the Gospels, the stories of Jesus, where we know what to expect, where we think we understand.

Would we be better to get rid of the Old Testament, which confuses us with its apparently vindictive and angry God, remote and unsympathetic to the concerns of ordinary human beings? Should we simply concentrate on the New Testament and all it has to say to us about the God of love and peace?

I'm not convinced. I'm not convinced because the Jesus we read about was shaped and formed by the Jewish Scriptures we know today as the Old Testament. The God of that Testament is the God that Jesus knows, the God of whom Jesus speaks.

If we ignore the Old Testament, then we are to some extent ignoring God, and we might just miss out on something precious, something that could bring us new knowledge, new understanding, something that could bring us into a new relationship with our God and Savior.

So it's back to Sodom and Gomorrah, back to God and Abraham as they look out over these two cities. God has just reaffirmed his promise to Abraham and Sarah that they will have a son, and Sarah has laughed. Now, as God looks over the cities of Sodom and Gomorrah, notorious for their wickedness, he remembers Abraham—one whom he has chosen, blessed, and called, but one who doubts, especially doubts the commonsense of this God who promises babies in old age.

God decides to share with Abraham the burden of the cities' future. God and an old man walk and talk together. It doesn't much sound like a remote, unsympathetic, vindictive, and angry God. This is a God who treats humans as friends, the God who walked with Adam and Eve in the garden and now walks with Abraham near the trees of Mamre. Far from being remote, this God engages with human beings, even if it would be easier not to bother. Why? Who knows what is in the mind of God?

It may be that this is a test for Abraham, that God wants to see if Abraham has caught on to what his God is really like. For the gods of the ancient world are nothing like the God of the Bible. The gods of the seasons, the gods of the crops—these are capricious and unpredictable, violent and vengeful. They have to be appeased through pleading and sacrifice.

But this God, this God seems different. This God is holy. This God makes promises. This God shares meals, takes time to get to know Abraham and Sarah, and sends the laughter of a newborn child to unsuspecting and elderly parents. This God is different.

And perhaps God is giving Abraham a chance to make sense of what is going on, to reason out what is different about this God. To think for himself until he learns to think like God.

It seems as though Abraham is trying to convince God that it would be unfair to kill the righteous alongside the unrighteous, as though Abraham is trying to work God around to Abraham's own way of thinking. But maybe God is working Abraham around to God's own way of thinking. And knowing Abraham to be a stubborn old man, God plays devil's advocate.

The conclusion they reach together is amazing. For it would not be unreasonable of God to destroy the cities, even with fifty righteous people living in them, because that's how it usually works. In everyday life, we are often judged guilty by association. We become accessories after the fact. All too often we hear stories of war, when all the people in a village are killed because of one rebel in their midst, or of an entire school class that is punished because one kid won't own up to some misdemeanor.

But here is a totally different scenario. Here, it seems, God entertains the idea that one might become *innocent* by association. The innocence of just fifty people, or even thirty, or even ten, might just be enough to save these cities. Does that remind you of one who was innocent, yet died for the sake of humanity? Not fifty, not thirty, not ten, but one is enough. One is enough to rescue the whole world, and us too.

Isn't this God whom we meet in Genesis the same God we meet in the Gospels, the same God of Jesus Christ? Surely yes. And because of that, we know that we too can converse with God, explore our world and the way we see God acting, even if it doesn't seem to make sense. Like Abraham we can bring our questions to God, even the deepest struggles we have with the way life seems to be, in all its unfairness and in all its joys. Until, perhaps, we learn to think like God.

For God loves us, loves us more than we can imagine, with the love of a father helping his daughter to tie her shoelaces or a mother helping her son struggle to forgive the friend who broke his toy car. Loving a child into maturity, into the fullness of all that the child is meant to be—all we are meant to be. God tenderly reaches a hand out to us, a hand we can grasp hold of. And find, in that grasp, the promise of life.

A character in the novel *Cold Sassy Tree* puts the question very well: "Ain't the best prayin' jest bein' with God and talkin' awhile, like He's a good friend; stead a-like he runs a store and you've come in a-hopin' to git a bargain?"[1]

Raewynne J. Whiteley is a Ph.D. student in homiletics at Princeton Theological Seminary and a pastoral associate at Trinity Church, Princeton New Jersey.

---

1. Olive Ann Burns, *Cold Sassy Tree* (New York: Dell, 1984), 362.

PROPER THIRTEEN

Toil for Joy

Ecclesiastes 1:12–14; 2:1–7, 11, 18–23; Colossians 3:5–17; Luke 12:13–21
C. Denise Yarbrough

IT IS EARLY morning, midweek in Toledo. A night nurse checks IVs on her patients, makes notations on charts, and prepares to leave as the morning shift arrives. The day nurse confers with her, and proceeds to visit each room, taking vital signs, greeting patients who are awake. In the ICU, a grieving family mourns the death of a loved one; on the labor and delivery floor a jubilant couple toasts the birth of their first child.

In another part of town, day care workers, on duty since 6:00 A.M., continue greeting sleepy, sometimes tearful children, as parents drop them off before heading toward jobs in offices, shops, factories, and schools. Schoolteachers scramble to get their own children out the door before rushing off to classrooms to prepare for their noisy broods. Cars stream out of quiet neighborhoods onto interstates and major city roads, as workers drive off, armed with an umpteenth cup of coffee, accompanied by radios updating them on world events. Road crews are all over the place, working at the endless task of repairing highways.

In residential neighborhoods joggers and exercise walkers chug around the streets. Downtown, the streets come to life as lawyers and government workers arrive, the library opens, and visitors pour into the riverfront. Another workday has begun, and workers are busy at their assigned tasks.

"What do mortals get from all the toil and strain with which they toil under the sun? For all their days are full of pain, and their work is a vexation; even at night their minds do not rest. This also is vanity." These haunting words are from the author of the book of Ecclesiastes, known by scholars as Qoheleth. A keen observer of the human condition, his reflections concerning the struggle to find meaning in daily life reverberate across the centuries with startling authenticity.

Despite its appearing to have a gloomy and pessimistic outlook, I love the book of Ecclesiastes. The passage we have heard is the only one appearing in the three-year lectionary cycle. That, I think, is a shame. Ecclesiastes is part of the wisdom tradition of ancient Israel, and it is full of keen insight concerning our place in the universe God created. This is the book in which appears the famous and beautiful poem "To everything there is a season."

Scholars believe that Qoheleth wrote between 450 and 350 B.C.E., in the Persian era. The economy was mercantile—money based and money driven. People worked hard, in urban centers. For the first time in Israelite history, average people were in debt. They were able to take financial risks that sometimes paid off and sometimes did not. With luck and hard work, people born poor could become rich. With bad luck, bad management, or a financial collapse, the rich could suddenly find themselves poor.

Similarities between Qoheleth's world and ours are hard to miss. Our mailboxes are stuffed with junk mail offering another credit card, encouraging us to finance home improvement projects, vacations, or new computers with a second mortgage. Television, radio, and print media bombard us with advertisements for products that will bring "the good life." Ads for financial planning services, insurance policies, and savings vehicles offer financial security and the prospect of passing our accumulated wealth on to the next generation. Not-for-profit organizations remind us to consider them in planning the disposition of our assets.

The quest for financial security consumes tremendous energy. Those retired and living on a fixed income, parents of teenagers, wondering how to save enough to put kids through college, young couples trying to save enough for a first home, persons of wealth, wondering how to manage it responsibly—all of us have to deal with issues Qoheleth faced. "What is all this about?" he asked. "Does it matter? Why am I doing all this anyway?"

As is often the case with our lectionary, today's reading stops at the author's gloomy question without letting us hear his answer. In the verses immediately following, Qoheleth says: "There is nothing better for mortals than to eat and drink, and find enjoyment in their toil. This also, I saw, is from the hand of God, for apart from him, who can eat or who can have enjoyment? For to the one who pleases him, God gives wisdom and knowledge and joy; but to the sinner he gives the work of gathering and heaping, only to give to the one who pleases God" (Ecclesiastes 2:24–26).

Notice: Qoheleth does not say that God rewards those who please God with wealth and riches, but, rather, with "wisdom and knowledge and joy." The fruits of a life with God are not material goods, but joy, wisdom, knowledge—fruits of the spirit that anyone, regardless of economic status, can acquire. In Luke's Gospel, Jesus warns the crowd: "One's life does not consist in the abundance of possessions." His parable concludes with God's sharp retort to the rich man, "You fool! This very night your life is being demanded of you. And the things you have prepared, whose will they be?"

Both Jesus and Qoheleth preach the same truth: that even in the midst of the humdrum, daily grind, one can—if one remains open and receptive to God—find joy and contentment through a contemplative approach to living. Qoheleth says: "This is what I have seen to be good: it is fitting to eat and drink and find enjoyment in all the toil with which one toils under the sun the few days of the life God gives us; for this is our lot"(Ecclesiastes 5:18). He calls us to life lived in the moment, for the moment. He invites us to gain perspective on work and daily lives, to step back and see them as part of a bigger picture in which the dominant figure is God. God is in control of your life and mine, so don't worry, he says. Enjoy each moment as it comes. When Qoheleth repeats the refrain "All is vanity," he is not voicing despair so much as being realistic—accepting the realities of the created order. The Hebrew word, *hebel*, translated *vanity*, means "vapor," or "breath." It connotes something real and important, but ephemeral and fleeting. Only God is not vanity. God is forever, and in surrendering to God, letting God control our destinies, we find joy and contentment.

Qoheleth's insight, repeated by Jesus, has been at the core of the mystical tradition in most major world religions for thousands of years. When I was at Holy Cross Monastery during my vacation, I read a book by a Buddhist monk called *Living Buddha, Living Christ*. Buddhists emphasize "mindfulness," a state of awareness and appreciation for the present moment. When Buddhists meditate, they work to achieve a state of mindfulness, a sense of being in the present moment, enjoying everything about that moment. The Christian mystical tradition has always pointed to the same truth: God is present in every particular moment of our lives, if we will take the time to become aware of that presence and leave ourselves open to it.

It takes practice and intentionality to remain open to God. Thich Nhat Hanh says, "The practice is to touch life deeply so that the Kingdom of God becomes a reality. This is not a matter of devotion. It is a matter of practice. . . . Is there a way to work in a meditative mood? The answer is clearly yes. We practice mindfulness of cooking, cleaning, sweeping, and washing. When we work this way we touch the ultimate dimension of reality."[1]

Our own tradition has always pointed to this truth as well. When St. Paul says, "Pray without ceasing," he does not suggest that we spend our lives on our knees, but rather that all we do in daily life become a prayer. That we become mindful of all our deeds as done in God's presence. The author of Colossians says, "Let the peace of Christ rule in your hearts, to which indeed you were called in the one body." When we cultivate a contemplative approach to daily living, we can enter the kingdom of God here and now, as we experience the presence of God permeating our mundane lives by transforming our hearts. In the midst of all with which we mortals toil under the sun, we will find the joy, wisdom, and knowledge, which are gifts from God, when we are mindful, aware, awake. As Jesus told the crowd, abundant life comes to those who are "rich toward God," rather than those who store up treasures for themselves.

As the sun sets over the city at the end of a long day, the workers return to their homes. They eat dinner, do household chores, visit with family and friends, tend to children and pets, watch TV, read, and finally go to bed to rest and prepare for the resumption of the daily round the next morning. Eat, drink, and find enjoyment in your toil. "For they will scarcely brood over the days of their lives, because God keeps them occupied with the joy of their hearts" (Ecclesiastes 5:20).

C. Denise Yarbrough is rector of the Church of the Transfiguration, Towaco, New Jersey.

---

1. *Living Buddha, Living Christ,* Thich Nhat Hanh (New York: G. P. Putnam's Sons, 1995), 38, 61.

PROPER FIFTEEN

Strengthening Weak Knees

Hebrews 12:1–14
Rhonda Smith McIntire

MANY OF you know my husband, Tim. Perhaps you don't know that he has weak knees. He does. Listen again to these words from the Letter to the Hebrews: "Lift your drooping hands and strengthen your weak knees, so that what is lame may not be put out of joint, but rather be healed."

Strengthen your weak knees so that there is healing instead of lameness.

That's what Tim did. During a basketball game with teenagers about a third his age, he heard a crunching/ripping/very weird sound in his knees. It was difficult for him to walk. He was, in effect, lame.

So, he went to an orthopedic doctor, who performed surgery, and a lame knee was healed.

That's what any of us would do, right? If we have an earache, we ask the doctor for antibiotics. If we're allergic to juniper berries, we take a decongestant. We have no hesitations at all about seeking medical remedies for bodily malfunctions like weak knees, because we trust modern science to guide us toward healing.

But, what do we do if the diagnosis isn't something like weak knees? What if the diagnosis is, instead, weak faith? Do we trust God to guide us toward healing?

We all know that, try as we might, a life of faith is *not* a constant progression. It is not beginning on the bottom floor and climbing steadily to the penthouse. No. A life of faith is more like a spiral that winds and curves and goes down as well as up. But this spiral is not necessarily a bad thing. In fact, psychologists tell us it is a good thing to grow in a spiral. Each step forward in psychological and spiritual growth *requires* times for regression in order to refuel and to internalize the growth changes honestly.

Your cathedral vestry has just returned from a two-day retreat several hours north of here. The vestry knows that weak knees are a possibility if vestry members spend every single meeting upstairs in the cathedral library, going over business item after business item. So, once a year, the vestry chooses to strengthen potential weak knees by retreating together, dreaming together, and visioning together in an entirely separate holy place.

One of you said to me recently, "All I do is work, and it doesn't feel like God is at my workplace." A signal to strengthen weak knees? I think so, and here's how: there's a Ministry Fair all set up in Kasemann Hall today. I promise you that you will feel God's presence if you involve yourself in LOGOS or Stephen Ministry or S.T.E.P or the choirs or Altar Guild or any of the cathedral ministries that welcome you and your spiraling faith.

It is important to pay attention to the words of today's epistle: "Lift your drooping hands and strengthen your weak knees . . . so that what is lame may not be put out of joint, but rather be healed." *Do something.* If your knees are weak because all you have done at the cathedral for the past five years is attend worship, then become a member of the St. Joseph Guild also. If your knees are weak because the Thrift Shop is the only place you've volunteered, then volunteer at the Gift Shop, too. If you've never attended the Sunday morning education hour, do it. Strengthen your weak knees. Don't let your faith become lame.

And, here's the most exciting part. If you are actively seeking to strengthen your faith, your journey will have an effect on the rest of us. Your healing will help my healing.

Scientists studying a colony of monkeys on a tiny island in Japan dumped truckloads of sweet potatoes on the shore. One day, something took place that had never before been observed. A young female monkey took her sweet potato down to the surf where she washed it. This improved the palatability of the food in two ways: agitation in the sea water removed sand and other debris, and an appetizing salt taste was added. That monkey soon taught the washing ritual to her mother and then to some playmates. The idea spread. Washing the sweet potatoes caught on. Then, one day, every single member of the colony was washing sweet potatoes in the sea.

And, there's more. Not long afterward, on a distant island, abruptly, and in the absence of any kind of communication between the colonies of monkeys, those on the second island were also washing their potatoes in the surf.

What I've just described is biologist Rupert Sheldrake's idea of "morphic resonance," which says that the behavior of animals and plants can be molded by the behavior of others across both space and time.

In his teachings recorded in the Gospels, Jesus often employs a teaching strategy that biblical scholars designate as "an argument from the lesser to the greater." "If God so clothes the grass of the field, which is alive today and tomorrow is thrown into the oven," says Jesus in the Sermon on the Mount, "will he not much more clothe you—you of little faith?" If this is the way God operates in the natural world, he argues, imagine how God might operate in matters of truly cosmic consequence.

Scientists are telling us that behavior, which includes faith and beliefs and ways of being, can be molded by the behavior of others throughout space and time. But this is what God has told us—from Abraham to Mary to Jesus: changes in the faith journey of all humanity can be brought about by changes in an individual faith journey. It is as unfathomable and as perfectly clear as this: Tim McIntire's weak knees will be strengthened when you seek healing.

Let it be so.

Rhonda Smith McIntire is canon residentiary of The Cathedral Church of St. John, Albuquerque, New Mexico.

PROPER SIXTEEN

Unnecessary Burdens

Luke 13:22–30
Claudia M. Wilson

A FEW DAYS ago I paid an annual visit to a friend. The journey is not that far, but I usually spend the night in order to avoid a late drive home. As I was packing my overnight bag, I thought back to all the packing I had done for business and vacation trips. Then I thought of all those people I have seen on airplanes who insist on bringing on board everything they possess as so-called "carry-on" baggage. You know—bulging hanging bag over the shoulder, suitcase in one hand, briefcase and shopping bag in the other, struggling sort of sideways down the aisle of the plane, bumping into things and other people as they go.

And then Jesus' words came to me: "Strive to enter through the narrow door." I began to think about the excess baggage we carry around that makes the narrow door a barrier rather than a gateway. I suppose one of the first things that comes to mind is, quite literally, possessions. Jesus is very clear in other parts of the Gospel about his attitude toward possessions. Simply put, they aren't good for us. "Sell your possessions, and give alms," we heard him tell his followers a few weeks ago. And we also heard him say, "Be on your guard against all kinds of greed; for one's life does not consist in the abundance of possessions." Elsewhere Jesus uses the example of the camel trying to get through the eye of a needle to describe the problems the rich will have in getting into the kingdom of heaven. (Talk about a narrow door!)

Possessions and the desire for them can be insidious things. We can fool ourselves into thinking that what we have is who we are, that self-worth is measured by material worth, that somehow money and possessions are a mark of intrinsic superiority. Possessions, and the effort we put into acquiring them, can separate us from our friends and neighbors, even from husbands, wives, and children, sisters and brothers. Possessions can make us very bulky, so bulky that no one can get really close to us, so bulky that we cannot reach out beyond them to grasp another's hand, so bulky that we cannot move from where we are.

But material possessions are not the only things that weigh us down, that make it difficult for us to get through the narrow door. We have other baggage with us as well, baggage that, unlike possessions, we cannot always see, but that is just as heavy and makes us just as bulky.

I speak now of sin and guilt, of anger and resentment, of fear and lack of trust. These are heavy baggage indeed, and most of us carry at least some of them around with us most of the time. Carrying them around is hard work; it takes a lot of energy, energy we could use for other things. And it takes time to get them all together every day and hoist them on our shoulders and grasp them in our hands. And there we are, struggling along through life like that traveler struggling down the narrow aisle of the airplane, knocking into the people on either side and then sitting uncomfortably with things around our feet, on our laps, and crammed into the overhead rack above us and on the other side of the aisle as well.

Do we really need these burdens? Do we really need to carry these things around with us? Do we really need to spend our time and energy nursing a grudge or finding ways to avoid that friend or neighbor to whom we are now not speaking because of some slight or misunderstanding? Is it better to hold on tightly to shopping bags full of anger at our parents, children, sisters, or brothers than to have hands free to reach out in an embrace? Is it better? I don't think so.

What's more, we do not have to live this way. We do not have to carry these burdens with us, day in and day out. Jesus tells us, "Forgive, and you will be forgiven." Jesus tells us, "Do not be afraid, little flock, for it is your Father's good pleasure to give you the kingdom." "Love one another, as I have loved you."

"Strive to enter through the narrow door," the door that is just wide enough for each of us as we truly are, without the excess baggage of sin and guilt, anger and resentment, fear and lack of trust. Without the various layers of protection we have put on. Without the persona we may have created for ourselves because we think that the persona is better or more presentable than we are. Without the illusion that money and possessions are a mark of superiority, a tribute to our own power and accomplishments, an essential embodiment of our identity.

The narrow door is wide enough for us, just as we are, as children of God, as the ones for whom Jesus died on the cross. Just as we are, created in the image of God, capable of love and devotion, of caring and nurturing. Just as we are, but not alone, trusting in God's love for us, listening for his voice when he calls us, walking in the way he would have us go. Jesus said, "Come to me, all you that are weary and are carrying heavy burdens, and I will give you rest."

We do not need those burdens. We can put them down. Then we can turn and offer helping hands to others as they struggle to put their burdens down as well. And then we can go through the narrow door, together. Just as we are, but not alone.

Claudia M. Wilson is deacon at St. John's Church, Getty Square, Yonkers, New York.

PROPER SEVENTEEN

"Oh, It's You Again!"

Ecclesiasticus 10:7–18; Hebrews 13:1–8; Luke 14:1, 7–14
Stephen Elkins-Williams

IN A RECENT interview, the renowned actor Sir Anthony Hopkins was reflecting on his star status. "When you're young," he said, "you crave power and fame. Now I know it's . . . no big deal. I get up and look into the mirror and say, 'Oh, it's you again.'"

I assume he smiles when he says that to himself (I hope he does) with a slight rueful shake of the head that implies, "I know who you are: a flawed human being who doesn't deserve all that comes your way, but life is a gift!"

If that is true, what a wonderful model for us: true humility grounded in gratitude and joy. But how difficult to imitate! How seriously we take ourselves. How we puff ourselves up, or tear ourselves down—forms of arrogance, both of these. How hard it is to look in the mirror and neither to frown nor to genuflect, but without pride or condemnation to smile and say, "Oh, it's you again."

"Arrogance is hateful to the Lord," Ecclesiasticus tells us. Hateful because it is untruth. Arrogance postulates its own reality, creates its own universe centered on itself, denies its limitations. Arrogance lives a lie.

The author of Ecclesiasticus does not want to let us do that. "The king of today will die tomorrow," he observes, adding graphically, "He inherits maggots and vermin and worms." "How can dust and ashes be proud?" Death is one of those limitations, perhaps *the* limitation, that our arrogance tries to deny. It only happens to others. It only happens after a very long life. It will not really happen to me. That is arrogance speaking, our re-creation of reality, our grasping for God-like power. It sets us in opposition to the true Creator, it separates us from God. "The beginning of human pride," Ecclesiasticus declares, "is to forsake the Lord; the heart has withdrawn from its Maker."

Arrogance is a heart disease, as deadly as any other. Its symptoms reveal that our hearts are not centered on God for whom they were created. Instead they are fatally centered on ourselves. Arrogance is easy to diagnose in someone else. We can see it, for one prominent example, in our president. He seems to have forgotten that the office he temporarily holds is a sacred trust, given to him for leadership and service, not for exploitation and self-aggrandizement. That mandate calls for honest truth and genuine repentance, not deception and spin control.

The infection of arrogance, however, is much harder to detect in ourselves. Like death itself, it seems something that happens only to someone else. Certainly the guests at the dinner in today's Gospel thought that, even though they were vying to sit in the places of honor. Jesus encourages them to take themselves less seriously and so allow others to do so as well. He also urges his host not just to satisfy social obligations and so serve himself, but to show genuine hospitality to those who truly need it. It is more blessed, as he says elsewhere, and less arrogant, to give than to receive.

Through Scripture Jesus addresses many such exhortations to each of us as an antidote to arrogance—the ones, for example, in today's reading from Hebrews. "Let mutual love continue. Do not neglect to show hospitality to strangers, for that some have entertained angels without knowing it. Remember those who are in prison, as though you were in prison with them; those who are being tortured, as though you yourselves were being tortured. Let marriage be held in honor by all, and let the marriage bed be kept undefiled. . . . Keep your lives free from the love of money, and be content with what you have."

These and other Scriptural counsels read easily and sound harmless, but they make great demands on us and are not easily lived. The arrogance in us that constantly urges us to put ourselves at the center of our universe, to view others with suspicion, and to use others for our own purposes causes us to fail frequently. As limited human beings, "sinner" is part of our identity.

When we sin, our arrogance seems to give us two choices. One is to deny it, to smooth things over, to excuse ourselves and so puff ourselves up some more. The other is to punish ourselves for it, to tear ourselves down over it, to use it to continue to take ourselves deadly seriously.

Our Baptismal Covenant gives us a third choice. "Whenever you fall into sin," it asks, will you "repent and return to the Lord?" Rather than continue to focus us on ourselves, genuine repentance will center us back on God. If "the beginning of man's pride is to depart from the Lord," the beginning of faith, humility, and love is to return to the Lord. Since "his heart has forsaken his Maker," now it must once again welcome the One for whom it is made.

That is not easy for us to do, especially time after time, day after day. We cannot believe that God is that patient, that understanding, that forgiving, but Scripture is full of assurances for our fears. The Epistle to the Hebrews declares that "God has said, 'I will never fail you nor forsake you.' Hence we can confidently say, 'The Lord is my helper, I will not be afraid.'" Even beyond God's word in Scripture, Jesus is the very incarnation of God's word, of God's forgiveness, of God's love. It is through faith in the crucified, resurrected Jesus that we know and can be assured of God's never-failing love. "I will never fail you nor forsake you."

Each time we need forgiveness, we can smile and say, not only to ourselves, but also, with relief and gratitude and adoration, to God, *"Oh, it's you again."*

*Stephen Elkins-Williams is rector of Chapel of the Holy Cross,
Chapel Hill, North Carolina.*

PROPER TWENTY-ONE

A Personal Lazarus

Luke 16:19–31
Barbara Kauber

THERE IS AN old Yiddish saying: "If you have money, you are wise and good-looking, and you can sing well, too." I am sure that the rich man was wise and good-looking. And undoubtedly he sang the lessons in synagogue every so often. He even was generous. Yes, generous. He had a beggar living at his gate, which means he was feeding the beggar, according to the requirements of the Law.

Nowhere does the Bible say that it is a sin to be rich. Jesus' story does not suggest that the rich man got his money by oppressing the poor or by robbing widows and orphans. The rich man fed the beggar at his door. The rich man knew the beggar's name. Lazarus was the rich man's personal beggar. When he was healthy enough to do it, Lazarus probably ran errands and carried messages for the rich man's household. After his death, the rich man wants Lazarus to run such an errand, to take a message to his brothers.

The rich man's request is the problem, of course. Even while he is parched with thirst in the flames of hell, he does not understand the relationship between himself and Lazarus. It's not just that Lazarus is now the chief guest at Abraham's table and the rich man is swallowing fire. The rich man was never able to see Lazarus as his brother, back when Lazarus was "his" beggar. Now he sees Lazarus as Abraham's beggar. To the rich man, Lazarus has changed masters. But he is still the beggar and messenger for higher-ranking folks. The torments of hell have not managed to wipe out the rich man's social definitions.

It really is okay to have money. And to be wise, good-looking, and able to sing well, too. What is not okay is to believe that we are better than somebody else.

Our nation is pretty generous to the needy. We have a lot of social welfare programs, and they do a lot of good even when they don't work perfectly. We have a lot of rich people who want to help those in need of housing, food, or education. Our churches and charitable foundations are busy offering help to meet human needs in this country and abroad. I do not know of a single person who is in favor of letting a child starve or grow up brain-damaged or deformed because of lack of proper care.

But we start getting uncharitable about poor, needy, and jobless people when we talk about them simply as "they." We depersonalize people and thereby manage to ignore specific injustices. We talk about welfare cheats, to justify cutting back on welfare, instead of getting to know families on welfare, many of whom do not cheat. We insist that every able-bodied person work. But what happens to a twenty-year-old kid with a girlfriend and a blind baby, who tries to make it on three minimum-wage jobs with twenty hours per week, each, without any health insurance? Congress has again rejected a proposed raise in minimum wage. Does any congressperson actually try to understand this kid? Does any congressperson live in the run-down old wooden building where the kid lives?

When Jesus tells his story of the rich man and Lazarus, I hear about a decent well-meaning rich guy who lacks just one thing. He never manages to meet Lazarus as a brother. He depersonalizes Lazarus. Jesus came, however, to personalize us.

Each of us cherishes Jesus, because Jesus cherishes us first. We know that Jesus our Lord is the one person in our entire world who always knows exactly who we are and yet loves us completely, just as we are. We are not just a sociological category to him. He is Savior for me, personally. For you, personally. In his lifetime, every person Jesus met was someone he reached out to personally. Now, in his resurrection, he reaches every person who has ever lived.

Salvation would not work for any of us if Jesus simply processed us all by groups, nationalities, denominations, income levels, political choices, sex, or sexual preference. No, Jesus redeems each of us personally, and each of us knows him in a distinctive way.

The rich man never managed to get the picture of God's reality. He never got to understand and recognize Lazarus as his brother before God. So all of his goodwill and his appropriate charity toward Lazarus could not help him. The rich man never shared Lazarus's situation. And so there is a deep, deep chasm between them that can never be bridged. It is the infinite gap between heaven and hell.

Each of us probably knows somebody we regard as not very well off, very educated, wise, clean, honest, or morally pure. We may not deliberately look down upon that person. But deep inside, if we are honest, we may feel a social distance. That person is your personal Lazarus. The one who may be the Christ for you, to teach you how to learn to love as God loves.

Our personal Lazarus is Jesus' personal gift to each one of us. I think Jesus gives each of us Lazarus because we need him so badly. As we learn to cherish and respect Lazarus, we also discover how Jesus loves us.

The other gift Jesus gives us through this story is the gift of being Lazarus for someone else. When someone wants to offer us a kindness, we can receive it with kindness. Elsewhere, Jesus says emphatically that if we do not allow him to serve us, we have no part in him. We need to wash Lazarus's feet. And we also need to allow our brother or sister in Christ to wash our feet. Jesus left that towel to all of us and to each of us.

It is not enough to give alms or to dole out unemployment benefits. We need to learn a kind of personal giving, so Lazarus truly becomes a brother or sister. It is not enough to receive help without gratitude, as if we were only getting what is owed us. We are brother or sister to the one who serves us. Whether I wash your feet or you wash mine, it is the Lord's towel we use. And it is the Lord's uniquely personal love that we celebrate, either as the rich man or as

Lazarus. For it is the Lord Jesus alone who conquers the infinite gap between Lazarus and the rich man, the chasm that separates heaven and hell.

Barbara Kauber is rector of St. Mark's Church, Newark, New York.

PROPER TWENTY-FIVE

Standing Outside—Invited In

Jeremiah 14:1–10, 19–22; Luke 18:9–14
Gordon J. De La Vars

OUR LORD'S parable about the Pharisee and the tax collector reminds me of something that happened many years ago, at the Catholic parish in Ohio where I was a member. A woman there had recently lost her husband, and shortly after his death, her only child, a daughter, had tried to take her own life. I remember that the girl was still in critical condition in our local hospital at the time.

The woman had been a regular churchgoer, an active member in the parish. Yet after her husband's death and her daughter's suicide attempt, she would not go into church. Instead, we would see her on Sundays standing at the side entrance by herself, smiling sadly and greeting others while they walked in. Despite the urging of the pastor, she would not attend the Mass, but would stand alone at the outside steps during the whole service, in all sorts of weather, Sunday after Sunday.

Sometimes during the Mass, as the congregation rose or knelt, prayed or sang, I would think about her. I would imagine her standing below the steps at the side of the church, so close that she could hear the words and music, the shuffling of feet and creaking of pews, but far away in her mind and heart, lost amid her sorrows and worries. What she thought about in her moments alone outside I could not know for sure. Was it shame that prevented her from coming into church? Was it anger with God for what he had allowed to happen to her and her family? Or did she suddenly feel unworthy to enter God's house and to pray with all of us "respectable" people?

This isn't, of course, a perfect match with the story Jesus tells in Luke's Gospel. The circumstances that prompted the woman to remain outside during Mass were not the same ones that compelled the tax collector to stand far off in the corner of the temple, beating his breast, and asking for God's mercy. And the attitude of my old congregation as a whole was not that of the self-righteous

Pharisee. In fact, I recall that several people tried to comfort the woman in her grief and distress, and we regularly remembered her daughter in the Prayers of the People. I'm sure someone at some point contacted a doctor.

It's just that I was moved then by her suffering, and it made me think of the sufferings of all those who struggle at the margins of our world. People who feel unworthy or unloved. People who, physically or symbolically, stand far off and alone, at the bottom of many church steps, as we may have done ourselves at times, with good reason. When we have felt too afraid to pray, too ashamed to look up to heaven. When we have sought mercy that we didn't think we deserved.

And we may have felt all of this not having done half of what the tax collector was probably guilty of! For if we are to understand the shock effect Jesus' story had on his first listeners, and if we are to understand the nature of God's mercy, we need to realize what a tax collector did in the time of Jesus and what a Pharisee sought to do. The tax collector, a Jew himself, was squeezing revenues out of his fellow citizens so that a foreign power could continue to occupy their land. He was also, as common practice, dipping into these revenues, lining his pockets while his countrymen scraped and saved up their last shekel.

The tax collector in Luke's Gospel would have been the kind of man capable of betraying a friend if it meant a profit. The kind of man who would keep two ledgers and juggle figures in commercial contracts. The kind of man who would cheat the elderly out of their pensions or collect high rents for tenement housing.

The Pharisee, in contrast, would have been a man passionately in love with his country, his people, and his faith. His strict adherence to religious law was meant to be an example to others and a beacon of hope in a time of oppression, a reminder that the sacred heritage had not been crushed. The Pharisee, although a prosperous businessman, would have sought justice for the downtrodden and equality between the different classes. People respected Pharisees not because they feared them, but because they knew that Pharisees cared deeply for Israel, for her traditions, her welfare, and her future.

But, as sometimes happens with good people, some of these Pharisees began to *believe* that they were good. The respect they enjoyed became familiar and anticipated. Too many press clippings, too many awards banquets! After a while even their faithfulness to the Law became self-conscious and artificial, so that instead of worshiping God, they were, without knowing it, worshiping *themselves* worshiping God. (It's an old religious illness.) The humility went out of their faith and was replaced by pride and contempt. They stood by themselves in the temple, away from their fellow men, aloof and self-contained.

And this is where our Lord catches up with them—or one of them at least, and with the tax collector, too. The repentant sinner goes home justified, because he knows he is a sinner—maybe a wretched one—and because he hopes against hope that God will find a way to release him from his sins and help him reform his life. But he might go home convinced that God has not heard him, and feel lonelier and more lost than ever.

The Pharisee, who has no reason to think of himself as acting in any other than a righteous way, returns to his home unjustified in the sight of God. As content as ever, as close to God, he thinks, as before, but in reality as far away from God as he imagined the tax collector to be.

And so our Lord, as he does often, assaults our sensibilities about what and who is righteous as he attacks the prejudices of his own audience, for they thought they knew the right person to cheer for. The right one to hiss at. The one who wore the white hat and the one who wore the black. And we are apt to ask the same questions as they did. How can a Pharisee, so clearly a man of God and a man of the people, turn out bad? Worse than that, how can a tax collector, a traitor, a parasite, society's refuse, turn out good?

Jesus switches hats on us, and it's a blessing that he does. Righteousness— conforming to God's will—is measured not by a life manifesting marks of holiness, but by a life of moments in which we ask God to make us holy. And these are moments when we may not expect God to listen. Moments when, in sorrow and bewilderment, in pain and anger, when feeling lost and alone, we wait for answers in the farthest corner of the temple, or even outside it. Moments when our hearts, weighed down by doubts and hurts and sins, are too heavy for us to bear. Moments when, unlike the Pharisee, we are not proud of what we've done, and when, like the tax collector, we don't know how to make it right.

But it is precisely in these moments that God finds us, for the outrageous quality of God's mercy is such that, when we believe ourselves farthest from him, we are actually nearest. When we feel ourselves most empty, we are most filled. When we think ourselves most wretched, we are most loved. For at these times we call on God, not to validate what we've done, but to acknowledge our dependence on God alone. Then, with nothing more than fragile trust, hope against hope, we repeat the words of the prophet Jeremiah: "You, O Lord, are in the midst of us, and we are called by your name; do not forsake us!" Before those words leave our lips, they are heard and acknowledged.

I don't remember what happened to the woman of my parish who stood outside the church on those Sundays long ago. I would like to think that those who tried to help her were successful and that our prayers for her and her daughter were answered. I would like to think that one day she returned to her home, feeling right with God. I would like to hope that she was able to discover somewhere in the tangle of her mind how the Lord was in her midst. Calling her by name, reminding her of his mercy, and inviting her—as God invites us, and all who come with humble and contrite hearts—to feed on the strength, the courage, and the glory of his grace.

Gordon J. De La Vars is rector of St. Paul's Church, Mayville, New York.

PROPER TWENTY-SEVEN

Burning Questions for God

Job 19:23–27; Luke 20:27–38
Michael A. Smith

AT ANY GIVEN point in time, I think all of us have one burning question we'd like to ask God. When I was six months old, if I had been able to talk, my question would surely have been, "Why strained carrots?"

As I grew older, my God questions grew and changed with me. At age two, I wanted to ask God where baby brothers come from, and how do I send one named Jimmy back there? By age three, as all parents know, God questions were coming in an endless flood. Why can't I fly like a bird? What makes a piano work? Where do dogs go when they're lost? Why do dogs bite? What is dad's razor for? Where is the North Pole? No doubt, I was every Sunday school teacher's dream.

In junior high, things began to change. Questions to God were no longer just innocent inquiries; they had become life and death appeals. Why does everyone at school hate me? What do I have to do to make Mom and Dad happy? Where are you, God, and how do I find you?

By adulthood, I had pretty much stopped asking questions of God. I had learned how the world was supposed to work, and I knew when the world was going bad. With this knowledge in hand, the questions I asked of God were really accusations, like the interrogation of a prosecuting attorney. "If you, God, are all powerful and all loving, why can't you stop my parents from getting a divorce? If you, God, have searched me and know my heart, why are you making me move from the one place I love? If you, God, satisfy the hungry with good things, why is my life so empty and meaningless?"

I suppose that in the technical sense I was still asking questions. But the "if" statements that preceded them gave me away. I was not really trying to grasp the mystery of God. I already knew what God was supposed to be doing, and God was not making the grade. When we say "if," we give ourselves away, and we stand in the company of Job. When we say "if," we come to God with our answers in hand. Answers we can put alongside Job's with pen and paper, answers we can engrave in rock with lead and iron. When we say "if," we're not really seeking answers. We already know the answers. What we're seeking is vindication. We want our Redeemer, our personal vindicator, to prove us right.

As Luke tells the Gospel story, Jesus has taken a long and roundabout way from Nazareth to Jerusalem. Luke scores no points for geography, but Jesus does get to Jerusalem a week or two before Passover. He makes a grand Palm Sunday entrance on a cloak-covered colt. And for a first order of business, he rebukes the moneychangers in the outer temple—not the smartest move if you want to win friends and influence people.

By the time Jesus arrives in Jerusalem, his reputation as a teacher has long preceded him. So he spends his remaining days there teaching in the temple. Surely Jesus expects that a lot of people will bring their burning questions to him for answers, or at least for vindication. He knows the days of debate will be long and frustrating. And I suppose he takes special steps to get ready. An extra serving of Quaker Oats at breakfast. Dr. Scholl inserts in his sandals. The full liter size of Ozarka water in his pouch. And one of those deluxe, folding stadium seats for the cold stone bleachers.

All sorts of people do come to him with questions, scribes and chief priests and Pharisees. And almost all of the questions they bring are traps: "By what authority are you doing these things?" "Who gave you this authority; is it divine or human?" "Is it lawful to pay taxes to the emperor or not?" They may not actually say the word, but if you listen closely, you can still hear the "if" in these questions. "If you are who you say you are (and we know you can't be), then let's see you stumble over this impossible question."

After long bouts of fancy footwork, Jesus finally faces the Sadducees. The power brokers. The guys in wing-tips and three-button banker suits. The no-nonsense literalists: if it's not written down in the Law and the prophets, then it's not true. The Sadducees know Jesus has been teaching about resurrection. They also know that the word *resurrection* is nowhere to be found in the law and the prophets. Resurrection cannot be true, and they have a sure-fire trap to prove their case.

The trap the Sadducees set for Jesus is their "one bride for seven brothers" question. Mosaic law says that a man must provide an heir to his brother's widow if she is childless. This is written in the law and is true. If this happens six times—or even twice—in a family of seven brothers, then resurrection cannot be true. If they are all resurrected, then the woman would have seven husbands. This kind of bigamy is a violation of God's law, so resurrection is not possible.

The Sadducees ask Jesus their question; but they already know the answer. They are only looking for vindication, and they are certain Jesus will trip and fall. But Jesus takes the Sadducees on. First he tells them that their ideas about resurrection are wrong. Resurrected life is a whole new way of life. Life without death. Life without marriage, because you no longer need marriage or pro-creation. Children of God in that age all live in blessed union with God their creator.

Jesus' next step is to beat the Sadducees at their own game. When God speaks to Moses at the burning bush, God tells Moses: "I am the God of Abraham. I am the God of Isaac. I am the God of Jacob." These words are written in the Law. They are true.

Using the Sadducees' own rules for reading Scripture, Jesus reminds them that God is the God of the living. God is not God of the dead. Since God is the God of the living, and God is the God of Abraham, Isaac, and Jacob—present tense—then Abraham, Isaac and Jacob must be alive. Since the books of the Law tell us that Abraham, Isaac, and Jacob died, and the books also tell us that they are now alive in God, then resurrection must be true.

I must say that when Jesus teaches, I prefer his parables over his logic lessons. But the Sadducees are big on logic, and when Jesus finishes they have nothing to say. No rebuttal whatsoever. In fact, everyone in the temple is so impressed that they pack up their empty traps and keep quiet. They won't be tripping Jesus up, at least in the daylight.

No doubt Jesus was exhausted after a few days of debate like this. And I think I now know why Jesus said more than once that the kingdom of heaven belongs to children. Children ask questions, real, genuine questions—no ifs, ands, or buts. Children ask questions because they really are hoping for answers. Children ask questions because they know that God is a mysterious adventure waiting to be explored. The kingdom of heaven belongs to children because children ask children's questions. And adults ask childish questions.

The Sadducees and the rest of us would do well to read the book of Job all the way through, and not to stop while Job is still demanding vindication. When Job and his mealy-mouthed friends get done talking, God finally gives Job an answer. God answers Job with a few questions of God's own: "Where were you when I laid the foundations of the earth? Can you bind the chains of the Pleiades, or loose the cords of Orion? Is it by your wisdom that the hawk soars, and spreads its wings toward the south?" And on and on and on.

In the end, Job has no more arguments with God: "I know that you can do all things, and that no purpose of yours can be thwarted. . . . I have uttered what I did not understand, things too wonderful for me, which I did not know. . . . I had heard of you by the hearing of the ear, but now my eye sees you."

God's answer to Job is to give Job a glimpse of divine reality. And Job comes back to himself. Job becomes a child again. It's not that Job finally gets the answers he wants or even the vindication he deserves. What Job finally gets is an assurance that whatever may come, whatever life brings, nothing can separate him from the love of God.

And in the three thousand years since the book of Job was written, no better answer to the question of God has been found. The really good news is that it's not answers we need. We need only become children of God again, and find our waiting home with Job in the loving arms of God.

Michael A. Smith is assistant rector of Emmanuel Episcopal Church, San Angelo, Texas.

PROPER TWENTY-EIGHT

The small god of Uncle Ralph

Malachi 3:13–4:2a, 5–6; Luke 21:5–19
Carolyn West

ONE SUMMER when I was growing up in the little Texas town of Burnet, our Methodist church sponsored a week-long revival. My parents felt obliged to support the effort, and so the Kern family attended services almost every night. After introducing himself to the adults, the evangelist turned to the children. In a sugary voice, he asked us to call him "Uncle Ralph" and his wife "Miss Melinda." This did little to make the long, boring sermon tolerable for my brother, Paul, and me. At midweek, Paul's best friend, Larry, wrote a message with his finger on the dusty side of the evangelists' trailer: "Paul Kern *hates* Uncle Ralph."

By the last night of the revival, most church members agreed with Paul. Uncle Ralph was a dud. Few souls had been reeled in at the altar calls, and all hopes rested on the last service. Uncle Ralph employed every scary bit of Scripture he could muster. He painted God as a fire-breathing exterminator. It was the 1950s, when fallout shelters were hatching under many suburban homes. Yet even his descriptions of a God poised to unleash a nuclear holocaust failed to move us phlegmatic Methodists from our seats.

Uncle Ralph invited us to come forward and "get right with God." Miss Melinda began her trembly, soul-wrenching organ music. Everyone still held back. Suddenly, in the middle of "The Old Rugged Cross," Miss Melinda stood up with a dramatic flourish, scanned the congregation, marched into the crowd, and stopped in front of me. "Young lady, are you saved?" she challenged. "Do you know what will happen to your soul when God sets the bomb off?" I did what any normal sixth grader would do. I started giggling. The more stricken she looked, the louder I giggled. Huge hair bouncing, Miss Melinda fled back to the organ. A jab from my father's elbow shocked me to my senses.

That's one way to react to news of the end times, the day of judgment, the destruction of the world as we know it. But who really knows the proper way to respond when we hear such doomsday predictions? Passages like the one I just read from the Gospel of Luke aren't usually picked to hang on our walls or to memorize as our favorites. How do we deal with them, seriously and responsibly?

The great and terrible Day of the Lord was a common image among the Jews. Long before Jesus' day, prophets like Malachi spoke of that day, burning like an oven, when the righteous would be tested and all evildoers would be burned to stubble. This kind of imagery was part of Jesus' mindset as a Jew and played a large part in his prophecies.

Less than forty years after Jesus spoke these words, his people would rebel against their Roman conquerors. Jesus foresaw this uprising, and its consequences, as inevitable. In A.D. 70, three Roman legions were sent to besiege the defiant city. Starvation, disease, and relentless slaughter followed, partly from the Roman siege and partly from Jews fighting each other for control behind the walls.

Tradition says Jerusalem finally fell on the same day it had been conquered more than seven hundred years earlier by the Babylonians. The city's walls were torn down and its buildings burned. The magnificent marble-and-gold temple was obliterated. The core of Jerusalem lay in ruins for at least thirty years, a ghost town where wild animals stalked through the ruins. The temple was never rebuilt; a mosque sits in its place today.

The first Christians lived through this destruction, but Luke and his community did not merely endure a Roman siege. Their entire lives were besieged by persecution for what they believed. "Do not be terrified," Luke remembered Jesus saying. "In the midst of the most unimaginable suffering I will give you courage. I will even give you brave words to speak; and God will still be with you."

Maybe we *should* be memorizing the words of this Gospel reading. Maybe we should be hanging them on our walls. Scripture like this recognizes that life is not always easy, that living faithfully under God is often difficult and unpopular, that somewhere at the end of time there will be judgment and accountability. But for those who persevere under siege, God's strength is always near, and the battle can eventually be won.

We come to church for many reasons, but often it is to find help living through our own everyday forms of siege. We lose a job, a mate, a child, a friend. We divorce, fall off the wagon, face a disease that could kill or cripple our bodies or our minds. We are judged through the blind eyes of prejudice. We struggle to raise children, or to grow up, in a dangerous world. The very moment when we almost lose hope is the moment we need assurance that, if we can just hang on, God will get us through. That is the moment when we need something written for people under siege.

The only part of the great temple to survive destruction was what may have been a small portion of its west wall. Through the years, millions of Jews—and others as well—have gone to lament their misfortunes and to pray for God's strength at what is called "The Wailing Wall." They write their prayers on small pieces of paper, fold them tightly, and stuff them into cracks between the stones. The stones are worn smooth with rubbing and are warmed by the sun. Leaning against this fragmented ruin feels like leaning against the bosom of God.

Whenever God is presented as cosmic bogeyman, whenever worshiping God is based primarily on fear, then we experience only the small, vengeful god of Uncle Ralph and Miss Melinda. We see a pygmy god, and catch no glimpse of the breadth and depth of the One who created us. We never get to know the great God of Malachi, Luke, and Jesus. The God present, even during the destruction. The God still present in the ruins. The God who says, "Do not be terrified. For you who revere my name the sun of righteousness shall rise, with healing in its wings."

Carolyn West is vicar of St. John's College Ministry, Murray, Kentucky.

■ 5

PREACHING IN PERSPECTIVE: BIBLICAL, HISTORICAL, THEOLOGICAL, AND SPIRITUAL ESSAYS

PREACHING JOHN—WORD AND WORDS
Robert W. Kysar

THE GOSPEL of John is of special interest to us preachers because it seems to be preaching in its own narrative way.[1] To some degree this is true of all the Gospels, but John has a special homiletical quality. This Gospel begins with a hymn dedicated to the Word, Logos, and that Word is the subject of the narrative sermon, which ends with the narrator telling us at 20:30–31:

Now Jesus did many other signs in the presence of his disciples, which are not written in this book. But these are written so that you may come to believe [or go on believing] that Jesus is the Messiah, the Son of God, and that through believing you may have life in his name.

The narrative leads readers to an experience of the life that is available in Christ.[2] With words, the evangelist brings us to a confrontation with the Word, Christ. Those words tell a story that contains both speech and actions. Words are the medium of narrative, of character, and of action, as well as of speech. There is a kind of self-consciousness about the way the evangelist proceeds. The Word became flesh and dwelt among us. Now the Word becomes *words* and dwells among us. In this Gospel, words take on a sacramental quality, for through words, God's grace comes to the reader and hearer.[3]

How does this Gospel use language to re-present the Christ-Word? I hope to respond to that question in only a preliminary way by exploring how the Johannine proclamation of the Word with words entails understanding the historical, literary, and theological nature of this Gospel. This article will sketch the nature of the fourth Gospel with special attention to how each feature—historical, literary, and theological—benefits the preacher. At the same time, I hope this discussion also makes clearer how the fourth evangelist preaches the message. My thesis is that John helps us understand both *what* to preach and *how* to preach it.

I. The Historical Origin of the Fourth Gospel

The field of research on the Gospel of John is voluminous and complicated, and here I can only summarize the most widely held view of the origin of the Gospel. A later section will give us opportunity to note how the new literary criticism in biblical studies enlightens John's style of proclamation. Preachers need, I believe, to be informed about the major movements afoot in Johannine studies.[4]

The origin of this Gospel has puzzled critics for centuries, and hypotheses for its setting are numerous. Yet in the last four decades a theory has emerged that has captured a great deal of attention and achieved considerable consensus. In brief, the proposal suggests that the fourth Gospel was written for a group of Christian Jews soon after they were separated from the synagogue in which they had worshiped. The clearest evidence for such a theory is found in the use of the word ἀποσυνάγωγος ("expelled" or "put out" of the synagogue) in 9:22, 12:42, and 16:2. After the separation of the messianic Jews from their sisters and brothers in the synagogue, the two groups engaged in a lively and sometimes vitriolic dialogue about their differences. J. Louis Martyn, one of the early proponents of this hypothesis, suggested that as a result of this dialogue between Christians and Jews, the Gospel is a two-level drama. At one level is the story of Jesus and his ministry, but, at a only slightly deeper level, readers see the story of the Johannine church and its experience.[5] The evangelist in effect does with the Jesus story something very much like what preachers set out to do each Sunday with the appointed passage(s). We elaborate the text but soon lead our listeners to consider another level at which the text intersects with our lives.

This theory for the origin of the Gospel of John has helped us in understanding several things about the document. As a consequence of this situation at the time of the writing of the Gospel, the Johannine community was trying to determine its identity, separated from but still in continuity with Judaism. If this hypothesis is sound, the question at stake for both the Johannine church and its sister synagogue was "Who are we?" Moreover, the theory enables us to comprehend the Gospel's view of Judaism and the Johannine sectarian, insider/outsider (us against them) language. Its preoccupation with Christ's identity also makes sense, since the major issue between the synagogue and the church was probably the question, "Who is Jesus?"

The most important contribution this proposal for the Gospel's origin makes to preaching is the light it sheds on the tone with which the fourth evangelist speaks of Jews and Judaism. The issue of John and Judaism is complex and controversial, but certainly "the Jews" (οἱ Ἰουδαῖοι) are most often presented in this Gospel as Jesus' opponents. Moreover, the evangelist clearly claims that Christianity is superior to Judaism (e.g., 1:17). The most poignant example of this anti-Jewish tone is 8:44 where Jesus declares to the Jews that they are children of the Devil and thereby demonizes them and their religion. The theory of the expulsion from the synagogue helps us recognize *the polemic quality of this language.* If the Gospel originated out of a clash between Christians and Jews, it is no wonder that the story includes attacks on the church's opponents. Polemic language was common between different groups in the ancient world and was often designed less to destroy an opponent than to bolster the reader's confidence.[6]

The fourth evangelist's proclamation of the Word in words is tainted with this polemical intent. Although not commendable, the polemic is understandable, since the proclamation of the Gospel always takes seriously the context of the community to which it is addressed. In that sense, the preached Word in John has an occasional character, fashioned for a particular situation in the life of the church. The same is true of the Gospel's attempt to strengthen the embattled community, to emphasize the people's unity, and to build their confidence.[6]

We preachers have a responsibility to help our congregations understand the occasion for which the Gospel was written. In particular we need to offer reasons for the harsh treatment of the Jews in John. Sermons offer important opportunities for such explanation and for neutralizing, insofar as possible, the use of the Gospel's language for anti-Semitic purposes today.

II. Theological Themes in John

With this brief discussion of the most important theory for the origin of the Gospel of John behind us, we turn to the theological nature of the Gospel.[7] This Gospel is saturated with theological thought and represents one of the major theologies of the entire New Testament. I mention here only two of the Johannine themes that I believe are most important for preachers.

The first is *Christology*, the core of Johannine theology. Everything arises from the question of who Christ is: pneumatology, eschatology, ecclesiolgy, soteriology, and all the rest. Even the understanding of God is christocentric, since everything John says about God entails God's relationship with Christ. God is Christ's Father. God is the sending One, who sends Christ. One knows God through knowing Christ. Like a hub of the wheel, all the theological spokes reach into christology and find their center there.

However, one of the amazing things about the christology of the fourth Gospel is that it is so very diverse we really should speak of *Christologies*.[8] The fourth evangelist describes Christ in many different ways, and does so without worrying about consistency. The heart of this problem is 1:14. On the one hand, "the Word became flesh" and, on the other hand, "we have seen his glory." How are we to reconcile human flesh and divine glory? How can flesh and glory reside in one person?[9]

Another good example is 5:19–25, in which Jesus speaks of his dependence on God. "The Son can do nothing on his own, but only what he sees the Father doing" (v. 19). How might we reconcile this statement of utter dependence with the christology of the prologue of the Gospel where Christ is called God's word and even God? The evangelist weaves together a number of very different christological statements without harmonizing them. Christ is the Word, God's own self, the revealer of God, a prophet or messenger (the one sent), and an agent of God.[10] John seems to say all these are helpful in some way and does not allow one to elbow the others out.

We can learn an important homiletical lesson from John's pluralistic christology: Christ's identity is forever a mystery that we need not try to solve. There are a variety of ways of speaking of Christ's relationship with God which are valid and need to be held together. Furthermore, the language to speak of Christ's identity is essentially metaphorical. In speaking of that identity, we have no option except to forge language based on our own experience. So, Christ is compared to a child in a close relationship with a parent, to an agent authorized to act on behalf of his or her sender, and to human self-expression (Word). The nature of christological language (and ultimately of theological language in general) encourages us to create our own contemporary metaphors for understanding Christ. Preachers ought not be shy about attempting that kind of contemporizing of language about the identity and work of Christ.

The relationship among the various christological categories employed by the fourth evangelist implies the second theme, namely, *paradox*. John's christology is paradoxical. The Gospel seems to say that truth is found not in one view but in several held together in tension with one another. Christ holds together the divine and the human without compromise (1:14), and claims to be one with God while still subservient to God (e.g., 10:30, 38 and 14:28). The multiplicity of Johannine christology is indicative of the paradoxical or many-faceted nature of Johannine theology. Out of this paradoxical christology, the fourth evangelist presents several sides to a number of other theological ideas. The most widely recognized Johannine paradoxical tension is between realized and futuristic eschatology (e.g., 5:21 and 5:24). The same double-sidedness is also found in the view of divine sovereignty (or election) and human freedom (6:67–70).

We also encounter paradox or double-sidedness in John's use of words with multiple meanings. This point anticipates what we should include in the discussion of Johannine language below, but merits consideration here. Sometimes paradoxical theological thought is encapsulated into single words or phrases. If you recognize the possibility that John's so-called double entendre is intentional, then it illustrates the paradoxical quality we have been discussing. That is to say, if in an instance of double meaning, both meanings make equal sense in terms of the evangelist's style and thought, then paradox is packed into a single word or phrase.

Chapter 3 contains several specimens of paradox in single words or phrases. The Greek word ἄνωθεν in verses 3 and 7 means both born "again" and born "from above." The word translated "wind" (πνεῦμα—vv. 5, 6, 8) can also mean both spirit and breath. "Lifted up" (ὕψωοεν—v. 14) can refer to both the enthronement of a king or a crucifixion. In each case, it is easy to argue that *both* meanings are proper and need to be included in the reading of this passage. Interpreters should not always assume the evangelist actually meant *one* of the two possible meanings and not the other. The fourth evangelist presents the many-sidedness of large theological themes in tiny word pictures.

What does all this mean for *preaching theological themes in John?* To begin with, how do we discern theological themes in this theologically rich Gospel? First, we should keep the whole of the Gospel before us when working on any one passage. Perhaps we may need to reread the whole of John to get a fresh perspective on a passage. Second, it helps if we remember that the author of the Gospel is not a contemporary systematic theologian! The Gospel's purpose is to nurture faith, not explicate theology. This means that we should not read John through the eyes of the creeds (for instance, what Christ's sonship means in John), for to do so may get us into more trouble than truth. Third, we ought to be aware that the Gospel is a community document, written for, and out of, a real Christian community with hurts, fears, and all the rest. The evangelist was writing on behalf of a community and addressing that community.

Finally, we do well to remember that the basic theme and claim of the Gospel is revelation. God has been revealed in Christ. Because of Christ, we know something about God we did not know before, since Christ "exegetes" the very heart of God (1:18). "Truth" in John probably means the truth of the revelation. The consistent theme of John is that in seeing and hearing Christ we see and hear God (e.g., 5:24 and 14:9–14). We are probably wise to ask of every text we read and preach on, how does this passage in some sense make God known?

Discerning theological themes in John leads us to some proposals for preaching them. One such proposal is that we *preach the paradoxes of John*. The church today, I believe, needs to take paradox more seriously, because we would profit from understanding that knowledge or truth is complex. Much to our dismay, there may not always be a single, simple answer. In our time, some try to reduce truth to easy, singular, uncomplicated statements, and we may be attracted to those who can tell us precisely what truth is.

I think John invites us to take a more complicated view. Truth is many-sided, paradoxical, and evasive. For example, John 6:60–71 portrays something important about faith. Yes, faith is decision for Christ, but it is also a gift, given by God. Both are true in our lives today: we know we have to embrace the gift of grace, yet there are times when we seem to believe without willing it, without being able within ourselves to believe.[11]

Furthermore, I propose that we *preach the sacramental quality of John*. I do not mean sacramental in the sense of baptism and Eucharist, although they are, of course, equally important. I have in mind the fact that John suggests that seeing and hearing a flesh and blood Jesus is our way of seeing and hearing God. God encounters us through the material world. This view cultivates a sacramental perspective on experience by taking the incarnational theology of the prologue seriously. It encourages our congregations to experience the consolation of the community as God's consolation, and the Christian colleague as the risen Christ. It is not that God once became flesh and dwelt among us, but that God is always becoming enfleshed in the community and hence dwelling among us.

To look at the other side of the issue (as John would want us to), we might also consider *preaching the otherness of Jesus*. The Gospel of John portrays Christ as radically other and not as the compassionate, warm, and gentle Jesus we would like. Perhaps it would be well from time to time to explore the otherness of Jesus, which in the fourth Gospel is presented in a number of ways.

Christ is said to descend and ascend (3:13). He is from above, not below and not of this world (8:23). All of this implies the allusive Christ and suggests that in Christ we encounter mystery. Perhaps we need a stronger sense of mystery in Christian worship and life today. Preaching his otherness may help us avoid domesticating Jesus, making him fit into our systems and presuppositions.

III. The Literary Features of John

The second major movement in Johannine scholarship, with which preachers could profitably be familiar, emphasizes the literary qualities of John. There is a new interest in the purely literary character of Scripture without primary reference to its historical origin. The whole of biblical studies has been influenced by what is sometimes called the "new literary criticism," and in the last couple of decades it has had an impact on Johannine studies. Generally this new literary concern concentrates on the text as we have it without dependence on theories about the origins of the biblical documents or their historical settings. Most literary critics do not, however, propose that we abandon historical criticism all together but only that we pay more attention to the features of the text as it stands. The movement includes such interpretative methods as reader response and narrative criticism.[12]

There are an increasing number of very fruitful studies of the literary qualities of John. It will suffice here to mention only a few examples of these studies and their importance for a homiletical interpretation of John.[13]

The first example of the success of literary criticism are the investigations of the narrative structure of John.[14] A number of scholars have identified "closures" in the whole of the Gospel. In the prologue, Christ (the Logos) is called God (1:1 and 18). Then the Gospel proper closes with Thomas's confession that Christ is both "Lord and God" (20:28). (Most scholars regard chapter 21 as an appendix to the Gospel.) The prologue claims that those who receive and believe in the Logos receive "power (or authority) to become children of God" (1:12). In John's crucifixion scene, Jesus entrusts his mother and the beloved disciple to each other as parent and child, thus creating a new family of God (19:26–27).[15] These bookends hold the narrative together and suggest the major thrust of the message of all that is between them.

Another example of the richness of the literary study of John is the work done on irony. There are many types of irony, of course, but in this case it is adequate to think of it as a situation in which characters say more than they realize they are saying. In the Gospel of John, it is usually the case that characters in the story do or say something they do not fully understand, while readers see and know something the characters do not. The Samaritan woman's question to Jesus in 4:12 ("Are you greater than our ancestor Jacob, who gave us the well . . . ?") is fraught with irony, since we readers know that of course Jesus is indeed greater. Pilate does not realize the full sense of the placard he has placed on Jesus' cross (19:19–22). Johannine irony has been studied with great care, with the result that we more fully appreciate the subtle skill with which the evangelist speaks to readers.[16]

The new literary interest in John has also resulted in studies of the characters in the narrative.[17] One fascinating proposal concerns the role of the unnamed characters in the Gospel story (e.g., the Samaritan woman and the beloved disciple). We might be inclined to think that leaving a character unnamed diminishes her or his importance. David Beck, however, persuasively argues that the fourth evangelist uses anonymous characters to foster the reader's identification with them. Since a character is without a name, we ourselves can more easily take that role in the story.[18] That proposal strengthens the impression that the evangelist leaves the beloved disciple unnamed in order to invite readers to think of themselves as such a disciple.[19]

A final example of the results of the new literary criticism in Johannine studies pertains to the narrative world of the Gospel. A narrative world is simply the world created by the storyteller and within which a story's characters live and the plot unfolds.[20] Authors invite readers into this world—the environment of the story—and ask them to accept that world as believable and true for the duration of the story. Every story creates such a world. Sometimes it is very much like our own real world (e.g., the novel *Primary Colors*) and sometimes very different (e.g., the *Star Wars* movies). The narrative world of the fourth Gospel is unique because it ushers readers into a milieu that, among other things, has two quite distinct realms—the above and the below—and in which there is a clear and sharp distinction between truth and falsehood. Culpepper writes:

> *The implicit purpose of the gospel narrative is to alter irrevocably the reader's perception of the real world. The narrative world of the gospel is therefore neither a window on the ministry of Jesus nor a window on the history of the Johannine community. Primarily at least, it is the literary creation of the evangelist, which is crafted with the purpose of leading readers to "see" the world as the evangelist sees it so that in reading the gospel they will be forced to test their perceptions and beliefs about the "real" world against the evangelist's perspective on the world they encountered in the gospel.*[21]

Preachers, I think, want to do the very same thing with their listeners as the evangelist does with the readers of the Gospel. We are interested in the story's world because it is both like and unlike our lived worlds. We try to entice our listeners into the biblical world (or more precisely, the world of the text on which we are preaching) and then demonstrate how that world is like our own but also challenges our worlds.

The new literary criticism cultivates an appreciation for the text itself—something preachers have long treasured. This movement makes at least two quite different contributions to preaching. First, the new literary criticism of Scripture suggests that we can concentrate on the text without being overly worried about its historical background. This is not to say that historical studies are made irrelevant by literary criticism, for that is clearly not the case. However, as preachers we always bump up against historical questions that are not solved and which we cannot solve. We must go ahead and preach the text without that historical bit of knowledge (e.g., was Paul the author of the pastoral epistles?). Without always answering such questions, literary criticism allows us to attend to and preach the text as we find it and frees us to preach without historical certainty.

Second, and more important, we can identify literary techniques in the Gospel story and try to replicate them in our sermons. For instance, the evangelist's ironic presentation of Christ's kingship might fashion a sermon for Christ the King Sunday. A sermon on the Samaritan woman might ask what her name was and invite listeners to name her with their own identity. Whatever literary quality of the Gospel one chooses, fashioning a sermon around that feature is biblical preaching at its best.

The theological themes of the fourth Gospel are entwined with its literary features. In particular, the Gospel advocates theological themes through its use of language. We have already seen how the evangelist's paradoxical style of theological thought is expressed in the use of words and phrases with multiple meanings. Moreover, our discussion included some remarks on the polemic quality of Johannine language. Now let's examine two other features of the language of this Gospel through which the Word is proclaimed in words, namely, the symbolic quality of the language and the nature of progression in the Johannine discourses.

As nearly everyone agrees, John's language is highly symbolic or metaphorical.[22] Words and phrases may refer to something more than their usual or obvious referent within the narrative. A good example is *water* and the way it points us below itself (e.g., 4:1–42). This feature adds riches beyond measure to the Johannnine text, but also presents a problem for interpreters. When shall we take a word, phrase, or action as symbolic, that is, as referring to something more (and greater) than its obvious referent? Because the fourth evangelist makes ample use of symbolic meaning, we are inclined to look for it everywhere. A case in point is the "blood and water" that flows from Jesus' side after the spear thrust (19:34). The obvious meaning is that Jesus is indeed dead. However, should we take these two fluids as representative of other realities? The best protection against making up symbolic references where none exists is simply to check it out elsewhere in the Gospel. Is water used symbolically elsewhere? To what does it refer there? How about "blood"? Is there any evidence that the evangelist elsewhere assigns it a symbolic significance? Attempting to be consistent with the evangelist's style as a whole may prevent our misuse of the text.

Turning to another feature of Johannine language, the discourses of the fourth Gospel seem to have been put together with little regard for logic. The narrative material flows with a natural logic; however, the structure of the discourses is one of the classic problems in Johannine studies and one that is not easily explained. There are a number of ways of reading the discourses, each of which is more helpful in some cases than in others.

Sometimes the discourses appear to proceed in a spiral. For example, in 17:6–19, verses 6–14 seem held together by the word "given," but the word "world" begins to appear with it (vv. 9, 11, 13, and 14). Then in verses 15–19 the sentences are linked with the word "world." In this case, there is a kind of spiraling effect, but there is clearer evidence of another way of spotting the progression of a discourse. In such passages, movement is occasioned more by connections between words than by ordinary logic. Perhaps we should not look for logic but for association of ideas and concepts. Another way of thinking of the progression of these passages is to consider each of them a stream of consciousness. You don't analyze a stream of consciousness, but you try to enter it and be carried along with it. You "go with the flow."

How does one go about *preaching John's language*? I offer two possibilities for taking advantage of the nature of Johannine language for homiletical purposes. First, I suggest we use the symbolic and metaphorical language by adapting it to our day. Relanguage John for contemporary listeners.[23] In this case, we allow John's language to excite our imaginations, and we "play" with the language to see what happens. For instance, the ambiguity of πνεῦμα in chapter 3 is really a condensed little metaphor using *wind* to enlighten the meaning of *spirit*. The spirit and the wind are the same. As is the case with the Spirit, you can see the evidence of the wind's presence but not the wind itself. The freedom of the wind, its strength, its changing directions all help us articulate the church's experience of the Holy Spirit. All this might inspire preachers to weave their own analogies using wind and spirit. Imagine a child flying a kite and learning the power and mystery of the wind. The language's metaphorical quality invites us to create metaphors for our day out of John's metaphors.

I also invite you to craft sermons around some of John's favorite words. For example, the evangelist is fond of the word *abide* (the verb μένω), and it is rich with possibilities for preaching. In John the word suggests relationship. The father abides in the Son (14:10), and the believers abide in Son (15:4). Relationship is the key to knowing God, and how we are related matters in terms of what we know. Relationships constitute the heart of our faith, and in them we discover the deeper dimensions of life, particularly life together.

Another example is the word *world* (κόσμος). The fourth evangelist often uses it in a negative sense to speak of the realm of evil and unbelief. The world hates Christ and the believers (15:18). However, on the other hand, God "so loved the world" that God sends the son (3:16) for the redemption of the world. Moreover, believers are sent into the world, as God sent Christ into the world (17:18 and 20:21). By examining this single word in its contexts in the fourth Gospel, we discover the essential ingredients of a theology of mission. The Christian community is distinct from the world, but in mission to the world. Driven by God's love for the creation, we are invited to engage the world with the gospel message.[25]

Conclusion

These matters do not exhaust the ways in which the fourth evangelist preaches the Word with words; however, perhaps they give us a starting point from which to examine individual passages in John in terms of how they preach. Still another point needs to be made in closing.

In the introduction, I suggested that the Gospel of John shows us both what to preach and how to preach it because the Gospel is itself a narrative sermon. In John's story of Jesus there is a dynamic relationship between narratives and discourses, so that the two literary forms team up to lead readers into the new life God offers us in Christ (e.g., 13:1–20). Story enacts words, and words represent actions; story interprets words, and words story. Actions are the Word.[26]

Consider what this means for the sermon. Actions and words are welded together. Gestures embody the message that is spoken in words. The preacher's very presence in some way enacts the words of the sermon, for God calls us to embody the message, to allow it to take control of our whole being, both our words and actions. When by the grace of God that happens, the Word is once again embodied in flesh and blood. By the grace of God, our words then are the Word.

Robert W. Kysar is Bandy Professor of Preaching and
New Testament Emeritus at the Candler School of Theology,
Emory University, Atlanta, Georgia.

---

1. This article is an adaptation of a presentation I made for the Preaching with Excellence program, June, 1999, and to whose participants I owe my profound thanks.

2. See Gail O'Day's excellent commentary on the Gospel of John in volume IX of *The New Interpreter's Bible: A Commentary in Twelve Volumes*, Leander E. Keck, general ed. (Nashville: Abingdon, 1995), 491–865, especially 852.

3. See Kysar, *John, the Maverick Gospel*, rev. ed. (Louisville: Westminster John Knox, 1993), 122–126.

4. For a general overview of recent Johannine scholarship, see Gerard S. Sloyan, *What Are They Saying About John?* (New York/Mahwah: Paulist, 1991).

5. J. Louis Martyn, *History and Theology in the Fourth Gospel* (New York: Harper and Row, 1968; rev. and enlarged ed., Nashville: Abingdon, 1979). See also Raymond E. Brown, S.S., *The Gospel According to John*, The Anchor Bible, vols. 29 and 29a (Garden City: Doubleday, 1966 and 1970) and *The Community of the Beloved Disciple: The Life, Loves, and Hates of an Individual Church in New Testament Times* (New York/Ramsey/Toronto: Paulist, 1979).

6. See Luke Timothy Johnson, "The New Testament's Anti-Jewish Slander and the Conventions of Ancient Polemic," *Journal of Biblical Literature*, 108 (1989), 419–441, and Craig A. Evans and Donald A. Hagner, eds., *Anti-Semitism and Early Chrisitanity: Issues of Polemic and Faith* (Minneapolis: Fortress, 1993).

7. A very good overview of Johannine theology is found in D. Moody Smith, *The Theology of the Gospel of John* (Cambridge: Cambridge University Press, 1995).

8. See Kysar, *John, the Maverick Gospel*, chapter 1.

9. This posed the classic conflict between Rudolf Bultmann and Ernst Käsemann. See Käsemann, "The Structure and Purpose of the Prologue to John's Gospel," *New Testament Questions of Today* (Philadelphia: Fortress, 1969), 138–167; and Bultmann, *The Gospel of John: A Commentary* (Philadelphia: Westminster, 1971), 60–72.

10. See Paul N. Anderson, *The Christology of the Fourth Gospel: Its Unity and Disunity in the Light of John 6* (Valley Forge: Trinity Press International, 1996).

11. Kysar, "The Dismantling of Decisional Faith: A Reading of John 6:25–71," *Critical Readings of John 6*, R. Alan Culpepper, ed., Biblical Interpretation Series 22 (Leiden/New York/Köln: Brill, 1997), 161–181.

12. Another important scholarly trend in Johannine studies is the new social science interpretation, e.g., Bruce J. Malina and Richard L. Rohrbaugh, *Social-Science Commentary on the Gospel of John* (Minneapolis: Fortress, 1998).

13. Consult R. Alan Culpepper, *Anatomy of the Fourth Gospel: A Study in Literary Design* (Philadelphia: Fortress, 1983); and Jeffrey Lloyd Staley, *The Print's First Kiss: A Rhetorical Investigation of the Implied Reader in the Fourth Gospel*, Society of Biblical Literature Dissertation Series 82 (Atlanta: Scholars, 1988).

14. The best narrative critical study of John is Mark W. G. Stibbe, *John as Storyteller: Narrative Criticism and the Fourth Gospel*, Society for New Testament Studies, Monograph Series 73 (Cambridge/New York: Cambridge University Press, 1992). See also Fernando F. Segovia, "The Journey(s) of the Word of God: A Reading of the Plot of the Fourth Gospel," *Semeia 53: The Fourth Gospel from a Literary Perspective*, R. Alan Culpepper and Fernando F. Segovia, eds. (Atlanta: Scholars, 1991), 23–54.

15. R. Alan Culpepper, "The Pivot of John's Prologue," *New Testament Studies* 27 (1980), 1–31.

16. For example, Paul D. Duke, *Irony in the Fourth Gospel* (Atlanta: John Knox Press, 1985); and Gail R. O'Day, *Revelation in the Fourth Gospel* (Philadelphia: Fortress, 1986).

17. For example, Sandra M. Schneiders, *The Revelatory Text: Interpreting the New Testament as Sacred Scripture* (New York: HarperCollins, 1991), 180–197; Culpepper, *Anatomy of the Fourth Gospel*, chapter 5; and Jeffrey Staley, "Stumbling in the Dark, Reaching for the Light: Reading Character in John 5 and 9," *Semeia* 53, 55–80.

18. David R. Beck, *The Discipleship Paradigm: Readers and Anonymous Characters in the Fourth Gospel*, Biblical Interpretation Series 27 (Leiden/New York/Cologne: Brill, 1997).

19. See Rudolf Schnackenburg, *The Gospel According to St. John* (New York: Crossroads, 1982), vol. 3, 375–388.

20. See Schneiders, *The Revelatory Text*, chapter 5; and Norman R. Petersen, *The Gospel of John and the Sociology of Light: Language and Characterization in the Fourth Gospel* (Valley Forge: Trinity Press International, 1993).

21. Culpepper, *Anatomy of the Fourth Gospel*, 4–5.

22. See Craig R. Koester, *Symbolism in the Fourth Gospel: Meaning, Mystery, Community* (Minneapolis: Fortress, 1995).

23. See Robert G. Hughes and Robert Kysar, *Preaching Doctrine for the Twenty-First Century* (Minneapolis: Fortress, 1997), 29–32.

24. See Brown, *Gospel According to St. John*, vol. I, 510–512.

25. See my discussion of 20:19–23 in *John*, Augsburg Commentary on the New Testament (Minneapolis: Augsburg, 1986), 302–305.

26. See Terence E. Fretheim, "Word of God," *The Anchor Bible Dictionary*, David Noel Freedman, editor-in-chief (New York/Long/Toronto/Sydney/Auckland: Doubleday, 1992), vol. 6, 961–968.

Reflections on Preaching Through the Ages

O. C. Edwards, Jr.

I HAVE SPENT the last sixteen years trying to write a history of Christian preaching, and I am approaching the end of my first draft. What follows is the perspective gained on the preaching enterprise through that effort. I begin with something that may be easy to forget in our daily preoccupation with our task: the *importance* of preaching. So let me remind you that, in their development and expansion, most of the significant movements in the history of the church have involved preaching.

This can be seen first of all in the way the Gospel spread after Pentecost. In A.D. 49, just sixteen years after the classical date assigned to the Crucifixion, the emperor Claudius ordered Jews out of Rome because of disturbances within their community resulting from the activity of Christian missionaries. In that short a time Christian preaching had moved from a backwater province of the empire to its very center and was having enough impact to come to the attention of the highest reaches of government. Fifteen years later, when the citizens of Rome believed the fire that had burned their city had been set by the emperor Nero to inspire him in poetic composition, he shifted the blame to the Christians, who in that short time had become the standard scapegoats on whom anything unpleasant could be blamed. Some very effective preaching must have been done to evangelize a Christian community in Rome large enough to have received so much public attention, even if it was largely negative.

It is certainly not coincidental that the period when Christianity finally displaced Greco-Roman religion as the official cult of the empire was a time when the greatest bishops and theologians of the church had achieved success as sophists and teachers of rhetoric before ordination. Then, too, the church's response to the unchurched populations of the newly founded cities in the High Middle Ages was to create the mendicant orders of friars, itinerant preachers to be sent where the need was greatest. It belabors the obvious to mention the Reformation as a preaching movement. And the examples can be rounded off without being anywhere near exhausted by noting that the abolitionist movement in the nineteenth and the civil rights movement in the twentieth century numbered preachers among their most effective leaders, and preaching as one of the major media through which they spread their message. Most of the great movements in the history of the church have depended on preaching to accomplish their purposes.

This is not even to mention the importance of preaching in the ordinary life of the church. In a justly famous passage in *The Shape of the Liturgy*, Dom Gregory Dix listed the occasions on which the people of God have found making Eucharist to be the most appropriate activity.[1] A list of the times when preaching has seemed the natural thing to do would both overlap his to a considerable extent and, if anything, be even longer. And what Dix said about

ordinary offerings of the Eucharist applies equally well to the preaching of sermons: *Best of all, week by week and month by month, on a hundred thousand*
successive Sundays, faithfully, unfailingly, across all the parishes of
Christendom, the pastors have done just this to make the plebs sancta Dei—
the holy common people of God.[2] That the same thing can be said of both the
Eucharist and preaching should surprise no one, because we know very well
that two main channels of grace in the church are Word and Sacrament. Of
the two, however, preaching has been the major means by which Christians have
been formed intellectually. It gives specificity to the grace the Eucharist com-
municates sacramentally. Many historical examples could be given of the grace
that has been communicated through preaching, but these are not necessary
here, because I am sure that all of us can document that proposition from our
own lives.

With such a reminder of the importance of preaching in the history of the
church, it is not surprising, though many would be surprised, that we have many
examples of the sermons preached during most periods in church history. A case
in point: for the years 1150 to 1350 a list of sermon manuscripts has been com-
piled that runs to nine volumes with a cumulative 7,300 pages.[3] If the average
number of sermons per page is consistent with a sample taken of over forty
pages, then more than eighty thousand sermons have been preserved in manuscript. Since this is one of the periods from which one could have expected
relatively few sermons to have survived, it can be taken as an indication of the
number of sermons from the past that are still in existence.

It will amaze no one that most of the sermons that have come down from
different periods of church history are from the homiletical equivalent of "the
rich and famous," but we can assume that then, as now, ordinary preaching
was very similar to that of the "tall steeple preachers" in form and content,
since it would all reflect the consciousness of the church at the time. It cannot
even be taken for granted that the sermons of the "giants of the pulpit" were
necessarily more eloquent, profound, or filled with spiritual insight, because
we have known too many excellent preachers whose reputation never reached
beyond a small circle. By the same token, many proclaimers of the Word most
esteemed in their own generation make a poor showing over the test of time.
Thus, while it can be said that ordinary preaching has been most important in
the life of the church, it nevertheless remains true that for most Christian generations, we have to infer what such preaching was like from what was done
by the better-known preachers whose sermons have come down to us.

An example of what can be inferred about ordinary preachers from the ones
whose sermons have not been lost is the qualities that have made all of them
effective. A list of those qualities can begin with what F. Van der Meer said
about his subject in *Augustine the Bishop*: "His real secret, which he shares
with all orators who really succeed in fascinating us, is that he had such an
enormous amount to say."[4] That reminds all teachers of preaching of the old
distinction between "sermons that have something to say and sermons that have
to say something." There is no doubt about which sort is more memorable, or,

perhaps more accurately, none about the sort for which one retains pleasant memories.

To break down the elements of "having something to say," it can be noted that all really effective preachers have at least three qualities in common. They all have a good mind, a rhetorical reflex, and personal holiness. *Rhetorical reflex* means a native sense of how to get one's point across when addressing a group; the meaning of the other two terms is obvious. It is likely that among the group of preachers who are respected in any given period there may be found all the possible ratios in which the relative strengths of these three elements may be combined. But to do preaching at its best, one needs each of these qualities in a high degree, because a lack on any one of the three will diminish the effect, and do so in a characteristic way.

In addition to the qualities of preachers, we have to think of the characteristics of the times in which they preached. There have been many different kinds of preaching in history and they were all probably related to what was going on in the society in which they arose. More will be said of this later; the only point to be made right now is that these movements all draw on contemporary standards of what makes public speaking effective, and tastes in that have changed rapidly at times. In most ages a factor in the formation of taste in oratory has been Greco-Roman rhetoric. That is not surprising, because that enterprise represents the best effort ever made to observe what did and did not work in public address and to create a vocabulary with which to communicate that information.

In a pure form, however, the criteria of classical rhetoric have never served well as standards for Christian preaching. The reason for this is that none of the three classical *genera dicendi* (basic forms of speech) provides for the explication of a text, and thus they provide no place for the interpretation of passages from the Bible that has been one of the most persistent elements in Christian preaching.

The way the text to be explicated is chosen has varied considerably over the centuries. Probably the use of a lectionary has been most common, but many preachers through the ages have seen virtue in preaching all the way through one biblical book before considering a passage from another (*lectio continua*), even though this method is as fixed and artificial as following a lectionary. Others preachers have chosen the passage or verse that seemed to be the portion of the Bible most relevant to their congregation at that moment, the result being either expository or textual preaching, depending on the length of the passage chosen. And some have chosen a subject, a topic, to speak about, which they authorized scripturally by citations from various parts of the Bible.[5]

However the passage is chosen, it is nevertheless the case that the way the text is explicated reflects the principles of biblical interpretation in vogue at the time. Or, more precisely, it reflects the hermeneutics of at least the community for which it was prepared, since at any given moment there is a variety of Christian communities, and each has its own characteristic method of discovering what a biblical passage means to and for them. Within this overall variation, there nevertheless have been methods that have prevailed within large portions of the Christian community. Among these, the most dramatic shift has undoubtedly been that from allegorical interpretation to use of the historical/ critical method. Even that, however, has not made as much difference as one might think. While use of the two methods would produce very different understandings of the original meaning of the passage, the way in which it is brought to bear on the life of the congregation would probably be very similar. The literal, grammatical, historical meaning of a biblical text is always the meaning it had for its first hearers or readers, and the relevance of the text to later congregations is necessarily always analogical.

That being so, it is disappointing that few sermons of the past can be read with much edification by most Christians today. That probably is more a matter of different concerns preoccupying the churches than it is the result of changed methods of biblical interpretation. In spite of this, it can still be seen that in every generation the church has been able to turn to the Bible for necessary insight into its own situation. Somehow, through preaching, the Bible speaks to the condition of the local community of the people of God, whenever and wherever they are assembled. This capacity of the Scriptures to give needed insight into such an immense variety of situations is undoubtedly much of what is meant by calling them *inspired.*

I will organize the rest of my observations in terms of the five tasks of a speaker recognized by Greco-Roman rhetoric: Invention, Disposition, Elocution or Style, Memory, and Delivery.

Invention

Invention consists of deciding what to say in a speech. Aristotle defined rhetoric as "an ability in each particular case to see the available means of persuasion."[6] Persuasion, as such, is not what we are trying to accomplish in all sermons; but preaching is motivated behavior; it is trying to accomplish something. A good list of the things we try to accomplish in preaching comes from Ronald E. Osborn: "The skillful preacher attempts to catch the hearers' interest from the start and to sustain it throughout, engaging their problems and concerns, passing on the tradition, guiding understanding, correcting false impressions, answering objections, projecting a vision, undertaking to persuade, imparting grace."[7]

To have a chance of meeting these goals, preachers need to be strategic in their invention: they need to figure where they want their congregations to arrive, identify the obstacles that stand in the way of their going there, and design a process to help them get by the roadblocks and arrive safely at their destination. Part of all such processes is a demonstration that what is proposed is consistent with whatever is accepted by members of the congregation as authoritative. Most Christians have been willing to assume that the Bible is normative for their belief, but the way its authority has been brought to bear has varied enormously. Thus the preacher whose invention involves an appeal to Bible must make it in accordance with the criteria acknowledged by those who will hear the sermon. While we all are probably familiar with some sort of proof-texting, that has by no means ever been the main way biblical warrant has been invoked for positions taken in sermons. Other appeals made in preaching have been to reason, emotion, and imagination. The variety of possible combinations of these appeals can be seen in the sermons of five revivalists.

Jonathan Edwards combined rigorous logic with acute psychological analysis to move people to love God's election of some to salvation and some to damnation.

The published sermons of *John Wesley* seem to be instructions in Christian doctrine (modeled as they were on the Church of England's *Book of Homilies*) but in actual delivery, the calm voice of reason was not all that was heard. Horace Walpole, a litterateur and a pioneer in the Gothic revival, has left an unsympathetic account of what it was like to hear him preach: "Wesley is a lean, elderly man, fresh-coloured, his hair smoothly combed, but with a soupçon of curl at the ends. Wondrous clean, but as evidently an actor as Garrick. He spoke his sermon, but so fast, and with so little accent, that I am sure he has often uttered it, for it was like a lesson; but towards the end he exalted his voice, and acted very ugly enthusiasm."[8]

George Whitefield, on other hand, preached in such a way that it was hard for people to remember afterwards what he had said, but they did remember that it was enormously moving, as Benjamin Franklin testified in his autobiography. He went to hear Whitefield intending not to give a penny to the orphanage in Georgia for which the preacher was trying to raise money, but he wound up emptying his pockets.

Charles Grandison Finney had been trained in law rather than theology, and he argued to get a conviction, except that instead of trying to convince jurors that the *defendant* was guilty, he set out to make his hearers feel that *they* were.

Dwight L. Moody's idea of a sermon has been compared to the report of one businessman to another.

Since all these such different styles of preaching were for the single purpose of converting sinners to Christianity, we can see that sermon invention for all the many purposes of preaching must have varied enormously.

Disposition

There has been equal variety in homiletical approaches to *Disposition*. Greco-Roman rhetoric recognized three basic types of speech (*genera dicendi*), each with its characteristic outline. These were: (1) the forensic speech, the sort made in a law court, designed to persuade an audience about what happened in the past; (2) the deliberative, the type given in a legislative assembly to recommend what ought to be done in the future; and (3) the epideictic, made on public occasions to "point with pride" or to "view with alarm" some person or activity in the present life of the community, the sort of speech made on ceremonial occasions. As noted earlier, sermons fit none of these three arrangements of a speech because none provides for the explication of a text, nor was there one standard outline into which classical homilies fall.[9] Looking down through history, one can find expository sermons with many different outlines.

Origen would comment verse by verse as he went along, tossing out exegetical information and doing allegorical interpretation in which his application occurred, commenting on the biblical text in the way that a grammarian teaching in a secondary school at the time would comment on a classical one. Sometimes he began with an introduction and sometimes not.[10]

Chrysostom would do literal exegesis with no effort at application until he got to the last verse he had time to talk about. Even then, the moral lesson he found did not always come too obviously from the verse just exegeted.

Puritans would go through three steps with each verse (or, sometimes, phrase): they would exegete it, state as a proposition the doctrine taught in it (confirming that proposition from other passages in the Bible), and then find applications to lives of the congregation, or, as they called them, "uses." Notice that this variety of disposition or outline occurs within a single basic type of sermon. Imagine how much greater the differences are when one considers the whole range of sermon forms. Incidentally, I think there are more forms of preaching today than in all previous Christian centuries put together. That is probably because there are more Christians, more preachers, and consequently more sermons than ever before. This indicates how radically *ad hoc* all Christian preaching is. Just as at Pentecost all heard the Good News in their own languages, everyone always needs to hear it not only in their own tongue, but in terms of the culture of which they are a part as well.

In classical rhetoric the concept of *Elocution* was not as inclusive as that of *Style* today. It was generally limited to figures of sound and thought, i.e., to figures of speech that had their appeal in the way they struck the ear (such as alliteration or rhyme) and those that pleased the mind (metaphor, for example). It was recognized, however, that there were three levels of style, each with its characteristic use or abstention from figures: the plain style to teach, the middle to please, and the grand to move.

There has been a pendulum swing through the ages in the church's attitude toward the use of these figures. Some have thought that only plain style, which eschewed such ornamentation, was consistent with the Gospel. Others have used great artistry to convey the Christian message. This alternation may be related to the dominance of the right brain or left brain in an individual or culture. It is certainly related to what Charles Williams has referred to as "the two chief approaches to God defined in Christian thought," the way of the rejection of images and that of the affirmation of them.[11] It is a matter for reflection, for example, that Gregory the Great (c. 540–604) was the first preacher in the history of the church to make much use of extended narratives to illustrate the points in his sermons, and his doing so was not widely imitated until the High Middle Ages when friars began using exempla.

I will combine *Memory* and *Delivery* with one of the few sweeping generalizations I can make about preaching through the ages: with rare exceptions, the most effective preachers have not preached from manuscripts. In not doing so they have to an extent honored the standard of the Greco-Roman rhetoricians who either memorized their orations or spoke them extemporaneously.[12]

This generalization can be documented by noting that Augustine wanted nothing to impede his ability to gauge audience reactions to what he was saying. If he saw ready comprehension, he would move along, but if he saw uncertainty on the faces of his auditors, he would go back over the point and offer analogies. Bernard of Clairvaux did much the same. Indeed, the standard was so established that Archbishop William Laud apologized for using "papers" when he preached from the scaffold where he was beheaded. While Spurgeon would think all week about his sermon for the coming Sunday, he would wait until after Saturday afternoon tea to draw up the outline that would be only thing he took into the pulpit. Henry Ward Beecher would have several ideas for sermons going around his mind at once and wouldn't decide on which to preach until Sunday morning after breakfast. There are exceptions that prove this rule like any other, exceptions of the stature of Tillotson and Fosdick; nevertheless, the generalization that most of the greatest preachers spoke without a manuscript is a safe one.

With that, the only things left to be said are warnings voiced by far greater authorities than the present one. First let us hear from Dante:

> *Christ his apostles did not thus address:*
> *Go forth and preach idle stories to all men,*
> *But taught them his true doctrine to profess.*
>
> *Forth with his shield the apostles sally then,*
> *None other than his word their lips escapes,*
> *This only is the sword they wield amain.*
>
> *But nowadays men preach with jokes and japes,*
> *And if they raise a laugh, their cowls all swell with pride*
> *They ask no more, the jackanapes.*[13]

Or, to draw on an even more exalted authority, listen to the second lesson for Morning Prayer on the Feast of Pentecost: "When I came to you, brothers and sisters, I did not come proclaiming the mystery of God to you in lofty words or wisdom. For I decided to know nothing among you except Jesus Christ, and him crucified. And I came to you in weakness and in fear and in much trembling. My speech and my proclamation were not with plausible words of wisdom, but with a demonstration of the Spirit and of power, so that your faith might rest not on human wisdom but on the power of God. Yet among the mature we do speak wisdom, though it is not a wisdom of this age or of the rulers of this age, who are doomed to perish. But we speak God's wisdom, secret and hidden, which God decreed before the ages for our glory. None of the rulers of this age understood this; for if they had, they would not have crucified the Lord of glory. But, as it is written, 'What no eye has seen, nor ear heard, nor the human heart conceived, what God has prepared for those who love him'—

these things God has revealed to us through the Spirit; for the Spirit searches everything, even the depths of God. For what human being knows what is truly human except the human spirit that is within? So also no one comprehends what is truly God's except the Spirit of God. Now we have received not the spirit of the world, but the Spirit that is from God, so that we may understand the gifts bestowed on us by God. And we speak of these things in words not taught by human wisdom but taught by the Spirit, interpreting spiritual things to those who are spiritual" (1 Corinthians 2:1–13).

> *O. C. Edwards, Jr., is emeritus professor of preaching at Seabury-Western Theological Seminary, Evanston, Illinois.*

---

1. Dom Gregory Dix, *The Shape of the Liturgy* (London: Dacre Press, 1945), 744.

2. Ibid. Emphasis his.

3. J.B. Schneyer, *Reportium der lateinischen Sermones des Mittelalters fur die Zeit von 1150–1350* ("Beitrdge zur Geschichte der Philosophie und Theologie des Mattelalters," Band XLIII, Heften 1–9; Munster: Aschendorffsche Verlagsbuchhandlung, 1969–1980).

4. *The Life and Work of a Father of a Church*, trans. Brian Battershaw and G. R. Lamb (London and New York: Sheed and Ward, 1961), 432.

5. In practice, however, these methods of choosing the text to be explicated do not automatically produce sermons of clearly different forms. Preachers following a lectionary, for instance, can do either expository or textual or even topical preaching.

6. Rhet. 1.2. The translation given is that of *Aristotle on Rhetoric, A Theory of Civil Discourse*, ed. George A. Kennedy (New York and Oxford: Oxford University Press, 1991), 36. The translation given in the Loeb Classics edition is: "the faculty of discovering the possible means of persuasion in reference to any subject whatever."

7. Ronald E. Osborn, *A History of Christian Preaching, Vol. 1, Folly of God: The Rise of Christian Preaching* (St. Louis, MO: Chalice Press, 1999), xiii.

8. I seem to have lost the reference for this, but I believe that Ronald Knox quoted it in the chapter on Wesley in his *Enthusiasm*.

9. To the extent that "homily" has a technical meaning, it refers to sermons following the pattern of verse-by-verse interpretation of a biblical passage—what is referred to today as "expository preaching."

10. When one was used, however, it was not an introduction in our sense, i.e., it did not necessarily "lead into" the topic that was to be discussed. Often it was a discussion of a moral issue that happened to be on his mind that was not always related to the passage being interpreted. Sometimes, however, it would relate that sermon to the one that had preceded it.

11. Charles Williams, *The Figure of Beatrice: A Study in Dante* (Cambridge: D.S. Brewer, a 1994 reprint of the original edition of 1943), 8.

12. Both traditions were highly honored. On the one hand, rhetoricians devised elaborate methods of memorization that are still called upon by anyone offering to help people improve their memories. On the other, itinerant sophists made glamorous careers of raising to an art form the schoolboy exercise of giving impromptu orations on topics set by their audience, speeches that observed all the rules of rhetoric, including periodic sentences, the figures, and frequent quotations from classical literature.

13. *Par. xxix*, 109–17, trans. Dorothy L. Sayers.

Living with Ambiguity as Faithfulness to Christ: Some Implications of Richard Hooker's Theology for an Anglican Homiletic

Thomas H. Troeger

"full of tongue and weak of braine"

Two parallel activities have drawn me to this topic: observing Christians who use the Bible to make absolute claims in the name of God, when in fact the truth is ambiguous, and reading works by and about Richard Hooker (c. 1554–1600), the great apologist for the Elizabethan Settlement of 1559. Hooker offered an alternative theological vision to biblicism, by which I mean a proof-text driven reading of the Scriptures, a "Literalism, which worships the text and gives it an inappropriate superiority over the spirit that animates it."[1]

My holding these two things in tandem—our current wave of biblicism and Hooker's theology—reveals that I am not writing an objective history of Hooker and his thought, if there is such a thing as "objectivity" in a postmodern age. I acknowledge from the start that this essay grows out of my pain and weariness at seeing the Scriptures and the name of God invoked to justify hostile judgments against gays, lesbians, various ethnic groups, women asserting their full and equal status with men, multiple patterns of family life, and other religions.

Although four centuries separate Hooker's era and ours, his work offers an historical perspective on our current religious entanglements and provides theological principles that can shape our preaching in ways that

- honor the Bible without idolizing it,
- keep us faithful to Christ as we live in an ambiguous world,
- affirm the dynamic nature of the church,
- claim the full range of cognitive and creative gifts with which God has endowed us, and
- open us to the new winds of the Holy Spirit.

This essay, then, is not a systematic treatment of Hooker's thought but rather an attempt to identify some of the implications of his theology for preaching in our time.

I am employing a dynamic understanding of tradition as I draw upon Hooker for our own day. Such dynamism assumes that later generations return to their progenitors not to replicate exactly what their ancestors thought and did, but to draw from their work new wisdom for a new age. To use the imagery of Brian Wren, who writes in the context of understanding the dynamism of the biblical witness, "tradition means not photocopying" what faithful people did in the past "but pushing forward in the direction they point."[2]

Although this is not an essay in hagiography, I am leaving aside any consideration of the weaknesses of Hooker's thought or person. I know it is the current fashion to search for the inadequacies and indiscretions of anyone who is a public figure or who is an honored worthy from the past. But I find the depth and breadth, the rigor and balance of Hooker's thought so salutary for the religious afflictions of our day that I will be drawing only upon the strength and grace of his work, leaving refutation and scandal hunting to others.

Just as the political and theological conflicts that raged about Hooker fed his apology for the Elizabethan Settlement, so the religious conflicts of our society are driving me to find a homiletic that is free of the moral arrogance and anti-intellectualism that so often accompany a narrowly biblicist theology. When Hooker writes about "this present age full of tongue and weake of braine,"[3] I find his words depressingly accurate about much of our current religious rhetoric.

I call what I am developing an "Anglican" homiletic since it is inspired by the work of one of our greatest Anglican thinkers, and since I hope it incorporates those qualities that I consider characteristic of Anglicanism at its best. Many of these qualities either flow from Hooker's thought or were inspired by the generous spirit of the man's witness. They include

- a sense of balance and proportion,
- an affirmation of the image of God in all persons,
- an appreciation for the aesthetic as a dimension of holiness,
- the centrality to Christian life of feeding upon Christ in the heart by faith with thanksgiving,
- liturgical practice in which worship is the common prayer of the whole people of God,
- incarnational theology that takes seriously the need to embody the Gospel in acts of justice and compassion, and
- an appreciation for the inheritance of ancient prayer traditions while remaining open to revision and the new work of the Holy Spirit.

Although I call it an Anglican homiletic, I would not honor the man who has inspired my work if I did not make it clear that I welcome all Christian preachers who want to consider what truth this homiletic may hold for them, and how it may help to counteract the oppressive and hostile use of religion in our day.

"ten times redoubled tokens of our unfainedlie reconciled love"

"The tone and breadth of thought in Hooker's writings reveal the sweetness of his temperament and the loving spirit with which he approached the world in general and his fellow-human beings in particular. Kindness and readiness to reconcile opposites were the dominant notes of his mind. He had a sharply developed power of criticism. But there is not the slightest sign of bitterness or arrogance in his criticism; only an assertion of disagreement. Hatred of any kind was, in fact, alien to his nature."[4]

This observation about Hooker's character is in itself significant to the development of a homiletic for our time. It reminds us that it is not thought alone that engages us, but the tone and spirit of the individual who expresses the thought. The person of Hooker suggests that an Anglican homiletic includes attention to the character of the preacher. Becoming a preacher involves cultivating the grace of being able to assert disagreement without "bitterness or arrogance." Such cultivation is part of a homiletic that tends to the heart and soul of the preacher. It nurtures the hope of reconciliation and mutual understanding. As Hooker himself writes at the conclusion of his preface to *The Laws*: "But our trust in the almightie is, that with us contentions are now at their highest floate, and that the day will come (for what cause of despaire is there) when the passions of former enmitie being allaied, we shal with ten times redoubled tokens of our unfainedlie reconciled love, shewe our selves each towards other the same which Joseph and the brethren of Joseph were at the time of their enterview in Aegypt."[5]

Hooker's generous tone is in part, as John N. Wall has demonstrated, a rhetorical strategy. Wall analyzes Hooker's style as "the developing of a voice or a perspective from which to present the arguments of the Lawes which will make them appear less threatening, less oppositional, more considered, more thought out, the positions of one truly open to persuasion that have been reached only after considering both sides rather than of an already convinced controversialist."[6]

Hooker's marginalia, penned on the copy of a work by his critics, reveal that he had little patience for fools: "Ignorant assee . . . Your godfathers and Godmothers have much to answere unto God for not seing you better Catechised. . . You rage yell and bellow as one that were carried besides him self."[7] We need to remember, however, that these comments were meant only for Hooker's own eyes. He did not stoop to such language in the public arena because he wanted to establish a genuinely persuasive voice for matters that he knew were crucial to the welfare of church and state. Hooker's rhetorical strategy is rooted in the seriousness of the situation and a need to loosen the rigid biblicism of his opponents.

But Hooker's generous rhetoric also arose from the essential decency of his character and from a deep conviction that grace is extended by God even to those who are in error about God. While Hooker's opponents demonized Rome and all its cohorts, insisting they were damned forever, Hooker preached a more gracious gospel. While acknowledging that he disagreed with the Romanists, Hooker explained in one of his sermons how he would like to assure them, saying: "Be of good comfort, you have to do with a merciful God, who will make the best of that little which you hold well, and not with a captious sophister, who gathereth the worst out of every thing in which you are mistaken."[8] Four centuries later some of this may sound condescending to our ears, but in the context of the vicious rhetoric that fueled the violence of his age, these were generous words.

A little later in the same sermon, Hooker returns to the theme and pours out his own heart: "Surely I must confess, that if it be an error to think that God may be merciful to save men even when they err, my greatest comfort is my error: were it not for the love I bear to this error, I would never wish to speak or to live."[9]

Thus Hooker's public voice represents more than the mastery of rhetoric and the politics of persuasion, as important as these are. Hooker's voice is also shaped by a conviction that God's grace extends even to those in error about God, and it is the preacher's obligation to give witness to the generosity of God toward all people. An Anglican homiletic drawn from the life and work of Hooker, would, therefore, acknowledge the impact of a theology of grace upon the preacher's character as well as the content and rhetoric of the preacher's sermons.

Of course, a homiletic that recognizes the impact of theology upon personal character reminds us not only of the grace that can fill the pulpit, but also the terror. An authoritarian theology may reinforce or draw out the tyrannical tendencies of an individual or community, thus creating one of the most dangerous weapons known to humanity: theological napalm that uses the name of God to justify hatred and violence. Theological napalm is manufactured through cognitive rigidities that are "without any feeling for the twilight zones of the mind" that can "do nothing with nuances or with half-grasped, fragmentary insights and oracular intuitions" because it is "all or nothing, white or black, God or the Devil."[10]

"wordes to be warie and fewe"

The defense against theological violence requires something deeper than the interpersonal nostrums of being nice to everyone. We need a theology that empowers us to live gracefully and faithfully in an ambiguous world. And that is precisely what Hooker provides.

In the first book *Of the Laws of Ecclesiastical Polity*, Hooker acknowledges "He that goeth about to perswade a multitude, that they are not so well governed as they ought to be, shall never want attentive and favourable hearers; because they know the manifold defects whereunto every kind of regiment is subject."[11] But Hooker is eager to move beyond superficial criticism and to understand those laws that make for the healthy and faithful governance of human life.

Deeply influenced by Thomistic thought,[12] Hooker uses the term *law* to designate the force, purpose, and shape of any finite reality: "That which doth assigne unto each thing the kinde, that which doth moderate the force and power, that which doth appoint the forme and measure of working, the same we terme a Lawe."[13]

The nature and character of God represent a unique species of law: "The being of God is a kinde of lawe to his working: for that perfection which God is, geveth perfection to that he doth."[14] And this peculiarity of the divine character has consequences for our speaking of God. It necessitates a kind of holy reserve. Although it is "life" to know God, "and joy to make mention of his name: yet our soundest knowledge is to know that we know him not as in deed he is, neither can know him: and our safest eloquence concernening him is our silence, when we confesse without confession that his glory is inexplicable, his greatnes above our capacitie and reach. He is above, and we upon earth, therefore it behoveth our wordes to be warie and fewe."[15]

In these early observations of Hooker we see themes that will not only continue to develop through his work, but that already suggest some starting principles for an Anglican homiletic. Such a homiletic is not afraid to draw upon our knowledge of the created order, because it is God who has created it according to God's purposes and laws. The implication of Hooker's thought is that to resort to Scripture alone, to become a biblicist, is to be less than trusting in the Creator to whom the Bible gives witness. It is unbiblical to be exclusively biblical.

But this expansion of the base of knowledge for a life of faith does not give us license to use God's name freely. We need, instead, to recognize that "our safest eloquence concerning [God] is our silence," and what words we do use are to be "warie and fewe." Hooker himself preached some profound sermons, but here we see where the depth of them comes from: a homiletic that refuses to wave God's name glibly like a banner for the preacher's judgments. How many holy wars and crusades might we be spared by a homiletic that honors the eloquence of silence about God and whose words are wary and few?

"no goodnesse desired which proceedeth not from God himself"

About the nature of humanity, however, Hooker is quite voluble and very balanced. He clearly understands "the will of man to be inwardly obstinate, rebellious, and averse from all obedience unto the sacred lawes of his nature," but Hooker blends this with a Platonic view that people want the good: "All men desire to leade in this world an happie life. That life is led most happily, wherein all virtue is exercised without impediment or let [hindrance]."[16]

For Hooker this desire for the good flows directly from God and the way that God has shaped creation: "sith [seeing that] there can bee no goodnesse desired which proceedth not from God himselfe, as from the supreme cause of all things; and every effect doth after a sort conteine, at least wise resemble the cause from which it proceedeth: all things in the world are saide in some sort to seeke the highest, and to covet more or lesse the participation of God himselfe."[17]

There are at least two implications for an Anglican homiletic here. The first is a subtly balanced doctrine of humanity, one which acknowledges our rebellious and obstinate character while at the same time realizing that God has created us to desire the good. Such a homiletic is simultaneously realistic about human evil and the human capacity to want and to do the good. This homiletic neither debilitates a sense of self-worth nor feeds the illusion that we are sinless.

Hooker acknowledges that whatever others teach us of the way of the Lord or that we learn ourselves cannot "prevail, where wickednes and malice have taken deepe roote."[18] However, by maintaining that God has created us with the desire and capacity to do good, Hooker avoids the religious tyranny that arises from a doctrine of total human depravity. Hooker realized that "the religious objectivity which expressed itself as the complete annihilation of human nature before God was really indistinguishable from a complete religious subjectivism: this dialectic enabled men to pass their personal prejudices and irrational convictions as divine commandments."[19]

The second implication for an Anglican homiletic flows from Hooker's conviction that each element of the created order "doth after a sort conteine, at least wise resemble the cause from which it proceedeth," namely God. Since there is evidence of the Creator in creation, it follows that the world and the people of the world and their stories are worthy homiletical materials, worthy media of revelation and insight. Just because it is not from the Bible does not mean it is not from God. This implies that an Anglican homiletic provides a much wider base of observation and experience for the creation of homilies than *sola scriptura*. This broad-based Anglican homiletic offers a theological understanding of why it is appropriate for the preacher to work with the discoveries of science, the wisdom of other religious traditions, and new theologies that have been vastly enriched by the histories and experiences of woman and the two-thirds world. We do not preach about these because they are trendy, but because we stand in a theological tradition open to discovering the imprint of God in ways that we had not previously honored.

"naturally induced to seek communion and fellowship with others"

Hooker's doctrine of humanity is not simply about the individual, but is thoroughly social, recognizing the necessity of law to the regulation of human relationships and the governance of community, both civil and ecclesiastical. His understanding of the social dimension is as balanced as his understanding of rebellion and desire for the good in the individual: "But for as much as we are not by our selves sufficient to furnish ourselves with competent store of things needfull for such a life as our nature doth desire, a life fit for the dignitie of man: therefore to supply those defects and imperfections, which are in us living, single, and solelie by our selves, we are naturally induced to seeke communion and fellowship with others."[20]

Hooker fully recognizes how structures of power can be corrupted and warped, but he simultaneously claims the potential for their correction and what they might become at their best: "But just as the just authoritie of civill courtes and Parliaments is not therefore to bee abolished, because sometime there is cunning used to frame them according to the private intents of men over-potent in the common welth: So the grievous abuse which hath bene of councels should rather cause men to studie how so gratious a thing may againe be reduced to that first perfection. . . ."[21]

Aware of how easy it is to take potshots at politicians and bureaucracies, Hooker goes for a much more sophisticated social analysis. He uses the metaphors of foundation, root, and wellspring to urge us to look deeper than the symptoms of social malaise because "that which hath greatest force in the very things we see, is notwithstanding it selfe oftentimes not seene."[22] His work is an attempt to do just this: to understand the deep roots of the blessings and distortions of our corporate life. His word for that is *Polity*, coming from the Greek *polis*, city, meaning governance in the broadest sense.

The implication for an Anglican homiletic is that our preaching is never just about the saving of individual souls, though that certainly matters. Our homiletic also leads us to address the good and the evil of our life together in community. Authentic Anglican preaching deals with politics, the politics of society and the politics of the church. It does not simply lambaste politicians and bishops and the inconsistencies and wrongs of their governance, and it does not push a narrow sectarian or partisan agenda. In his opening sentences, Hooker acknowledges how easy and popular this strategy is. But his thought calls instead for a homiletic that helps us to acknowledge the injustices while working to claim the best possibilities of our life together as community.

"all things necessary unto salvation"

Hooker's appreciation for creation and what we can discover through nature and through the deep analysis of our social structures does not lead to a lessening of belief in the revelation of the Scriptures. Hooker describes the Scriptures as the way by which God has "further made knowne, such supernatural lawes as do serve for mens direction."[23] Although the word *supernatural* has come through the hyperbole of the mass media to mean spectacular, incredible, magical phenomena, Hooker employs the more restrained meaning that was characteristic of his era, when, according to the *Oxford English Dictionary*, the word meant "belonging to a higher realm or system than that of nature . . . [so that for example Hooker writes about] Eccl. Pol. I. xi. ~ 3 'Those supernatuarall passions of joy, peace, and delight.'"[24]

To understand the "supernatural lawes" by which the scriptures provide us "direction," Hooker analyzes three kinds of desire that are part of human nature: the "sensuall," the "intellectuall" and "lastly a spirituall and divine [desire], consisting in those things wheunto we tend by supernatural meanes here, but cannot here attaine unto them."[25] Hooker describes the Scriptures as the way that God speaks most clearly and definitively to this last desire, the highest and holiest hope of the heart. In the Bible "God him self is the teacher of the truth, wherby is made knowen the supernaturall way of salvation and law for them to live in that shal be saved."[26]

Hooker's thought here implies a homiletic that holds a high doctrine of Scripture, but without succumbing to biblicism. There are at least four ways that Hooker's thought works against making an idol of the Bible while profoundly honoring its witness.

First, although Hooker quotes Scripture, and sometimes refutes the position of others based on a close reading of a biblical text, he does not get lost in exegetical convolutions. He reads the Scriptures in a manner that draws him toward the realities to which the Scriptures give witness. The chief object of faith never becomes the Bible itself. Hooker writes: "Concerning faith the principall object whereof is that eternall veritie which hath discovered the treasures of hidden wisedome in Chirst; concerning hope the highest object whereof is that everlasting goodness which in Christ doth quicken the dead; concerning charitie the finall object wherof is that incomprehensible bewtien which shineth in the countenance of Christ the sonne of the living God."[27] These "vertues," as Hooker calls them, lead ultimately to "endless union, the misterie wherof is higher then the reach of the thoughts of men; concerning that faith hope and charitie without which there can be no salvation."[28]

The living, risen Christ, a mystery greater than our thought, is the saving reality to whom the Scriptures give witness. This implies a homiletic that in the name of Christ refuses to succumb to biblicism, a homiletic that takes seriously that Christ is alive now, a homiletic that invites us to follow Christ into territories the biblical writers never even imagined. It is a homiletic that reinforces the injunction of the *Book of Common Prayer* to "feed on Christ in our hearts with thanksgiving."

The *second* aspect of Hooker's doctrine of Scripture that works to avoid biblicism is his refusal to set up reason and Scripture as antithetical. Writing as he did in the sixteenth century, Hooker often struggles with the epistemological question of the relationship between Scripture and reason or Scripture and nature. It is important to note here that "reason" for Hooker is a far wider faculty of human knowing than the word would later come to denote in the Enlightenment. Although it includes our capacity for rational thought processes, *reason* for Hooker means much more than this. Because the sciences of cognition and neurology were not so developed in his day, Hooker knew nothing of our current theories of multiple intelligences and dual hemispheric functioning. Nevertheless, the holism of human consciousness that we now associate with such thinking suggests something of the spirit of what Hooker means by *reason*. Reason for him is nothing less than "the imprint of the divine countenance on man, [and] can and ought to be relied on. It is the proper guide to the discovery of that law according to which man must regulate the conduct of his natural life if he wishes to avoid sin, i.e., if he wishes to conform to the divinely ordained order of the Universe. By following reason man is ultimately following God and exercising his rational autonomy only apparently. He is really only co-operating with God, for nothing can be done or can happen except by virtue of God's efficacy, or without the perpetual aid and concurrence of the supreme cause of all things."[29]

Furthermore, Hooker finds that "many naturall or rational lawes are set down in holy scripture."[30] Scripture itself honors reason. Because reason can function to help us know the truth both in and outside of Scripture, we are rescued from an ironclad, literal appeal to the Bible. The high affirmation of reason, understood in Hooker's holistic use of the term, means we are to be responsible readers and interpreters of the Scripture. Proof texting is not a faithful use of the Bible because it ignores the gift of reason that God implants in us and employs in the Scriptures. Faithfulness to God requires the faithful use of the reason that God has given us.

Hooker's thought implies a homiletic that eschews an uncritical appeal to the Bible. An Anglican homiletic welcomes biblical scholarship, including the more recent developments in feminist and cultural interpretation, as a way of honoring God who has implanted the gift of reason in us and in the Bible.

The *third* principle of Hooker that guards against biblicism is his careful analysis about the ends and limits of different kinds of knowledge. He writes about "The sufficiencie of scripture unto the end for which it was instituted."[31] Hooker here draws upon his belief that "all kindes of knowledge have their certaine boundes and limits; each of them presupposeth many necessary things learned in other sciences and knowne before hand."[32] Hooker uses this principle to analyze the purpose of Scripture and to affirm unconditionally that it fills its specific function namely to reveal to us "all things necessary unto salvation."[33]

A *fourth* guard against biblicism is Hooker's understanding of the continuing work of the Holy Spirit. The Spirit is directing us into truth and goodness in the same way that the Spirit worked upon the biblical writers: "the selfsame Spirit, which revealeth the things that God hath set down in his law, may also be thought to aid and direct men in finding out by the light of reason what laws are expedient to be made for the guiding of his Church, over and besides them that are in Scripture (Lawes III.8.18)."[34] To chain human enquiry and reflection to the bounds of Scripture is unscriptural because the Scriptures are a witness to the ever-living Spirit who works in and through and among us.

"nature and scripture doe serve in such full sort"

Although Scripture reveals the highest knowledge to which we aspire, it is not the only knowledge that we seek and need. Since various kinds of knowledge may be shaped by other purposes, there is no need to whack the Scriptures out of shape to force them to meet an end for which they are not intended. Thus scientific discovery is not limited by the Scriptures, because the end of the holy writers is to reveal what is necessary for salvation. Their purpose is not to chart the motions of the planets or the legislative details of the ideal polity for church and state.

Hooker's philosophy of the ends of knowledge, including biblical knowledge, rescues us from the intellectual repression of biblicism or the political ideology that it often fosters. We do not turn to the Scriptures to answer questions that they were never intended to answer. Hooker understands that such distorted theology follows from "a desire to enlarge the necessarie use of the word of God; which desire hath begotten an error enlarging it further then (as we are perswaded) soundnes of truth will beare. For whereas God hath left sundry kindes of lawes unto men, and by all those lawes the actions of men are in some sort directed: they [Hooker's opponents] hold that one only lawe, the scriptures, must be the rule to direct in all thinges, even so farre as to the taking up of a rush or strawe."[35]

By way of contrast, Hooker's thought allows for a homiletic wide open to the curiosity of the intellect: "Hooker as a Christian neither would nor could deny the authority of faith; but he saw that if human society was to be saved from chaos, faith had to be synthesized with reason."[36]

At the same time Hooker never lets the intellect forget the profoundest question of human existence: what is our relationship to our creator? We are free to explore and to think in novel ways, yet the question of salvation keeps calling us to consider the ramifications of our explorations and innovations. The Scriptures and the end for which they are written do not suppress our thought but rescue us from the hubris of believing that our accomplishments are the source of our salvation. Instead of the distortions of an arrogant biblicism or an arrogant reason we end with an understanding of the complementary functions of Scripture and reason. They are to be taken together, not either one completely by itself or without the other: "It sufficeth therefore that nature and scripture doe serve in such full sort, that they both joyntly and not severallye eyther of them be so complete, that unto everlasting felicitie wee neede not the knowledge of any thing more than these two, may easily furnish our mindes with on all sides. . . ."[37]

"unto everlasting felicitie"

Based on what I have explored so far, it becomes clear that there is at least one other characteristic of Hooker's thought that has implications for an Anglican homiletic: namely, the way he is thoroughly immersed not only in the Scriptures, but in the philosophical and theological thought of the West. Hooker is a man of broad and deep learning, and his strong affirmation of reason liberates him to draw upon that learning for the purposes of illuminating the human condition in the light of the truth of God. This implies that an Anglican homiletic is not content only to draw upon the Scriptures, but to draw upon truth wherever it be found. An Anglican homiletic celebrates the witness of the saints, the traditions and history of the Church, and new realms of human experience and knowledge. Far from being unbiblical, such preaching is highly biblical: for it respects the limits of the Bible and honors the God whom the Bible honors. John Michael Christopher Bryan puts the matter succinctly when he observes: "The Puritan claim, *'That Scripture is the only rule of all things which in this life may be done by men,'* was intended piously, as Hooker generously recognized (*Lawes II.1.2*). In fact, it was unscriptural in the deepest sense, being contrary to the spirit and the methods of those who (under God) created Scripture, and of those who (under God) defined its canons."[38]

Let me then summarize some implications of Richard Hooker's thought for an Anglican homiletic as they have emerged in this essay. Such a homiletic is marked by these characteristics:

- attention to the character and tone of the preacher,
- the belief that it is unbiblical to be exclusively biblical,
- a holy reserve that refuses to wave God's name glibly like a banner for the preacher's judgments,

- a subtly balanced doctrine of humanity that acknowledges our rebellious character while at the same time realizing that God has created us to desire and do the good,
- the positive affirmation of creating homilies that draw from a much wider base of knowledge and experience than Scripture alone,
- a readiness to address the politics of society and the politics of the church but without becoming narrowly sectarian or partisan,
- holding a high doctrine of Scripture but without succumbing to biblicism so that the chief object of faith never becomes the Bible itself,
- a faith centered in the living Christ,
- a willingness to follow Christ into territories the biblical writers never even imagined,
- an understanding that the Spirit is still working to lead us into goodness and truth even as the Spirit did the same with the biblical writers,
- a refusal to set up reason and Scripture as antithetical, an insistence that they are instead complementary and mutually necessary to one another,
- a refusal to accept an uncritical appeal to the Bible,
- a refusal to use the Scriptures to answer questions that they were never intended to answer,
- a faith that is wide open to intellectual curiosity, and
- an eagerness to draw upon truth wherever it be found.

I do not consider the list to be complete. It is rather a beginning point for a homiletic that I would like to see us develop for the Church, for our classes, for ecumenical discussions, and for religious discourse in the public arena. If Anglican preachers have little sense of the homiletic that characterizes their tradition, then they will be easy targets for those who want to push a biblicist agenda and its accompanying terrors of anti-intellectualism, simplemindedness, and repression.

I have begun with Hooker because in the pilgrimage from my childhood Calvinism to Anglicanism, I kept reading that he was the greatest theologian that Anglicanism has produced, and every time I came upon quotations from Hooker I was startled by their incisive and cogent meaning for our own time. That drove me to read the man himself as well as literature about his person and his thought. And when I did this I found myself thinking, again and again, how helpful Hooker was to me as a person who loves Christ and who finds that love expanded and deepened by great thought and art. But even more important, I found myself thinking that if only Hooker's depth and balance, civility and grace were a part of our public religious discourse, our debates about values and pluralism might be less shrill and more filled with wisdom.

I do not mean to deify the man—he would be the first to confess his own weaknesses—but rather to suggest that Hooker's manner and thought model for us how the Anglican tradition can answer the direction of the Spirit in our own age: the call to give witness to Christ in a way that engages all the gifts that God has given us and that is hospitable and generous toward every member of our pluralistic, global community.[39]

Thomas H. Troeger is the Ralph E. and Norma E. Peck Professor of Preaching and Communications at Iliff School of Theology, Denver, Colorado.

1. Peter J. Gomes, *The Good Book: Reading the Bible with Mind and Heart* (New York: William Morrow and Company, 1996), 64.

2. Brian Wren, *What Language Shall I Borrow?* (New York: Crossroad, 1989), 133.

3. Richard Hooker, *Of the Laws of Ecclesiastical Polity* in three volumes in *The Folger Library Edition of The Works of Richard Hooker* (Cambridge, Massachusetts: The Belknap Press of Harvard University Press, 1977), Vol. I, bk. 1, 83.

4. Peter Munz, *The Place of Hooker in the History of Thought* (Westport, Connecticut: Greenwood Press, Publishers, 1971), 14.

5. Hooker, Vol. I preface, 53.

6. John N. Wall, "Hooker's 'Faire Speeche'" in Donald S. Armentrout, ed., *This Sacred History: Anglican Reflections for John Booty* (Cambridge, Massachusetts: Cowley Publications, 1990), 131.

7. Quoted by Wall in *This Sacred History*, 131.

8. Quoted by Isaac Walton, *The Life of Mr. Richard Hooker,* as reprinted in John Keble, *The Works of that Learned and Judicious Divine, Mr. Richard Hooker,* Vol. I (Oxford: Clarendon Press, 1874), 56.

9. Walton, 57.

10. Perry Miller, *The New England Mind: The Seventeenth Century* (New York: Macmillan, 1939), p. 45. Quoted in Munz, p. 22.

11. Hooker, Vol. I, bk. 1, 56.

12. Munz charts the influence of Thomas Aquinas on Hooker, often footnoting his summations with parallel references to Hooker and Aquinas.

13. Hooker, Vol. I, bk. 1, 58.

14. Hooker, Vol. I, bk. 1, 59.

15. *Ibid.*

16. Hooker, Vol. I, bk. 1, 96–97.

17. Hooker, Vol. I, bk. 1, 73.

18. Hooker, Vol. I, bk. 1, 98.

19. Munz, 37.

20. Hooker, Vol. I, bk. 1, 96.

21. Hooker, Vol. I, bk. 1, 109.

22. Hooker, Vol. I, bk. 1, 57.

23. Hooker, Vol. I, bk. 1, 110.

24. *Oxford English Dictionary*, second edition, prepared by J.A. Simpson and E.S.C. Weiner. Oxford: Oxford University Press (Clarendon Press, New York, 1991), 5, 233.

25. Hooker, Vol. I, bk. 1, 114.

26. Hooker, Vol. I, bk. 1, 117.

27. Hooker, Vol. I, bk. 1, 119.

28. *Ibid.*

29. Munz, 53–54.

30. Hooker, Vol. I, bk. 1, 119.

31. Hooker, Vol. I, bk. 1, 125.

32. *Ibid.*

33. *Ibid.*

34. John Michael Christopher Bryan, "The Judicious Mr. Hooker and the Early Christians," in Armentrout, 145.

35. Hooker, Vol. I, bk. 2, 145.

36. Munz, 40.

37. Hooker, Vol. I, bk. 1, 129.

38. John Michael Christopher Bryan, 159.

39. Among many other works that influenced this article, even if I do not cite specific quotations from them, are the following: John Booty, ed., *The Godly Kingdom of Tudor England: Great Books of the English Reformation* (Wilton, Conn.: Morehouse-Barlow Company, Inc., 1981). John R. H. Moorman, *The Anglican Spiritual Tradition* (Springfield, Ill.: Templegate Publishers, 1983). Geoffrey Rowell, ed., *The English Religious Tradition and the Genius of Anglicanism* (Nashville: Abingdon Press, 1992). William J. Wold, ed., *The Spirit of Anglicanism* (Harrisburg, Pa.: Morehouse Publishing, 1979). I am also indebted to my research assistant, Nature Johnston, who checked out the meaning of Hooker's Elizabethan diction for me and gave me glosses I have worked into the text of the article.

"That We May Delight in Your Will and Walk in Your Ways"

A. Katherine Grieb

THE LONGER I teach New Testament interpretation to seminary students, the more interested I have become in the question of the integrity of the preacher. In part, this is a practical concern: congregations listen more attentively to someone whose personal holiness is exemplary. In part, it is also a theological issue: I am convinced that sound exegesis depends as much on the obedient discernment of the heart as it does on the disciplined imagination of the intellect. The reflections offered here are my current attempt to sort out what it means to be a servant of the Word of God in parishes and seminaries in the Episcopal Church in the United States of America today.

In this endeavor, I am not primarily concerned with the interpretation of specific texts about peace, justice, or social concern, such as Amos 5, or Matthew 25, although, as everyone knows, the Bible is full of texts like these, and they show up regularly in the lectionary. Nor am I primarily concerned with the general process of reading Scripture, or with reading Scripture using a particular hermeneutic, say the hermeneutical privilege of the poor, although, as everyone *should* know, the Bible says more about the disparity of wealth and poverty than it says about any other ethical issue, and therefore there is a great deal for the preacher to say about that.

In these comments, I am primarily concerned with something even more basic: the conditions conducive to becoming a hearer of the Word of God, a discerner of the will of God, within a specific community—a preacher and/or teacher of the ways of God to those who would follow them. You will recognize my title, "That we may delight in your will and walk in your ways," as a phrase that belongs to the prayer at the end of the confession of sin. It asks for God's merciful guidance to enable the church to serve in a way that glorifies God's name—not a bad place for a preacher to begin to speak.

In the interests of rendering to God what is God's, let me also use something from Caesar, and state that these comments are, like Gaul, divided into three parts. Part one deals with the vocation of the preacher. Part two deals with spiritual disciplines needed for preaching. Part three deals with preaching in but not of the world.

1. "Everyone is searching for you": The Vocation of the Preacher

In the morning, while it was still very dark, [Jesus] got up and went out to a deserted place, and there he prayed. And Simon and his companions hunted for him. [The Greek work has the connotation of "tracking him down," the way someone might track an escaped prisoner with dogs.] *When they found him, they said to him, "Everyone is searching for you." He answered, "Let us go on to the neighboring towns, so that I may proclaim the message there also; for that is what I came out to do." And he went throughout Galilee, proclaiming the message in their synagogues and casting out demons"* (Mark 1:35–39).

When the computer dating service at Episcopal Church Center matches parish profiles and clergy profiles, the amount of agreement on one topic is remarkable. Almost every candidate for rector or assistant or associate indicates that preaching is a major priority. Almost every parish puts "excellence in preaching" at the top of its list of desired qualifications. If historians of twentieth-century American Anglicanism were to base their judgments on that information alone, surely the level of interest in preaching and support for excellence in preaching would appear to be at an all-time high.

But, when the new rector sits down with the senior warden (or when the new assistant sits down with the rector), and they talk about the weekly schedule of the parish and the expectations about how the clergy will spend their time, it is clear that these much valued, excellent sermons are supposed to appear like Athena, full-grown from the head of Zeus. The preacher who politely insists on a full day to read, research, listen, meditate, pray, and write about the lessons for that Sunday is often considered either naive or gamey. Maybe that's how it is *supposed* to work, but it never actually *does* work that way, so why pretend that it does?

"Everyone is searching for you" when you are doing parish ministry or college or hospital or prison chaplaincy or teaching in a Christian school or seminary. Pastoral care is a bottomless pit; you could always do more. The adult education programs also expand to fit the time allotted for them. The liturgy could always use more preparation. The next vestry meeting needs to be planned. You promised the youth group that you would help in the soup kitchen or with the Habitat for Humanity work day. And we haven't even talked about the dysfunctional parishioner who wants to take up all your time for some other less helpful agenda.

Sometimes when I find myself in that setting, it's hard to remember whom I'm working for, whom I'm accountable to. I forget to listen to the wisdom of the psalmist: "For God alone my soul waits in silence" (Psalm 62:1).

Jesus made sure that he had desert time, time in a deserted place, time to wait in silence for God alone. There, Mark tells us, he prayed. Almost as if to respect the intimacy of that time spent between Jesus and God, Mark tells us nothing else about it, but shifts our attention away from Jesus and his praying to Simon Peter and his companions, who are hunting Jesus down. Nevertheless, the alert reader notices that when they find him, something has changed. Something has happened in that interval of praying, talking, listening, waiting for God in silence—something that has shown Jesus what the next step is for him. And it isn't more of the same thing in the same place.

It doesn't seem to matter to Jesus that he has been enormously successful, that he is driving the crowds wild, that his ratings have gone up dramatically. It also doesn't seem to matter to Jesus that his coworkers and colleagues are ready to ride that tide to its logical conclusion. We get the impression that if Jesus had not gone off into the desert, he might have been right with them, doing the obvious, good, expected thing to do.

But listening to God in the silence, Jesus has heard a word telling him to move in a new direction. He has heard a clarifiying word about his call, his vocation—what God wants him to say and do. He has had long enough (enough time to work it through and to get it right) to get clear about what God wanted. So, when Peter and the rest arrive, he knows exactly what he has come out to do. "Let us go on to the neighboring towns, so that I may proclaim the message there also; for that is what I came out to do." And he goes throughout Galilee, proclaiming the word and casting out demons.

Preachers who follow Jesus are constantly facing vocational issues. The fresh Word of God, the right Word for right now, is given in the desert place. The still small voice is needed for the Word to grow. The most powerful preachers of social justice are the ones who have had time to pray and to think.

> Oh my people, what have I done to thee.
> Where shall the word be found, where will the word
> Resound? Not here, there is not enough silence.[1]

2. "A sower went out to sow": Spiritual Disciplines Needed for Preaching

"Listen! A sower went out to sow. And as he sowed, some seed fell on the path, and the birds came and ate it up. Other seed fell on rocky ground, where it did not have much soil, and it sprang up quickly, since it had no depth of soil. And

when the sun rose, it was scorched; and since it had no root, it withered away. Other seed fell among thorns, and the thorns grew up and choked it, and it yielded no grain. Other seed fell into good soil and brought forth grain, growing up and increasing and yielding thirty and sixty and a hundredfold." And he said, "Let anyone with ears to hear listen!" (Mark 4:3–9).

Of course, this parable raises hard questions for *all* hearers of the Word, but when I think about the spiritual disciplines necessary to preach and teach the Word of God, it is the soil of the *preacher* that concerns me. If the Word of God finds no root in us, how are we to implant it in the hearts of God's people?

Moreover, while we may need to ask ourselves about the perils of the path and of the rocky ground, I find myself more worried about the thorns that grow up in the wheat and choke it to death. Later, these are identified as "the cares of the world and the desire for wealth." How does that work? How do they choke the seed so that it yields no grain?

Perhaps the best example of willful exegesis (or, rather, flagrant eisegesis) is the concoction of the infamous "camel's gate" at Jerusalem—a bit of spurious geography invented sometime in the Middle Ages to allow that rich camel to go through the eye of a needle, after all, in spite of Jesus' warning. You remember the story of the rich man—sometimes called the rich young ruler—who was eager to follow Jesus, thought he had kept all the commandments from his youth, and eagerly sought the more advanced course in discipleship. Mark tells us that Jesus, looked at him and said to him, in love, "You lack only one thing; go and sell everything you have and give it to the poor and then come and follow me." Sadly the man turned away, for, the Evangelist tells us, he had many possessions. The disciples are dumbfounded when Jesus says, "How hard it is for the rich to enter into the kingdom."

They are even more astonished when Jesus tells them that it is harder for a rich man to get into heaven than for a camel to get through the eye of a needle! This is a joke, a hyperbole, like the one about taking the log out of your own eye so that you can see better to take the speck out of your brother's eye. In truth, it has been such an effective joke that nervous disciples throughout the centuries have continued to worry about it. One of these was worried enough to invent the camel's gate at Jerusalem.

There are at least two versions of this invention. In one, the gate is so low that the camel, as it *stands* there in front of the gate could not possibly get through it. The camel has to get down *on its knees* in order to get through, thus showing appropriate humility. Application: so a rich man who is appropriately humble might be able to get into the kingdom after all. In the other, more familiar version, the gate is so thin that the camel, fully loaded with all its baggage, could not possibly get through it. But, if the owner of all that baggage takes it off temporarily, the camel can get through the gate after all. Then, presumably, the baggage is reloaded. Application: so the rich man with his fully loaded camel has entered Jerusalem after all, having first shown sufficient detachment with respect to his wealth that he can let go of it—for a few minutes, at least.

What desperate things we will do to avoid hearing a hard text! The literalism with which this exegete took Jesus' joke and the concoction of such an elaborate escape route are almost as funny as the joke itself. Talk about "walking a mile for a Camel," this revisionist history is addictive behavior at its best (or worst). But the more I think about how this fable has been passed down from one generation of preachers to another since its invention—as a supposedly helpful way to deal with that troublesome passage, the more I feel a great sadness for the wealth-encumbered church that will never get past the eye of that text—in part, because its preachers have "solved the problem" for people who would otherwise have to deal with the force of Jesus' joke and who might be challenged by his wit to amend their lives.

If we don't have the money thing right, if we who preach are not faithful in our dealings with money, if we are not so truly identified with the poor that we can get the joke, we will never be able to preach a text like that. Each of us in our own ways will invent a camel's gate to get out of the tight spot.

We are called to holy living—necessarily—in order to be faithful preachers for the Holy One of Israel. The Bible will supply us with numerous occasions for reflecting on issues of wealth and poverty together with the people in our churches. But before we can urge, suggest, or even hint that members of our congregations might be called to give of themselves and of their means, we must be giving sacrificially ourselves. Before we join Paul in urging them "not to be conformed to this world, but to be transformed by the renewal of their minds" into the mind of Christ, in order to "perceive what is right and excellent and good," we ourselves must be visibly uninterested in conspicuous consumption and other worldly behavior—lest those dreadful words be said to us: "Preacher, I can't hear what you *say*, because what you *are* is speaking too loudly."

If those of us in the Episcopal Church, where politeness is still a cardinal virtue, may be protected from ever actually hearing those words, we still need to remember that, whenever they are rightly thought by someone, a human heart may have just excused itself from the jurisdiction of God's Word—because of us.

3. "Living as if not": Preaching In but Not Of the World

Paul writes to the church at Corinth: *I mean, brothers and sisters, the appointed time has grown short; from now on, let even those who have wives be as though they had none, and those who mourn as though they were not mourning, and those who rejoice as though they were not rejoicing, and those who buy as though they had no possessions, and those who deal with the world as though they had no dealings with it. For the present form of this world is passing away* (1 Corinthians 7:29–31).

Paul's words seem unreasonable to many Christians because we find it difficult to agree with his basic assumptions that the appointed time has grown short and that the present form of the world is passing away. Albert Schweitzer was not the only one to describe the demanding statements of Paul (and of Jesus before him) as characteristic of an "interim ethics," and thereby to consign them to the apostolic era now safely past. Moreover, as Max Weber noted, such loss of eschatological horizon and apocalyptic fervor is consistent with the routinization of charisma. The more the church becomes institutionalized, the more the early exciting message of the Gospel gives way to the *status quo ante*. How can we twenty-first-century Christians remember that the Lord will come like a thief in the night, at the time when we least expect it? How can we learn to live in Advent again? How can we put aside the many things that distract and trouble us (like Martha) and listen for the one thing that matters most of all?

Perhaps our best strategy is to remind ourselves that to confess *Jesus* as Lord means, among other things, to confess that *we* are *not*. As Paul says, "You are not your own; you belong to God." Living in the presence of God (*coram Deo*) means that all aspects of our lives are necessarily under the Lordship of Christ. The most important question in Christian ethics is not "What ought I to do?" (Immanuel Kant's question), but rather "Who is my Lord?"

One could argue that the two best indicators of lordship in our lives are the way we spend our time and the way we spend our money. Therefore, two disciplines of self-examination will tell us a lot about what our commitments truly are—a periodic review of our calendars and of our checkbooks *sub specie aeternitate*, from God's point of view, as best we are able to discern it. That's why it is not just "a good idea" for the preacher to go out to a deserted place, to claim prayer and preparation time for preaching. It may be the *only* way that we can hear the prophetic word; the word that is distinctly God's Word for the people we serve, and for ourselves as one of them. Otherwise we tend to do whatever the people around us think we should be doing. Moreover, it is not just a good thing to do to discipline our spending/buying/giving practices. It may be the *only* way we can hear the Word of God as a word of freedom, and as Gospel. I must have actually done it; I must have reformed my own giving practices before I can speak about that freedom from within it, as one whom the Lord has set free.

That is why the preacher's prayer for inspiration is also a prayer for conversion to a deeper level of confession of the Lordship of Jesus Christ, as in the Collect for Purity:

> *Almighty God, to You all hearts are open, all desires are known, and from You no secrets are hid; Cleanse the thoughts of our hearts by the inspiration of your Holy Spirit, that we may perfectly love You and worthily magnify your holy Name, through Jesus Christ our Lord.*

Let me close with a personal word. The most valuable thing I own is not any of the wedding presents, none of the family furniture, not the computer and all its files, not even (gasp) my books. It is a hat, a gift from a former parishioner when I left the parish. Polly made me a red stovepipe hat with the label "honest Kate" (like honest Abe) on it. When I looked puzzled, she told me she had made it for me because she could always count on me to tell the truth in the pulpit. You can see why that's the most valuable thing I own. I mention it here (in an article directed to preachers) not because I think it *is* true, but because I *want* it to be true—not only for me, but also for each of you. Indeed, it is dangerous not to tell the truth in the pulpit—the truth as we see it, of course, in all our finitude and our brokenness. But yes, to tell that truth from the pulpit. It is, after all, the Word of God that we are meant to be expounding and proclaiming, just as it is God to whom we will have to render an account for what is said about God in that Word and through that Word.

But God's ways are not our ways and God's thoughts are not our thoughts, as Isaiah makes clear. For as the heavens are high above the earth, so are God's ways higher than our ways and God's thoughts higher than our thoughts. It takes time to hear the Word of God, and to understand what it is we are to say about it—to *this* people, at *this* time, in *this* place. The geography of the human heart is such that it takes time for God to convert us in the sermon-writing process. Preaching has to do with the conversion of the preacher first.

The Word often comes not so much like a friend as like "friendly fire." It comes as the coal of fire that burns our lips and cleanses us so that we can speak to people who, like ourselves, are caught in various forms of violence against the earth, injustice toward our neighbors, and failure to love God. "For freedom Christ has set us free!" It is our joyful task to invite others into that same freedom through the proclamation of the Gospel of God. And like Isaiah, we will find ourselves better prepared to do that after some time in the temple.

Most merciful God, we confess that we have sinned against You. . . . For the sake of your son Jesus Christ, have mercy on us and forgive us; that we may delight in your will, and walk in your ways, to the glory of your Name.

A. Katherine Grieb is associate professor of New Testament at Virginia Theological Seminary and teaches at the Servant Leadership School of the Church of the Savior. She preaches regularly at St. Stephen & the Incarnation, a lay-led parish in the inner city of Washington, D.C.

---

1. Excerpt from "Ash Wednesday" in *Collected Poems 1909–1962*, copyright © 1930 and renewed 1958 by T.S. Eliot, reprinted by permission of Harcourt, Inc., Orlando, FLorida.

EVENSONG

Adding Our "More"

Deuteronomy 5:22–33; Luke 16:19–31
Roger Alling

WHEN IT was time for the Ten Commandments God gave quite a speech. The speech was not given quietly with "a still, small voice." Oh, no! This speech came with a multimedia light and sound show designed to knock your socks off: fire, thunderous clouds, deep gloom, loud voice. Powerful stuff. God gave a strong message, not to be ignored. God gave a definitive word. When the speech ended, the Deuteronomist writes, "he added no more."

You would think it would be enough, would you not? Certainly the preacher was on the first-string team. The setting was more impressive than the pulpit in our finest cathedrals. The special effects attending the sermon would put our best choirs, organs, and orchestras and all of our efforts at liturgical staging to shame.

Why, the congregation for this sermon was so impressed by the whole show that when it was over they were surprised that they were still alive. And yet, it was not enough. The message was not heard, nor were the commandments obeyed. God had decided to "add nothing more," but that turned out to be wishful thinking.

All preachers, God included, find out that saying it once rarely gets the job done. Even with fire, clouds, and deep gloom. *More* will be added because it *must* be added. Communication is not complete until the message is received and followed. And that is never a simple matter.

Some people seem to be morally deaf, while others are criminally blind. Some people can't see important things that are right in front of their faces. Dives, the character in Jesus' parable, was one of these people. As he whiles away his days with sumptuous meals, his neighbor Lazarus wastes away in privation and distress. Never once is Dives's plenty challenged by Lazarus's poverty. Dives and Lazarus live in close proximity, but they inhabit different worlds.

Then both men die, and find that "inhabiting different worlds" remains the one thing they still have in common. Lazarus, at last, finds comfort in the bosom of Abraham. Dives is shocked to find that he now is in the place of torment.

But old habits die hard for Dives. He still thinks he can order room service. And who better than Lazarus to fetch him some water? Abraham intervenes, and Dives discovers just how grim and hopeless his situation has become.

It is hard to like Dives very much. He is unattractive, surly, and demanding. It is easy to think that he has got what's coming to him. He does, however, have one redeeming quality. He cares about his family back home. Even though it is late in the day, Dives wants to give them a message and send them a sermon. He knows that they are living the fat, sassy life. If they're not careful they are going to die and end up right where he is.

What's to be done? How can Dives get the message across, so that these brothers will mend their ways and save their souls? Dives comes up with an idea. He puts this suggestion to Abraham: "Why not send Lazarus back from the dead to warn my five brothers about the jeopardy of their situation? Lazarus can tell them that, if they continue to live blind and deaf to the needs of others, they will go to hell! That will work! Lazarus's coming back from the dead will be very impressive. A message under those circumstances will really get their attention."

Abraham thinks about this for a moment, and then he responds. "No need for that," he says. "These brothers of yours don't need a show like that. They already have what they need. They have Moses and the prophets. If these brothers of yours can't hear Moses and the prophets, they won't be able to hear anyone, even if he should return from the dead."

Someone has returned from the dead, as I am sure that you have heard. And we have to ask ourselves if *even that* has been enough. Has the message been received and heard? Have the commandments been obeyed? Does "more" have to be added? Is preaching part of that "more"? And if so, how do I figure in that?

Let me share with you my favorite verses from today's Deuteronomy lesson. They are the preaching contract that the people of Israel grant to Moses after God's great sermon. They read as follows: "Go near, you yourself, and hear all that the LORD our God will say. Then tell everything that the LORD our God tells you, and we will listen and do it."

I want a contract like that. It is so complete and so hopeful. The congregation would be asking me to do just what I should. What's more, they would promise to take seriously what I say, to hear God's words through mine. And, miracle of miracles, they would even be promising to form their lives under the guidance of what they hear. Wow! Is there a budding preacher anywhere who could ask for a better contract?

But preaching, we know, is not that easy or that automatic. The criminally blind and deaf we shall *always* have with us, and sometimes they will *be* us. When our preaching is empty, the emptiness may be in us. Sometimes it may be in those who hear us. We have to keep trying, and so do those who listen to us.

We do not lose heart. We believe that God has called us to this work and will be with us as we preach. Preaching, we will learn, is not something that we do by ourselves. Preaching is a community matter. Sisters and brothers will help us as we grow. So will God.

We believe passionately in preaching. We are delighted that all of you are here this week and are excited about the growth and learning that is to come. God still speaks in the fire, in the cloud, and in the deep gloom. Christ Jesus has been raised from the dead, and has commissioned the Church to carry the Gospel to the ends of the earth.

The powerful manifestations of God, and the Resurrection of Jesus are all necessary. And yet they not sufficient for the task that lies before us. You and I are not finished. More must be added. This week, I hope, will help us add our "more" to the effort in which we are engaged.

Roger Alling is co-editor of this volume.

VISITATION OF THE BLESSED VIRGIN MARY

Pregnant with the Word

Luke 1:39–49
Linda L. Clader

IT DIDN'T happen all that long ago. I was sitting in the faculty lounge at school, eating a turkey sandwich. Across from me, eating an egg salad sandwich, was Jane Menten, my friend and the director of our field education program. We had been relaxing, eating our lunches, and chatting about this and that.

Just then, there was a voice at the door. We turned toward the sound. There, framed in the doorway, was a young woman, one of our second-year students. She was standing in her blue chambray dress, a dress she wore a lot in these latter days so as not to spend too much money on maternity clothes. All over the skirt of the dress were wet splotches. Her eyes were round, and her voice was breathy with wonder, fear, and joy. "I think my water just broke!" she said "It happened in the dean's office!"

My friend Jane left her lunch where it was, took the student to call her husband, and then saw that she got to her apartment. I just stayed in the faculty lounge and finished my lunch. Now and then I glanced over at Jane's egg salad sandwich with two bites taken out of it, and I prayed for Heath, for her husband, Peter, and for the baby who was on the way.

It was okay with me that Jane went with Heath and I didn't. I'm not a mom. I've never been through what Heath was experiencing. But Jane is a mom. She has two kids, teenagers now. And at times like this, it makes sense to turn to someone who has, as we say, "been there and done that." Somebody older and wiser, maybe a parent, a mentor, a guide. If there isn't a family member at hand to take that role, we choose someone else to guide us, and that someone *becomes* family of a sort, through the relationship created by the sharing. Do you suppose it was anything like that when Mary hurried through the hill country to the home of her kinswoman Elizabeth?

It's early evening. Elizabeth comes out of her house into the courtyard, carrying a cooking pot she's filled with a vegetable stew for dinner. She puts down the pot and carefully lowers herself down next to the fire. She pokes the coals to make sure they're ready. Just then, at the edge of her vision, she sees a movement. She looks up to the open door of the courtyard. There she sees a young woman, framed by the doorway. The veil over her head is arranged neatly, but there are streaks of dust on it, and there's dust on her skirt, too—a lot of dust. The young woman's eyes are round, and her voice is breathy as she says, "Elizabeth! I'm going to have a baby!"

Elizabeth freezes for a second. She looks in amazement at Mary. Then she begins to move. She takes hold of the corner of the house where she has been sitting and drags herself to her feet. Then she walks to where Mary is standing.

Only then does Mary take in what she is seeing: her cousin Elizabeth is pregnant, too, just as the angel has said—almost seven months pregnant. Tears well up in Mary's eyes, and she steps toward Elizabeth. Elizabeth takes a step toward Mary, and the child inside her gives her a good kick. The Spirit of God fills her with wonder and awe, and she cries out a blessing. The two women embrace, and they talk excitedly about what has happened to them. They sing. They weep. They praise God for mercy, for miracles, for freedom, for the promise of great things to come.

I'd like to know a lot more about the relationship between Elizabeth and Mary. For instance, when Mary learned that she would bear the Son of the Most High, why did she go to Elizabeth, rather than to her own mother?

Of course, Luke doesn't tell us any of that, because he's doing his own thing. The scholars say Luke is using the two annunciation stories to build up to the miraculous births of John and Jesus. He's using the birth stories themselves to sound the trumpets for the beginning of their ministries of prophecy, healing, and liberation. What seems to interest Luke is having the two boys, John and Jesus, encounter each other, in a way, before they are born. Fair enough.

But there they are, Mary and Elizabeth, both pregnant. And they are embracing in wonder and joy. Sharing stories about angels, singing about God's faithfulness to Israel and about God's faithfulness to *them*, two lowly women. Luke lets them sing a long time, and he doesn't let anybody come around and rebuke them for making too much noise or for calling attention to themselves.

The scholars also say that you're not supposed to make anything of the fact that the Gospel says Mary stayed with Elizabeth about three more months. You're not supposed to do the calculations and figure out that Mary would have had to be present when John was born. It's not part of what's important to the narrative, say the scholars.

But I just can't let go of this picture: the younger woman standing in the doorway of the older woman's home, in wonder, fear, and joy, looking for the support of someone older and wiser, a mentor, a guide. And the young woman finds, instead, an older woman who is also pregnant for the first time. The older woman is filled with the same wonder, fear, and joy, so they become sisters in the awesome miracle of it. They become sisters as the Holy Spirit, dwelling in one of them, greets the Holy Spirit dwelling in the other. They rejoice together, and together they sing a song.

That's the picture I can't let go of. And, of course, you already know why this picture is such a powerful one for me. Because it describes so beautifully where a professor of preaching lives. It's such a wonderful, awesome thing to encounter someone who is pregnant with the Word of God. And a preaching professor gets to meet people like that almost every day. People like you.

The preaching professor knows that it's her job to be the guide, the older, wiser one, the mentor, the one who has been there and done that before. But the wonderful thing about this job I have is that those students who come to me pregnant with the Word of God help me to give birth, too. The songs I hear from them give me the music for the unsung songs of my own heart. The Holy Spirit dwelling in them calls forth the Holy Spirit dwelling in me.

Now, it's just possible that there are one or two people in this room who are secretly afraid that everybody *else* is pregnant with the Word of God except *them*. Their stomachs are in knots, and their hands are a little sweaty, because they're secretly afraid that somebody made a mistake choosing them to come here this week. Afraid they only got to come because the dean or somebody liked them. It's even possible that some of the faculty at this conference are afraid of something like that.

But just to draw out this pregnancy metaphor as far as it can go—maybe beyond where it should go—let me say that that feeling in the pit of the stomach is part of the natural process. Morning sickness goes with pregnancy, even when you're talking about being pregnant with the Word of God.

All of us gathered here at this conference are pregnant with the Word. We're Mary—young and humble, awestruck by an encounter with an angel. And we're Elizabeth—getting along in years, and suddenly renewed by a miracle from God. We come seeking someone else's experience to guide us, and we stay to play the midwife as they give birth.

Nobody's really the old hand, it turns out. And nobody's really the rank beginner. Because—talk about old hands—the One who dwells in us is the Word that has never been silent since before the world began! And talk about rank beginners—the One who gives us voice is the Holy Spirit that is forever young, forever fresh, forever new!

Let's trust that. Let's trust that in each other.

Linda L. Clader is associate professor of homiletics at the Church Divinity School of the Pacific, Berkeley, California.

VISITATION OF THE BLESSED VIRGIN MARY—EVENSONG

Word-Bearing Prophets

Zechariah 2:10–13; John 3:25–30
Susan Gaumer

A NUMBER of years ago, in the middle of a hot afternoon in South Louisiana, in a windowless room in our diocesan office, I was immersed in the daunting task of sorting through an old audiovisual library. There were large reels of film and dozens of filmstrips, faded to red in little plastic containers. The experience had the quality of an archeological dig. I was considering tossing the whole lot when something caught my eye—a box of filmstrips entitled *Old Testament Prophets*. Individual titles were emblazoned on the cover—*Moses, Amos, Samuel, Elijah, Jeremiah, Ezekiel,* and others.

What caught my eye was the last one on the list: *John the Baptist.* I hadn't yet been to seminary, but I was quite sure I'd met John walking around in the early pages of the New Testament, not the Old. What was he doing here? I read through the tedious scripts of these audiovisual dinosaurs until I found the one for John. "He was a prophet in the Old Testament tradition," it said, "who pointed the way to Jesus." I guessed "tradition" meant something like "style."

A thought came into my mind—a sort of fantasy struck me, one that I have revisited over and over again since that afternoon. What had been boring and mundane suddenly became fascinating. With apologies to the discrete integrity of the Hebrew Scriptures, there in my vision was John striding determinedly from the Old Testament to the New, waving good-bye to Malachi, scaling Apocryphal peaks on the way (because that was the way my Bible was laid out), traipsing over the Maccabean hills, waving to Sirach and Tobit, by-passing Matthew (even fantasies are true to source theory), finally bursting in upon the opening pages of Mark, shouting "Prepare the way!" and "Repent!" John sounded, for all the world, like Amos or Jeremiah, as he branched out into Luke, Matthew, and John. I was thoroughly enchanted. The bearer of God's message in the fine old Hebrew style, trudging right into the New Covenant and making himself at home. It had a certain appeal.

Years later I was to revisit this image one morning in seminary. We were looking at prophetic call narratives in Hebrew Scripture. You know the pattern: God gets the attention of the prophet-to-be and states the task. The person says, "You must mean someone else; I couldn't possibly do that." Then God says, "I'll help you; but I'm not letting you off the hook." So the prophet utters the fateful words, "Here I am!" And that's that. A done deal. Moses, Samuel, Isaiah—perhaps you recognize this pattern in some deep way!

I was pondering all this, when suddenly we were led to the first chapter of Luke. And there—lo and behold—was another prophetic call narrative, fitting the pattern exactly. This time an angel sought out a young Hebrew girl (hardly prophet material). And, after a fervent "How can this be?" she gave herself over to God with the fateful words "Here I am. Let it be with me according to your word." I realized suddenly that Mary was a prophet! A bearer of God's Word, God's incarnate word in her case. Amazing! Life-changing!

Until that moment, I hadn't really thought much about the Virgin Mary. Maybe "resonated with her" or "engaged her" is a better way to say it. In the Roman Catholic world where I live, Mary is still usually portrayed as a distant, cool, loving, but totally unflappable perfect mother—a paragon of all I'm not.

With the flesh and bones, determination and strong character I've associated with prophecy, I began to like Mary, even to admire her. I got interested in what she is really about. The words of the Magnificat began to sound even more powerful, and I began to believe she actually uttered them. I began to see injustice and God's deep caring for the poor through her eyes, through what it must have been for her to live out her prophetic call faithfully: flee to Egypt, raise a Messiah, watch her son die, stick with the other disciples, and begin to be the Church.

As Mary came alive for me, I grew less critical of devotion to her. I wept when I saw a teenage Hispanic couple hold their newborn infant up to her statue in a cathedral in San Antonio. I delighted in discovering her picture, painted in a child-like way, on a wall behind a sacristy door in an up-to-date, post-Vatican II conference center, where no plaster images adorned the halls—a folk-art Theotokos behind the door. Someone had missed Mary and painted her there. Her image still bore God's Word to that hungry soul: *Stella Maris*, Our Lady Star of the Sea, with sparklers, fireworks bursting around her head.

I read recently about Muslims who worship an icon of Mary, in hopes her prayers will bring them babies, about a team of Syrian cosmonauts who prayed to her for safe travel in space. On their return, those Muslims sacrificed a sheep in her honor.

What resonance Mary has in this world! The Word she still bears goes out, way beyond known Christian circles. Mary's message is power—Christ's power to love, to change, to forgive, to witness to God's passion about human life. In her, God's voice cannot be silenced. One day my old fantasy returned, and I realized for the first time that John hadn't made that trek alone. Mary had been with him the whole way, bringing with her Hannah's great song, embodying strong reminiscences of Samuel, also called as a child into the ministry of bearing God's Word to the world. Second-century noncanonical writings equate Mary with Samuel, so her prophetic call even has a tradition. No wonder she still speaks to us with such strength.

We've remembered today Mary's apostolic visit to her cousin, which revealed the Good News that Zechariah's prophecy was being fulfilled in her: God dwelling in our midst by becoming human life, with all the richness and complexity we know that to be about. We know that, for Mary, bearing that Word to the world was a most difficult and dangerous task. And that it still is.

We've encountered the adult John being confronted by people confused about his role. But John was not confused. He was clear that his ministry was to point to Jesus, whatever the cost to himself. John knew the *fulfillment* of the *prophecy*'s the thing, *not* the *prophet*. The truth is, each one of us is called into this prophetic tradition with John and Mary. We're called to be the ones who say, "Prepare the way!" and "Repent!" over and over again. To the point that we, too, really hear those words, and begin to live them.

You and I are already challenged with the task of traipsing from one part of Holy Scripture to another, climbing the hills, descending the valleys. All with an open heart and a critical eye for the details that define the terrain—a prayerful and humbling endeavor.

We're invited into those holy moments when someone shares having caught sight of the presence of God in their lives, when someone offers up a baby, a hope, a dream, a disappointment, or a failure. Then, most especially, we must yield ourselves and point to the One in whom all holiness happens.

On days when we feel like quaint folk art hidden behind a sacristy door, we remember we're in good company. For God has called you and me, like Mary and John, to make God's Living Word heard in this world—in how we live, in what we do, in who we are, in how we preach. A dangerous calling, but a worthy one.

To respond in faith we may adopt the words of Mary, but we cannot pick and choose; we must use them all: "Here I am. Let it be with me according to your Word." Here I am. Let it be with you and me according to the Word of God.

Susan Gaumer is rector of St. Andrew's Church, New Orleans, Louisiana.

PROPER 4, YEAR A

"Oops! I Forgot!"

Romans 3:21–25a, 28; Matthew 7:21–27
J. Donald Waring

IT'S BEEN ten years now since I graduated from General Seminary in New York, but I still remember the preaching class I took my senior year. One afternoon a friend of mine was scheduled to preach. The dozen or so class members and I dispersed ourselves around the Chapel of the Good Shepherd, and my friend climbed into the imposing pulpit to give us the Word. All seemed to go well; and when the preacher was finished he descended from the pulpit to receive comments and critiques on his work. The other students and I, knowing that we ourselves would soon be subjected to the same experience, were kind and congratulatory with our feedback. We praised the preacher for his eloquent yet affable delivery. We complimented him on his interesting references to recent archeological digs in the Holy Land. We thanked him for his informative speculations about what life was really like for the Israelites in the days of the judges. This was the stuff of the Gospel! The preacher seemed to sit straighter and straighter in his pew as he received the lauds of this mutual affirmation society.

Finally it was saintly old Professor Bennett's turn to comment. He got right to the point: "Do you realize," he said to the student, "that not one single time in your entire sermon did you mention Jesus Christ?" Then a turncoat evangelical student chimed in: "You're right, Professor Bennett. His Jesus count was zero!" The student froze. Then his brow furrowed. Then his shoulders slumped. Then he rustled through his papers hoping to find those five little letters, J E S U S, somewhere in his text. They were nowhere to be found. He looked up with only this to say in his defense: "Oops. I forgot."

Jesus told a parable about a man who forgot. He was a man who set himself to the task of building a house. It would be a beach house. We might imagine that it would be the loveliest house on the beach: a three-car garage, a first-floor master retreat with walk-in closets, private bathrooms for all the kids, a "great room" complete with necessary cathedral ceilings, and, of course, the obligatory living room that no one will ever use. The man poured himself into the planning and building of his house; he spared no expense for the finest of materials. He did much of the work with his own two hands, and he finished the job just in time for the summer season. When he moved his family in, they were the envy of the beach community. By all outward appearances, the house was magnificent. But when the summer was over, "the rain fell, and the floods came, and the winds blew and beat against that house, and it fell—and great was its fall." And what might the foolish man who built his house upon the sand have to say in his defense? "Oops. I forgot the foundation."

In the same section of Matthew's Gospel, Jesus tells about some other people who make a critical oversight. They are relentless doers of good deeds: busy, important, action-oriented people who, in the name of Jesus, speak words of prophecy, cast out demons, and do many mighty works. They pour themselves into their charitable and religious activities. But come the great day of the Lord, their fate is anything but enviable. Jesus tells them to depart from his presence. Why? Perhaps they were overly proud of their accomplishments; they were just a bit too full of themselves and their self-described "mighty works."

Matthew, however, seems to suggest another reason for their exclusion: they forgot the one thing that was needful. In all their anxious, troubled rushing about to save the world in the name of Jesus, they forgot to be still and encounter Jesus themselves. "I never knew you," are the chilling words they hear on the lips of the One they neglected to meet. "Oops. We forgot," is about all we can imagine they could say in their defense.

What is the human capacity for forgetfulness? A story is told about a man and wife watching television. The husband announced he was going to the kitchen for a bowl of ice cream. His wife told him he'd better write that down since he'd forget by the time he got to the kitchen. He scoffed at such a thought. Sure enough, as he was on his way to the kitchen the phone rang. After a short conversation he hung up, went to the kitchen, found some leftover soup in the refrigerator, and brought out two bowls, one for himself and one for his wife. The woman looked at the soup and scolded the man: "See, I knew you'd forget." The man was puzzled. "What did I forget?" he asked. His wife replied, "I told you to bring some crackers with the soup!"

Perhaps our capacity to forget is not as great as this couple's. Or perhaps it is. Jesus seemed to think we have a fatal habit of forgetfulness and that this poses a spiritual problem for us. He told stories about forgetful people. You know them: An unmerciful servant is forgiven a multimillion-dollar debt. But he forgets, and goes out and beats up a man who owes him a few dollars (Matthew 18). Five foolish bridesmaids forget to bring enough oil for their lamps (Matthew 25). A wedding guest forgets to put on the proper garment (Matthew 22). A priest and a Levite forget their duties when they happen upon a man lying in the road beaten and bleeding (Luke 10). An unfaithful servant forgets that the master of the house is returning (Luke 12). And today, a man building a house forgets that the whole contraption needs a foundation (Matthew 7). What do these forgotten elements of the parables represent? They represent the one thing that is essential, yet goes overlooked: the forgiveness, the wedding garment, the oil, the foundation, the beaten man, the master of the house—all of these represent Jesus. For many of the players in the parables, their Jesus count is zero! Oops. They forgot.

We, too, forget. We forget our need for Jesus Christ. In the living of our lives and the building of our houses we forget that the human foundation is cracked and broken. It is ultimately unable to support the weight of existence. Yet we build upon it anyway, deceiving ourselves as if we had no sin. We may even pull off a few mighty works. But we wonder: why—why have I fallen short of the glory of God? Why have I not reached God? As preachers of the Gospel, what are we saying to people who are reaching for God? In these past ten years, I've learned to ask myself a question or two when I think a sermon is ready to go: Am I guilty of that critical oversight? Have I forgotten the grace of our Lord Jesus Christ? Am I suggesting to people that they need, and must, and really ought to do this and that mighty work? Never mind the foundation: build that house; be all you can be!

Sometimes, if I am honest with myself, I don't like the answer I get. I've turned the Gospel of grace into a work of Law. It's not that my "Jesus count" is particularly low, mind you. Neither was it low for the doers of good deeds. In fact, their "Jesus count" was rather high. You see, it's easy to preach about Jesus as if he were a new dispenser of an even tougher version of the law: "Try harder, pray longer, think positively" is what we are tempted to say in the name of Jesus. I remember one sermon in which I caught myself "calling" people to do six different things! Watch out for that phrase, "we are called." A whole gaggle of Pharisees can come riding into a sermon upon it! And what bad news that is, because no matter how strongly you build a house upon the sandy shores of human effort or the broken foundation of human potential, when the rains come and the winds blow its fall will be great.

So who can stand? Can anyone stand, let alone reach God? Today's reading from Romans is the apostle Paul's great statement of the atonement. He speaks of salvation for all as a gift of God's grace, through the redemption that is in Jesus Christ, whom God put forward. It is manifested apart from the Law, and we receive it by faith. In other words, we don't do it, we don't earn it, we don't work for it. We just have to trust it. It is accomplished; it is finished.

Indeed, Matthew's parable suggests that the builder of the house doesn't need to build a foundation. Not even that work is his responsibility. The foundation is already there; the strong rock lies just beneath the sand. All that the builder needed to do was sink down and connect with the cornerstone of the castle that would keep him safe (Psalm 31). But he forgot. Perhaps he never knew. What about those of us who claim to preach the Gospel on Sunday mornings? Will we "put forward" faith in our Lord Jesus Christ, or will we leave people thinking that our attempts at mighty works are sufficient to save?

Years ago three men were out duck hunting on a cold December morning, all wearing waist-high rubber waders. On the way to the duck blind, somehow the small, flat-bottomed boat they were in capsized and threw them into the cold water of the lake. They each thrashed about in a frenzy of activity, trying to swim ashore, trying to stay afloat, exhausting every ounce of energy to save themselves. Eventually, all three succumbed to the frigid waters. What was truly tragic about this accident was that the area of the lake where the men drowned was less than five feet deep. Perhaps they never knew. Perhaps in their panic they forgot. How sad that no one was there to remind them—to remind them that if they would just stop their frantic, frenzied attempt to stay afloat and save themselves, they would stand on solid ground. No one was there to tell them that if they would allow their feet to sink, they would live. No one was there to remind them to be still and to rest on the firm foundation of their salvation.[1]

Jesus said, "Not everyone who says to me 'Lord, Lord,' will enter the kingdom of heaven, but only the one who does the will of my Father in heaven." And this is the will of our Father in heaven: to sink down and connect with the cornerstone of the castle that will keep us safe. It is to know Jesus and, in knowing him, to love him. And in loving him, to serve him. And in serving him, to dwell in the house of the Lord forever.

J. Donald Waring is rector of St. Thomas Episcopal Church,
Terrace Park, Ohio.

---

1. The story of the fishermen is told by J. Keith Miller, in his book, *Hope in the Fast Lane* (San Francisco: Harper and Row, 1987), 128.

Paul, the Problematic "Preaching Parent"

2 Corinthians 6:3–7:1
Mitties McDonald DeChamplain

I AM CONVINCED that if we were to take a quick survey or straw poll this evening to determine our top three "preaching parents," the apostle Paul would *not* make most lists. Partly, for some of us, because it would sound a bit presumptuous or boastful to say so. Somehow the claim "Well, I really am a chip off the old Pauline apostolic block when I preach" seems painfully lacking in humility.

But there is another reason many of us do not claim Paul as a preaching parent. I have never put him on my list, because I have more or less avoided preaching from his writings. I got heavy doses of Paul in my early fundamental Bible church days more than twenty-five years ago. And as you can well imagine, not all of his sayings had a life-giving effect on me. Please don't hear me wrong. I received a great sufficiency of love and grace in that church (mediated by letters of Paul, not incidentally), but what I retained for a very long time were impossible exhortations to a rigid piety that I was incapable of embodying. Overexposure to literal interpretations of certain Pauline writings can actually make it difficult to remember that he was the consummate preacher of the Good News of God in Jesus Christ.

To put a more concrete and human face on my sermon, today's passage has an inescapably harsh and haunting ring to my ears, given how Paul's words were put to use in my early formation as a Christian. I was in my twenties, a member of a very large independent Bible church, and dating a *non-Christian* (the assumed state of anyone who did not attend church—preferably that church—regularly). Everyone there was worried about me and about the state of my faith and future. An intervention was needed! The ideal opportunity for the face-off came when I was hospitalized for a tonsillectomy in April of 1974. I can laugh about it now, but imagine how it felt to be a twenty-six-year-old woman confined to a hospital bed in a pediatrics ward, no less. Imagine me—speechless—with a ruptured jaw and a sore throat that left me feeling as though I had swallowed the gates of hell! And then imagine the senior pastor of my church, arriving at the hospital to make his inevitable pastoral call, with Bible tucked under his arm, storming into the pediatrics ward, dodging three-year-olds riding tricycles down the corridors on his way into my room.

It won't take any imagination to figure out what happened next. There I sat in bed, unable to speak or respond. The pastor opened his Bible, pointed it directly at me, and began to read: *Do not be mismatched with unbelievers. For what partnership is there between righteousness and lawlessness? Or what fellowship is there between light and darkness? What agreement does Christ have with Belial? Or what does a believer share with an unbeliever?*

One proof text between the eyes, a stern warning about the dangers of dating non-Christians, a prayer for me—and the pastor was gone. It was as close to a spiritual knockout punch as I have ever received. The sore throat and stiff jaw went away in a couple of weeks, and I was able to speak. But I did not really find my spiritual voice again until I became a confirmed Episcopalian in 1980. I did not even know I had a "preaching voice" until I was in my mid-thirties, and then I was hired at Fuller Theological Seminary to help other women and men discover their own preaching voices. Is it any wonder that so many people have a love/hate relationship with the apostle Paul?

While I was on the faculty at Fuller Seminary I began to make peace with Paul. Not Paul, the ghostly, ghastly preaching parent, so often quoted to keep my sisters and me silent in church and subservient in ministry. As one of my friends likes to say, *that* Paul is an apostle only a mother could love! No, I prefer the *real* Paul (homiletical warts, cultural biases, and all) who managed throughout his ministry *to prefer nothing whatever to Christ*. The real Paul is the one who—in season and out of season—remained so radically dependent on God that he was radically available, by the mercies of God, to the Church. The real Paul, by right, is preaching parent to us all, to all who proclaim the Gospel and all who seek the truth.

In fact, I think it is fair to say that the apostle Paul's preaching, to use the homiletical phrase for the day from Don Waring's earlier sermon, had one of the highest "Jesus counts" in all of salvation history. And when we consider that before the start of his preaching life, Pauls's—or should I say, "Saul's"?—Jesus count was subzero, his journey into Christ becomes all the more remarkable a story for preachers to consider. He had a *curriculum vita* to die for, with impeccable credentials. Most of it appears in the third chapter of his letter to the Philippians: circumcised on the eighth day, a member of the people of Israel, of the tribe of Benjamin, a Hebrew born of Hebrews; as to the Law, a Pharisee; as to zeal, a persecutor of the Church; as to righteousness under the Law, blameless.

Saul even had a beach house, where he could literally walk out the front patio door and sit in the sand! But as we all know well from Scripture, Saul's world as he knew it crumbled—not on a sandy beach, but on a dusty road to Damascus. And when the "transparent flame of love's free duty"[1] flashed around him that day in the face of Jesus Christ, Saul's savage voice, his proud heart, his stubborn will were put to flight forever. And he got a new name, a new identity, a new purpose, a new voice.

The text and subtext for every sermon of Paul's were simple: Jesus Christ, the crucified one. Paul was perpetually pregnant with the Word. He spoke, he thought, he wrote, and he acted in the name of Jesus. And for the sake of that Word, that Logos, whom Paul knew to be the reason for everything that is,

Paul was willing to go anywhere and to preach in any way necessary to get the only Word worth knowing across to people.

Paul's passionate, ongoing relationship with the church in Corinth is a brilliant witness to his faithful ministry of truth telling for the sake of the Gospel. One commentator tartly observes: "For anyone operating under the naïve presumption that joining a Christian church is a good way to meet all the best people and cultivate smooth social relations, a reading of Paul's Corinthian correspondence is the prescribed cure. But however much trouble the Corinthians were to each other and to Paul, they prove to be a cornucopia of blessing to us, for they triggered some of Paul's most profound and vigorous writing [and preaching]."[2]

Today's lesson is a representative example of how Paul used all that there was to use to speak the truth in love and to keep the Church open to the reconciling work of Christ.

Paul's detractors in Corinth were challenging his authority as a preacher and apostle. They kept asserting that Paul's "pregnancy" with the Word was a false one. In reply, Paul did what he had to do. He opened wide his heart to the Corinthians. He did not blame or accuse, defend or excuse himself. But with steadfast love he reminded them what preachers who are punch-drunk with the Gospel of Jesus Christ must be willing to do for Christ's sake. He is clear that true preachers don't take the beach house by the sea! Paul knew that the whole truth had to be communicated, not only with our lips but also with our lives. So he says: *Lest our ministry be brought into discredit, we avoid giving any offence in anything. As God's ministers, we try to recommend ourselves in all circumstances by our steadfast endurance: in affliction, hardship, and distress; when flogged, imprisoned, mobbed; overworked, sleepless, starving. We recommend ourselves by innocent behaviour and grasp of truth, by patience and kindliness, by gifts of the Holy Spirit, by unaffected love, by declaring the truth, by the power of God. We wield the weapons of righteousness in right hand and left. Honour and dishonour, praise and blame, are alike our lot: we are the impostors who speak the truth, the unknown men whom all men know; dying we still live on; disciplined by suffering, we are not done to death; in our sorrows we have always cause for joy; poor ourselves, we bring wealth to many; penniless, we own the world.*[3]

Paul knew that the secret of Christian living and true excellence in preaching were the same: *preferring nothing whatever to Christ.* He was a believer in using all the media of brain, will, and body to draw as unreservedly as possible into relationship with the other. Paul knew as well as anybody the whole truth about preachers—that, like everybody else, we are fragile creatures who shatter pretty easily under challenge or criticism, or the cut and thrust of ordinary ministry. So he is bold to say earlier in this same letter, *We have this treasure in clay jars, so that it may be made clear that this extraordinary power belongs to God and does not come from us.*

I am convinced that it must have been the ravishing beauty of Paul's preaching on the love and mercy of Christ that would, in another generation, prompt

Martin Luther to write, "God rides the lame horse, and God carves the rotten wood." It has never been God's way to choose perfect, unblemished creatures to do God's work of grace in the world. God chooses people like Saul, like you and me, flawed and cracked. Out of our intrinsic weakness, the holiness of God breaks surface in us from time to time.

Our world today summons us more than ever to labor, love, and give our whole selves with abandon for the sake of the Gospel. We are the ones who, after Paul's example, now "go for broke" in our preaching for Christ's sake. We are willing, for Christ's sake, to be seen and seen through. We must open wide our hearts to preach the Good News. We are the keepers of the dream— God's dream, Paul's dream, the Church's dream—of a "world redeemed by Christ-like love; all life in Christ made new."[4] And some day, what we preach, by the mercies of God, shall be so. All life in Christ made new. Let it be. Let it be. Let it be.

Mitties McDonald DeChamplain is Trinity Church Professor of Preaching at The General Theological Seminary, New York City.

---

1. From the Phos Hilaron in *Enriching Our Worship* (New York: Church Publishing Incorporated, 1998).

2. See Eugene Peterson's introduction to 2 Corinthians in *The Message: The New Testament in Contemporary English* (Colorado Springs, Colorado: NAVPRESS, 1993), 368.

3. *Revised English Bible*, 2 Corinthians 6:3–10.

4. From Hymn #705, *The Hymnal, 1982* (New York: Church Publishing, 1985).

For the Preaching of the Gospel

Coming to the Cliff

Romans 10:5–17; Matthew 10:5–22
Anne K. Bartlett

Oh God of Light and Love, you sent your Word for the creation of the world and for our redemption in your Son, Jesus Christ. Bless us as we preach and hear your Word proclaimed. Speak to us and through us, that your name may be glorified, now and forever.

When I received the schedule for this conference, the first thing I did was to find when I would preach, and on what texts. "A Votive for the Preaching of the Gospel." I wasn't aware we *had* a votive for the preaching of the Gospel. Printed right there on the schedule was an unfamiliar collect, addressed to our

God of light and love, acknowledging God's Word sent for creation and for our redemption. A bidding to be blessed as preachers and as hearers of the Word proclaimed. A petition that God speak to us, and through us, for the glorifying of God's Holy Name. A *wonderful* collect, rich in layers of meaning; and I knew I had never laid eyes upon it before, because I *would* have remembered it.

Then I turned to the Scriptures appointed for this Votive of the Preaching of the Gospel, and my spirits soared. What great texts to preach on! The Gospel is Matthew's version of how Jesus sent out the disciples, two by two, to preach and to heal. He tells them to travel light. He tells them how to comport themselves, what to say ("Say this: The kingdom of heaven has come near"). He tells them what to do when they run into indifference, into hostility, into danger.

The Epistle is even better. Here is Paul himself, writing about the preaching task. He quotes reassuring words from Deuteronomy, words about the Word being near us, on our lips and in our hearts. Words about what we are to say— we who are sent to be preachers, with our beautiful feet, bearing such Good News for the all the world. "Preach this," writes Paul. "Proclaim Jesus is Lord, and God has raised him from the dead." Alleluia, Amen! I basked again in Paul's eloquent, strengthening words defining the preacher's task and purpose: we are sent to proclaim so that others might hear, and believe, and so be saved.

How did I get so lucky—to preach about preaching to preachers on the day appointed for A Votive for the Preaching of the Gospel (which, somehow, I had not heard, nor ever seen; *how* had I missed it)? So I called Roger and asked him about the collect. And he said, "Do you like it? I wrote it."

Ah, yes, Roger, I like it. Very much. Thank you. And I believe the church needs this votive, so let's all take it back to where we came from, or to where we are going, and use it, spread it widely.

My first reaction was delight. Exhilaration, even. The sermon could be a call to arms, a festive celebration of our calling. That's how my experience began, but it soon changed—deepened, darkened. I found myself led into an uneasy exploration of the interior life of a preacher, as I know it. I cannot speak for anyone else. But I find I need to add my voice to Matthew's, and to Paul's, and to Roger's. To try to speak my experience of the task to which we are called. To speak as honestly as I know how of what it's like to be a preacher of the Word, from the inside out.

> *Come to the edge of the cliff, he said.*
> *Oh, no, we're afraid, they cried.*
> *Come to the edge of the cliff, he said.*
> *Oh, no, we're afraid, they cried.*
> *Come to the edge of the cliff, he said.*[1]

The truth is—my truth is—the preaching task is terrifying. How dare we? How dare we climb into these pulpits, open our mouths, and speak of things so far beyond our understanding. To speak of *God*, for heaven's sake? How dare we do that?

How often it has happened. The Gospel has been read, the book put back on the altar. I'm in position at the pulpit. I've said my little prayer as a final incantation (like a baseball pitcher on the mound, giving one last obsessive tug of his cap). The congregation has sat down and settled in. In that tiny moment of expectant silence that I must break, that I am called to break—how often I most desperately wish to say *nothing. Not one word.* I want simply to stare back, then shrug my shoulders, and mutely raise my hands in recognition that *any* word at all is inadequate, absurd. And then, if I could, I would turn, climb down, go back to my chair. And we could all just sit there, as the Quakers do, and wait for the silence to be broken. Or not.

Come to the edge of the cliff, he said.
Oh, no, we're afraid, they cried.

Way down deep in preachers lurks this fear of coming the edge of the cliff, of daring to open our mouths at all. And the fear is well founded. We know the truth that there *are* no words with which to articulate the Mystery. The task is impossible. Let's begin with that. What's really scary is to hear a preacher who has no fear, who pretends to know the mind of God, who speaks without a stammer, without a hesitation, with no humility before the Holy One. When we declare we don't know very much at all, we are both cunning and correct. We should choose our words with care and reverence and with restraint. In our pulpits, we preachers stand out like lightning rods. And at any moment, if we're not careful, we could be struck with a bolt of divine displeasure that, in a flash, would burn us to a crisp. I'm surprised it hasn't happened to me yet. Lord knows I've deserved it.

But we have been called to this task. We are preachers. We have been sent. We are to speak.

Come to the edge of the cliff, he said.
Oh, no, we're afraid, we cried.
Come to the edge of the cliff.
I'm calling you by name.

There's another fear that's not as holy as the creaturely caution to say anything at all of God. This secondary fear is the fear of self-exposure. When we stand up to preach, we reveal ourselves. It can't be helped. We have this treasure in earthly vessels. When we preach, the Word comes through our flesh and blood. We get mixed up in it, try though we might to keep ourselves hidden and out of sight.

But it doesn't work that way. And the dangers are twofold. On the one hand, if we try to hide for fear of being seen or for fear of failure, then our words are flat and lifeless, because we do not inhabit them. We are not really "there," and everybody knows it. That's when we stand way back from the edge, for fear of seeming foolish, or a phony, or foolhardy; in any case, irrational. So we try to hide ourselves from the congregation. We try to hide even from the eyes of God. And the truth is not in us.

Worse is the flip side of this fear, the tendency to exhibitionism that some of us reveal. We like too much to be seen and so we preach ourselves instead of Christ.

Either way our fear of being revealed as the fools we are surely are makes us anxious. In our anxiety, we forget what it is we are to be about, and instead we seek the approval of those to whom we have been sent. This preaching life exposes our souls, not only to the world, but also even to ourselves, so that we may see just how vast and bottomless is our pathetic need to be *liked*. "Loved your sermon!" Ah.

The truth is, we were not called to entertain. We were not called to be witty or even particularly bright. We're sent to preach Christ, and him crucified. We're sent to tell all the world that the Risen One is Lord. We're sent to proclaim that the kingdom is near, that God is close at hand, close as a heartbeat, close as our breath. We have been sent out like scouts, and our mission is to report back what we have seen and heard. That report is what we call a sermon.

That's when Matthew's words wake us up, remind us what it is we are to be about. When we proclaim what we have been sent to say, we are warned to expect indifference, not affirmation, to expect resistance, even the occasional hostility. We're preachers, for God's sake, not performers. The question isn't "Did they like it?" The question is "Did I preach the Gospel truth?" Be shrewd as a snake and innocent as doves, dear ones, because this terrain is full of land mines for your soul. Approval may be the most dangerous trap of all.

Come to the edge of the cliff, he said.
Oh, no, we're afraid, they cried.
Come to the edge of the cliff, he said.
Oh, no, we're afraid, they cried.
Come anyway, he said.
They came. He pushed.
They flew.

So I entered into these texts appointed for A Votive for the Preaching of the Gospel, first with delight and then with increasing apprehension, trepidation. Aware of dangers lurking in this call, I moved (or, more accurately, *was* moved) to yet another place inside of them, a place of grace that feels like free fall. A place where our feet no longer touch the solid ground and suddenly we're over the edge, beyond our fears. (Did we jump? Or were we pushed? It's hard to say.) This, too, is part of what it is to be a preacher; and I want to find words to tell it, because here is where I've found God's grace.

I believe that most of us who are called to preach *need* to preach, not for others but for our own soul's sake. Here's what I mean. You seasoned preachers, tell me if this is as true for you as it is for me. Sometimes when I'm preaching, I am aware of being released from all self-consciousness, while in the same moment (as I preach) I feel more truly who I really am than I have ever been. Does this make sense? In preaching free fall we fly in that perfect freedom of this service. We lose self-consciousness, we lose our selves, so that, in God's grace, our true selves may be found.

Let me come at it another way. The Hindus speak of a system of centers in our bodies, the seven chakras, each sensitive to a particular spiritual task, as well as energetically affecting certain parts of the body. The fifth chakra, they say, is located at the base of the throat and affects what happens in the neck, the throat, the jaws, the mouth, and the lips. Here in the throat is said to be where our will resides, between the head and heart. To be spiritually mature, the Hindus say, is to let loose of our own will so that it may be aligned with God's will. We Christians might speak of this as being conformed to Christ. That's what happens when our wills are surrendered to the Spirit, our heads and hearts lined up right, and from our own throats come words that speak God's Word. So conformed, we trust the Voice who calls us. We go over the edge, and fly. In the process we preachers are healed and sanctified a sermon at a time.

Here's my point: I don't think being called to preach has a thing to do with our supposed "gifts." I think it's how God keeps us close, we who are so prone to wander. Preaching makes us enter into sacred story. It helps us see ourselves as the flawed and fragile, fearful creatures that we are—yet so well beloved that God trusts us with the Holy Word and bids us preach.

Bids us preach, because that is how God has chosen to save us. For such as us, perhaps there is no other way.

Anne K. Bartlett is associate rector of St. John the Baptist Episcopal Church, Portland, Oregon.

---

1. Different forms of the poem used in this sermon have appeared in a variety of places. The source is unknown. From various renderings, the author has modified the wording for her purposes in this sermon.

Never the Point of the Story

2 Corinthians 7:2–16
Timothy Mulder

WALKING BACK to the dorm Saturday night after our first session, I had a vision—of sorts. The sign that had greeted us at the student union, "WELCOME EPISCOPAL PREACHING PROGRAM," had been changed to: "WARNING: EPISCOPAL PREACHING FRANKENSTEINS IN THE MAKING."

Behind the sign was a room with the glow of laboratory lights streaming from its windows. Peeking through the doors, one could observe homiletical alchemists piecing together a being who could craft words like Barbara Brown Taylor, paint prophetic visions like Walter Brueggemann, tell stories like Fred Craddock, and light spiritual fires the way Jim Forbes does. I felt myself getting excited. Could I ever become a preacher like that? Will that happen at this conference? Will we be able to create super preachers for the Episcopal Church? Are there secrets to this art of preaching that, if known, will draw the modern masses to Christ, even as Peter's sermon did on that first Pentecost?

But then I woke up.

Preaching styles shift almost as rapidly as hemlines. And just about the time we get our wardrobe changed around, we realize that we can't pull off that style in the way that Gwyneth Paltrow, Harrison Ford, Fred Craddock, Barbara Taylor can.

But this week I have met one preacher whom I might resemble. And maybe you, too. I say might because we know so little about him. A letter in the New Testament bears his name, but the letter was written *to* him, rather than *about* him. I've never heard him mentioned in a preaching class. His name is Titus. Titus who? We don't know. He's a fairly insignificant character in this letter to the Corinthians. What did he look like? We don't know. What did he sound like? He's never quoted anywhere, so how *would* we know? What was his most memorable sermon? No one remembers. So why might he be our model for a preacher?

All we know is that Paul sent Titus into the middle of a conflict, just as every preacher (or for that matter, every Christian) is sent into the middle of a conflict. A division had occurred in the Corinthian church. A faction led by one of its leaders had turned the community against Paul and his teachings. In response, Paul had fired off a stern letter. We're not sure what it said, but we know he had second thoughts after he dropped it in the mail.

I'm glad Paul didn't tell us what the conflict was about. It could have been as trivial as the Altar Guild wanting red candles at Christmas, or as significant as denying the Eucharist to baptized children. His silence on the specifics allows us to apply our own situation to his experience. Whatever it was, we know that it threatened to bring the relationship between Paul and the Corinthians to an end. Paul wanted the relationship to be restored. He was afraid that it might be lost forever. But more than fear or institutional survival was at stake.

This week, hundreds of miles from home, I have become aware once again how my life is no longer complete by itself. I am no longer simply Tim Mulder. A part of me is the woman I love, and who loves me, and the two children with whom we share life. Although I am having a wonderful time with all of you, I do not want even to try to imagine how dreadful life would be if I were not able to return to them on Friday. The depth and joy of a relationship that moves us beyond ourselves is beyond description. Perhaps it is akin to what Jesus had in mind when he talked with Nicodemus about being born a second time. Perhaps it approaches the joy of God in the created order, or of Paul in regard to the churches he started. And if such joy, then what intense sorrow at the prospect of *breaking* such a relationship! Or even worse, of its demise! It was not fear that motivated Paul so much as unwillingness to let go of such joy. For this is the joy of life that goes beyond itself. This is the joy of affirming that we are incomplete, but necessary, parts of one body. It was into this conflict that Paul sent Titus.

If you don't want to spend your days in the land of conflict, then don't become a preacher. Preaching exists because there is a conflict. In fact, the Church exists in the world *because* there is unresolved conflict. Conflict is an ever-present reminder that the reign of God is not yet complete. If it can be said that "where there is smoke, there's fire," then it is equally true that "where there is conflict, there is pain."

Of all the things our modern age has mastered, I doubt we have become more expert in anything than in our ability to deceive one another by making our lives look so perfect. From the manicure of our suburban lawns, to the titles on our business cards, to the way we hold the hymnal on Sunday morning— *we look good*. But I never go into worship any more without assuming that I am walking into a room *full* of pain—pain living in hope.

Titus was sent into the Corinthian conflict for one reason: to see if there was any hope. Hope for Paul and hope for the future of a Christian witness in Corinth. The preacher is, above all else, a conduit of hope.

Barbara Brown Taylor has likened the preacher to Cyrano de Bergerac. You remember him—that less-than-handsome Frenchman who passed messages between two would-be lovers? Sometimes the messages came from one direction, sometimes from the other. Sometimes the preacher passes on a word from God, sometimes from the people to God. I like Taylor's image, but, in my experience, it is not always words of love that the preacher gets handed to pass on.

Her lip was trembling as she walked into my study. A tear dropped before she even sat down. "He hurts us and he frightens us. I can't take it any longer. I don't dare leave my children alone with him." Why had she come to church to say those things? Because she has hope that the preacher will marshal the Body of Christ to surround her with love and hold her up with their support— and will call on the Lord not to abandon this woman and her children.

A man at a cocktail party tells me, "I don't believe the stuff you talk about, but I keep coming." "Why?" I ask. "I don't know," he flippantly replies, "maybe it's just my insurance policy." What hope lies buried in his heart like the golf ball under the pile of fall leaves? The preacher will have to spend the time to look under every pile with that man, until what once was lost can now be found.

A mother stands with her four children in the hallway. I'm running late, but the look in her eyes says that this matters. "My husband and I have been married fifteen years. We could never agree on which one of our churches to go to, so we didn't do anything. Tell me: is it too late to enroll my son in the confirmation class, my teenage daughter in the senior high program, and the twins in Sunday school?" Beneath her question I hear another: "Is there hope for me and my children? Is it too late for them to learn, not only the stories, but the life of Jesus, and to love him and to know his love?" The preacher is there to assure her that *now* is the acceptable time, that *now* the reign of God can begin among her family.

Bob lies in the intensive care unit. He will die soon, but now he wants to pray. So do his wife, his children, and a few friends who have gathered. We hold hands. We pray about our hope, hope in the One whose love will not let us go, not even at the grave.

In town the lawyer argues for her client, the firefighter races to a call, the teacher leans over a desk. And when they find their way to their pew on Sunday morning, they pray that their lives will make a difference. They do because they enflesh the hope of Jesus who walks with us, and talks with us, and tells us we are his own.

Christians live in the midst of conflict, but if we bear any distinguishing mark, it is that we are a people of hope. Each week we gather in hope, looking for hope. And someone has been sent there to pass the notes, the messages, the words. What is true for the preacher in the community of faith is equally true for the Christian in the world. At my ordination my mother said to me, in the manner of an ancient rabbi, "Tim, just love your people. Love them in Jesus' name, and all the rest will be commentary." Pastoral care and preaching blend into one the way hot fudge and vanilla ice cream do after a while in the same bowl.

Titus went to share life with the people of Corinth. He could well be our new patron saint for preachers. No one knows or remembers what he said. He was never the point of the story, but the story cannot be told without him. Because, in the end, Christ was glorified, Paul rejoiced, the church carried on, and hope was rewarded.

Timothy Mulder is rector of St. John's on the Mountain,
Bernardsville, New Jersey.

THE MARTYRS OF UGANDA

Martyrs and Metanarratives

Matthew 24:9–13; Hebrews 10:32–39
John A. Dally

DAVID SAID, "All men are liars." David was a man. Therefore, David was a liar. Therefore, all men are not liars. We hear this false syllogism and sense at once that there is something wrong with it, but we cannot say immediately just what it is. So it is with the stories that surround the martyrs of Uganda. They cannot logically all be true, but it is nearly impossible to sort out the false parts.

This much is beyond doubt: On June 3, 1886, thirty-two men ranging in age from thirteen to twenty-five, all recent converts to Anglican or Roman Catholic Christianity, were put to death at Namugongo by order of the *kabaka*, the king of Buganda, as the region was then known. That they died bravely and with complete confidence in their God is unquestioned. That their noble deaths led to the rapid growth of Christianity in Buganda is amply attested by the thousands of Anglican and Roman Catholic Christians who populate Uganda today. That these young men died for the sake of the Gospel, however, is less clear.

Mwanga, the kabaka of Buganda, was an absolute monarch who saw his sovereignty being eaten away by the encroachment of foreign powers, most often preceded or accompanied by their missionaries. His father, Mutesa, had willingly received the first Roman Catholic missionaries to arrive on his soil and was equally glad to hear the Anglicans who soon followed, though he remained perplexed about whether Christianity was one religion or two. By his son Mwanga's time, the Islamic missionaries had also set up shop in Buganda, so the king had three foreign religions to compare to his own, all competing for his allegiance. But this was not to be a merely philosophical choice. Behind the Roman Catholic missionaries lay the territorial amibitions of France. Behind the Anglicans, the rapidly expanding empire of Great Britain. And behind the Muslims, the explicit desire of the khedive of Cairo to annex a land Stanley had called "the jewel of Africa." No one except the missionaries really cared which religion Mwanga picked, so long as the choice paved the way for their access to Buganda's rich natural resources.

Mwanga was faced with a choice similar to that which had confronted Kamehameha of Hawaii some twenty years earlier. Kamehameha gave his royal preference to the faith of the British missionaries because he was afraid that the Americans wanted only to build a naval station at Pearl Harbor, overthrow his monarchy, and annex his island kingdom to the United States. He was right.

Unlike Kamehameha, Mwanga was without doubt a despotic ruler, but he was certainly pushed to the edge by the prospect of seeing his country carved into pieces and carried away by foreign powers. He decided to put a stop to it. By decreeing the death of African converts to Anglican and Roman Catholic Christianity, Mwanga was trying (vainly, as it turned out) to repulse the invasion of his country by Britain and France. He killed converts to Islam, too, but the church does not see fit to commemorate those deaths.

And so we have a complicated story here, one that becomes more so as soon as we go beneath its surface. Surrounding the story of the Ugandan martyrs, you see, are metanarratives that critique Mwanga's sexuality. And here our false syllogism begins.

One of these metanarratives states that Mwanga had tried to sodomize each of these thirty-two men and put them to death because, in the name of Jesus, they refused his advances. The other story is that the missionaries outraged Mwanga by baptizing the pages of his court but not him, because he refused to give up his many wives and because he had murdered contenders for his throne upon his accession, thus proving himself a barbarian.

If the first story (which I found on four different websites dedicated to the martyrs of Uganda) is true, then these male martyrs are joined to a long history of female saints of the church who were tortured, mutilated, executed—and subsequently canonized—for nothing more nor less than refusing sexual intercourse to a non-Christian. The story of Mwanga's homosexuality was cited by a Ugandan bishop at Lambeth last year as a basis for critiquing the phenomenon of homosexuality in Western culture. So this story has wide circulation.

When I consulted the four African priests who teach or study at Seabury for their opinion, however, they said that the story was a concoction of the missionaries and that it was Mwanga's excessive *heterosexuality* that led to the breakdown in relations. I continued my research and found this story also confirmed by several different websites.

If this second story is true, it is deeply ironic that Western missionaries would refuse Mwanga baptism. After all, they used a Bible that recounts the many wives of David and Solomon and portrays these monarchs as slaughtering all their enemies to ensure the safety of their thrones. "Why do you see the speck in your neighbor's eye, but do not notice the log in your own eye?" Jesus asks (Matthew 7:3).

This feast of the martyrs of Uganda should remind us all of the degree to which the history of the spread of Christianity is a history of Western cultural imperialism, particularly with respect to the management of gender and sexuality. Instead of preaching Christ, and him crucified, too many Western missionaries said, "Cover yourselves." Instead of proclaiming a God who loves the human race enough to die for it, too many Western missionaries said, "Put away your wives." Is it any wonder that the stern critique of gender and sexuality we spread throughout the world in the name of Jesus should now be returning to critique us in that same name?

But the fact that the whole world is now arguing about gender and sexuality should make us prick up our theological ears. The global awakening of women's consciousness is, without doubt, the single greatest influence in our lifetimes on the Gospel that you and I will preach—surfacing, as it does, the fundamental unheard story of the other half of the human race. It gives the lie to our claims of universality and calls into question the adequacy of our theological vision to date. It signals the end of the glorification of violence and of a God who blesses it. It is the beginning of the end of our fear of difference.

In the twenty-six years I have been an Episcopalian, the church has generated tremendous heat, and virtually no light, arguing about the role of women and the place of gay men and lesbians in the Church and in the world. It seems our forebears have drained our imaginations of any response to gender and sexuality except prohibition or license. But Scripture invites us to view our genderedness and our sexuality not as a subject for prohibition or license, but as a source of revelation—an opportunity to catch a glimpse of the face of God. "Then God said, 'Let us make humankind in our image, according to our likeness'. . . [I]n the image of God he created them; male and female" (Genesis 1:26–27).

What if the missionaries to Uganda had been able to recognize the image of God in the many wives of the kabaka? What if each of these women had been washed in the waters of baptism and proclaimed a daughter of the New Covenant? Isn't it possible that we wouldn't have to mourn the death of these thirty-two young men today? And what if you and I could begin to admit that nice people *do* have bodies and that, because of these bodies, they experience the world differently, and thus offer to others a unique piece of the divine image?

Of course, it would be much easier to retreat to our earlier understandings and roles, to leave men and women in their separate niches,[1] the men with the tools, the women with the babies. But it doesn't work. And, truth be told, it never did—as the troubled history of male-female relations attests.

The writer of Hebrews knows exactly how we feel. He or she writes to a community of Jewish Christians who are finding it too damned hard to hold their old and new identities together. As Jews they knew their place in the empire; as Christians they have lost all their former privileges. They want to go back to the way it was. But the writer argues passionately that God is never "back," but always "ahead," birthing them into a new reality.

The author of Hebrews offers us similar encouragement. Don't shrink back from the challenges before you. Press on to reveal the fullness of God's image in the faces of a redeemed humanity. Offer to a divided people the news that reconciliation is possible. Teach them to pray, "Holy and gracious One, in your infinite love you made us for yourself, and, when we had fallen into sin and become subject to evil and death, you in your mercy sent Jesus Christ, your only and eternal child, to reconcile us to you." Proclaim the end of humanity's last great divide in the table of the Christ, who—though embodied as a man—rejected every cultural norm of gender in his day, called a new family about him to do the will of God, and recognized a piece of the divine countenance in every human being he met.

Tell this good story. Celebrate the sacraments of the New Covenant of reconciliation. And give thanks for the mercy of God that the end has not yet come.

John A. Dally is professor of Christian communication and Director of Extension Education at Seabury-Western Theological Seminary, Evanston, and vicar of St. Dunstan of Canterbury Parish, Westchester, Illinois.

1. This homily was preached in a chapel in which statues of the Virgin Mary (holding the infant Jesus) and Saint Joseph (holding a carpenter's tools) occupied separate niches on either side of the apse.

EVENSONG

The Nag

Psalm 59; Luke 18:1–8
Katharine Jefferts Schori

TWENTY YEARS ago this summer, I went off to climb a mountain in central Washington. Mount Stuart is close to ten thousand feet high. The route we chose was a technical one, requiring a day's hike in, and a cold night, bivouacked at the base of the climb. The next morning there were a number of near-vertical and hair-raising pitches before we finally got to the summit. Then we had to climb down the other side of the mountain and hike back out to the trailhead—before it got dark.

This was my first really serious mountaineering, and it seemed like a glorious thing to do. I went on this trip with the guy I was going to marry in another month and a friend of his. I was probably in the best aerobic shape of my life—feeling lean and mean, and ready for anything. I was running regularly. I'd even run a marathon that spring. But I spent the first day watching the dust of those two guys far out ahead of me. They seemed to have made some kind of unconscious pact to have a race up that blasted mountain.

Once we roped up on the technical part, it wasn't so bad. Neither of them could get more than a rope's length away, and we took turns following the leader up the rock. It was appropriately tense and thrilling. And the view from the top *was* spectacular. But the leader wouldn't let us rest there—too far to the trailhead for more than five minutes on top.

We left the summit and went down into hell—four thousand feet of vertical down-climbing. Something like taking the stairs down from the top of the

Empire State Building—twice—and taking the steps two at a time. Big long steps down, and we had to do it in a controlled way or we would have tumbled off the side of the mountain. By the time we were halfway down, my knees were quivering like Jell-O. Climbers call it "sewing-machine leg." And the worst part was that I had to keep up, because I didn't know where we were going. I coped by getting snarly—at the leader, his friend, at the mountain, at whatever was in range. I held it together until we got to the bottom. Lo and behold, they were actually *waiting* for me! And then came the plan: "We're going to climb over that ridge and down the other side. We're not going by the trail because it's too late. It'll be dark if we don't hurry." I dissolved.

The trip seemed like a glorious thing to do, but I wasn't prepared for the drudgery, the altitude-induced headache, the pain, the tears of frustration, the embarrassment of tears, and not being able to keep up. It's like giving birth. Once you get through it, you forget the pain . . . most of it. . .

The widow in Luke's Gospel story has been on a mountaineering trip for years. She's been going to the courthouse to do something like a Middle Eastern sit-in. She parks herself outside the judge's office door, or sits in the back of his courtroom, and buttonholes him every time he leaves. That judge can't go into his office, or out for lunch, without running into her. She probably whines "Give me justice" twenty times a week. Maybe she makes friends with the judge's mother and his wife, hoping that they will help to turn his heart. Finally she gets down on her knees in the middle of his courtroom and tugs on his robe every time he comes near. "Give me justice. Give me justice." Finally he listens, as the Greek says, "so she won't give me a black eye."

This woman is probably the best example in the Gospels of the helpless widow—nobody around her seems to be the least bit concerned with her plight. But her persistence finally makes the rest of the community do the work of justice. Despite what he says, the judge gives her justice, because he's worried about what everybody else will think. He's concerned about the stain on his reputation.

I used to know a woman like that widow. She was a deacon in my home parish. She was a living example of that kind of persistence, both in her twelve-year journey to the diaconate, and in her hard-fought battle with breast cancer. She took this parable as an icon of her journey; then she started a religious order that she called the "Order of the Importunate Woman."

The charter went like this: "An ecumenical order of women. However, not wishing to be sexist, we will admit men as associates. The purpose of this Order is to succor and nurture the many women who work tirelessly in the churches of this country, yet frequently feel that, to really accomplish anything, they must nag, nag, nag."

She even did some heraldry and designed a shield: "The shield . . . blue and purple fields [a reference to the judge's black eye?], divided by a silver band, on which are three pairs of red lips. Surmounted by the motto, 'Nag, Nag, Nag.'"

Nagging was a great virtue in Cece's life. She incarnated for us a faithful belief in justice, even when it looks rationally impossible. And she showed us the willingness to keep fighting for it. Cece was the one in the parish who started the sewing guild to provide warm clothing for children. She was the one who organized dinners and invited the residents from the senior housing project across the street. She was the one who called the welfare agency to get the names of families who needed a little extra and then organized a collection of toiletries and birthday presents. She was the one who put a banner up on the church lawn every time there was a nuclear weapons test, asking people to pray for an end to the arms race. She was the steamroller, the Sherman tank, who badgered other people into action.

Should we call this story of the widow the parable of the Importunate Preacher? We're certainly meant to nag every unjust system in sight—and keep on nagging—for human dignity and the end of poverty—and justice. That's certainly what we mean when we pray, "Your kingdom come." But sometimes when we say those words it feels like we're only nagging God. It's possible to keep saying that prayer in the privacy of our closets and not do much to make it happen.

But that prayer is also an opportunity to let God nag *us*. It's just possible that sometimes we are the judge who doesn't want a black eye. Do we avoid preaching the just word until we get nagged into it? Sometimes grace comes in the form of a steamroller who won't let us run away.

Who's kneeling on our doorstep? What nags at us? Is it the rest of creation, crying "misuse"? Is it the abused children who've been too long ignored? Is it the forgotten elders, or the poor of other nations, or the migrant laborers of our own? Which one stirs *your* passions, who pushes *your* buttons? That's your importunate widow, and she is a gift to you. Much like Dame Wisdom, who cries, "You who thirst for justice, turn aside. Meet me here, sitting in your way."

Turn around and embrace that Nag. Pick her up and put her on your back. Let her get her hooks into you—she is wisdom in another guise. Let her cry for justice become your own.

Preaching is both about nagging and being nagged. Sometimes it's climbing up the mountain, step by step, to the glorious view from the top. We have a good sense of where we're going, and companions to egg us on, and the whole thing is an exhilarating challenge. But once we've been to the mountaintop, we have to come down.

Sometimes, we get to fly. Other times, preaching is more like the exhausted and painful process of climbing down the mountain. Our knees shake, and we have no idea where the next sermon is going to come from. Our knees quiver when we see that guy in the front pew with his arms crossed, shaking his head. The work feels solitary, like the widow prophet crying in the wilderness, and we despair that anyone will ever listen. We are confronted with our own weakness, and frustration, and sheer inability at every step. Sometimes we even get ornery. There are times, coming down the trail, when we're going to find ourselves saying, "O God, no! Not one more sermon!" How are we possibly going to get to the bottom of this mountain, let alone up the next one?

And yet, when the Son of Man comes, will he find that kind of persistent faith? Where is the oomph we need to keep going? Where are we going to find the strength to keep preaching justice, week after exhausting week?

Some of you know Bobbie McFerrin. In his *Medicine Music*, he and his father sing, "Strengthen up those weakened knees. . . ." It's about discipline. "For those who have been trained by it, no discipline seems pleasant at the time, but painful. Strengthen up your feeble arms, strengthen up those weakened knees, fix your mind on things above. . . ."

The strength for climbing mountains comes from the disciplined training of our bodies and minds. It takes hard aerobic exercise—learning to use all the breath we can muster. It takes the discipline of learning to live with sore feet and aching knees.

The strength for nagging after justice comes from the discipline of listening for the still, small voice. Strength comes from being fed at this table. Strength may come as the grace-filled steamroller, like the one charging through the widow's reluctant community. Sometimes we discover real strength only when we reach the end of our own resources.

"My eyes are fixed on you, O my Strength. . . . To you, O my Strength, will I sing."

We preachers are made of dust: sewing-machine legs, tears of frustration, and faint hearts. The marrow in our bones, the strength in our beautiful feet, the ability to keep nagging—those are the delicate fruit of knowing God, the inspiration that breathes life into the dust.

Take a deep breath—and then breathe in some more—we're going to need all the breath we can muster for this journey. Breathe deeply. Let that nagging Holy Spirit down into your bones and muscles and the very smallest capillaries. Breathe deeply. And start climbing down the mountain, one foot after the other, one knee-straining step after another. God's justice lies that way, over the next mountain!

Katharine Jefferts Schori is pastoral associate at the Church of the Good Samaritan, Corvallis, Oregon.

Justin Martyr

Preaching as Apology

1 Corinthians 1:18–25; John 12:44–50
David J. Schlafer

WELL, IT'S all but over, and we are out of here. Some of us are long gone, in fact. The rest of us have bags packed and engines running. I would have preferred a grand climactic liturgy, just as I would have preferred a conference free of glitches. (I build lots of organizational fantasy castles.)

The first of this week's notable glitches was the eleventh-hour loss of a staff member and a consequent need to change the worship/preaching schedule. That change, in turn, produced a corresponding shuffle of days, lessons, and liturgical occasions.

As the designated pinch-hitting preacher for this final day, with apology in hand, I paid a visit to Justin Martyr (whom we should have recognized last Tuesday). "Justin," I began, "I'm very sorry to have to ask you this—but would you be willing for us to transfer your feast from Tuesday until Friday?"

Justin chuckled. "Hey!" he replied. "I'll be more than glad to take anything you give me. Most folks don't notice me at all!" With a twinkle in his eye he continued, "Transferring my feast won't give you the liturgical finale you *want*. But it just might give you the conference closure you *need*." "How's that?" I asked, without a clue. "My witness to the Gospel was to offer an *apology*," he said. "*Apologetics* is what your conference—what *all* preaching is about."

I winced when I heard the "A" word, for I have, as they say, "a history" with "apologetics." I learned early on, of course, that apologetics has nothing to do with making excuses or begging forgiveness. Offering an "apology" means giving a defense—countering questions about *truth* with reasons for *belief*.

My first encounter with apologetics was an evening's crash course in my church youth group. We sat around a table, a group of teenagers, with Bibles and a one-page handout before us. "Here are some objections often raised against Christianity," the handout announced, "and a biblical bomb you can use to explode each one."

This apologetic enterprise seemed a bit curious. Quite apart from whether it was *appropriate* to employ Scripture texts as objection-detonators, there was another, more practical question. Would there be anyone around to believe anything after the "bombs" went off?

Yet, even though I wasn't much impressed with this particular set of tactics, there was something in the goal of apologetics that deeply appealed to me. I really did want to know the answers to questions about religious belief. Most babies, upon being thumped immediately after birth, draw a big breath and holler, "Waaah!" I drew a big breath, and hollered, "*Why?*" Ever since I can remember, I have wanted reasons—*good* reasons. For belief in God, I wanted to give the best reasons—reasons beyond a shadow of a doubt.

My concern was not always welcome in my church. Time and again, First Corinthians One was used as a "bomb": "the wisdom of God is foolishness to the world; the 'wisdom' of the world is foolishness to God." After the explosions, however, my questions continued. If I didn't have the resources to convince other people of Chrisitanity's odd-sounding claims, how could I believe them myself? I suspected Paul's assertions about wisdoms—human and divine—were an "apology," all right. An *excuse*—an *inexcusable* excuse.

Over an extended journey into apologetics, I have come to think that Paul's words have been misperceived by his anti-intellectualist interpreters. But Paul's point is a sharp one, nonetheless. To those who have no context for understanding it, Paul says, the Gospel sounds like sheer insanity. It sounds, in their ears, not so much false, as meaningless—utterly absurd. The message of the Cross, for the uncomprehending mind, does not even rise to the dignity of error. "A crucified Christ is the savior of the world." That claim has about as much intelligibility as the sentence: "Tall blue ideas sleep furiously." It simply doesn't compute. There is no point even in arguing about it.

In John's Gospel this morning, such a scenario is played out *live*, and it comes to a crashing end as follows: "Although [Jesus] had performed so many signs in their presence, they did not believe in him." A proliferation of signs was not sufficient—even seeing is not believing. Which is, perhaps, why, at the end of the day, John's Jesus wraps up his whole ministry of sign and discourse with a simple assertion: "I have come as light into the world, so that everyone who believes in me should not remain in darkness." End of argument. Apologetics abandoned altogether in favor of a simple affirmation of the Gospel.

Except that a nagging question still remains—so how does a preacher proceed in making simple declarations of saving grace to a world that finds them incomprehensible, that has no context in which to consider them? And all at once, the question of apologetics reemerges, more urgent than before. How is a preacher to name the Light, so that it can be seen for what it is?

Many apologetic strategies have been employed in Christian preaching across the ages. The various forms these "reasoned defenses" take, however, are by no means equivalent in meaning or equal in value. "Apologetics" has sometimes meant *mowing down, digging in, patching up,* or *making over.*

Reasoning can be employed in an attempt to blast an infidel's objection to bits. The ideology left standing after the analytical carnage is the ideology that wins.

Reasoning can be called in to build an impenetrable fortress for the faithful. Perhaps the alien ideas and practices that assail and assault the faithful can be warded off and the inhabitants of the fortress kept safe until the next seige.

Reasoning can be cranked up in a "deferred maintenance campaign." Beliefs tend to wear down over time, to crumble when left unattended. Maybe they can be put back together again.

Reasoning can be marshaled to repackage, repolish, and remarket a belief system, according to the best guesses of what will attract current consumer interest. "What would you *like* to believe—that's all we are *really* trying to sell!"

Against all such forms of "apologetics," Paul's stern words to the Corinthians apply with telling force: *Foolishness! It won't work; because it shouldn't work.* God's wisdom is caricatured by, not contained in or conveyed through, such human folly.

But there are other ways to do apologetics. Apologetics need not entail mowing down, digging in, patching up, or making over. The work of apologetics can be directed toward *setting forth, clearing away,* and *reaching out.*

What C. S. Lewis did in *Mere Christianity*, is, in a way, what each of the Gospel writers did in their distinctive faith communities—to *set forth*, clearly, comprehensively, coherently the simple riches and the complex simplicity of the Gospel. Not to beat down, browbeat, or get the better of objections or opponents, but simply to shed light, to "name grace" in ways that help people see it.

We honor Justin Martyr for his apologetic work, the work of *clearing away* misconceptions that cast illusory shadows along the arduous trail toward faith. In his day, Roman citizens understood a commitment to the Reign of God as inherently distracting to political duty, and disloyal to social order. "Not so," said Justin in one of his *Apologies*, "let me show you why."

To minds steeped in the philosophy of Greece, a "Word made Flesh" was "a circular square." "Christian belief is not inherently irrational," said Justin, in his other *Apology*. "Let me show you what can be said to remove that misconception."

"Christian teaching distorts and demeans the Word of YHWH that we read with reverence," said sincere second-century Jewish believers. "That stumbling block can be cleared away," thought Justin, and wrote his *Dialogue with Trypho* to address this profound concern.

And, because of Justin's apologetic work, Romans, Greeks, and Jews were able to see the Light who was obscured by their objections.

"I came not to judge the world, but to save it," says John's Jesus, even after sign upon sign had been disregarded and denounced, *reaching out,* embodying his *apologia,* in a uplifted and uplifting way, drawing all the world unto himself. "Greater works shall you do," Jesus says to his apprentice apologists, "because I go to my Father."

Setting forth, clearing away, reaching out—against such forms of apologetics, St. Paul has no objection. That, after all, is what Paul the preacher is about.

Think of major points of growth, significant changes of direction in the course of your own life. Who has helped you—and how—in those teachable moments, those times of transition? Has it happened when you have been battered, bribed, or bought off? I doubt it very seriously. For me, it has been when a sensitive apologist has served my learning, has nurtured in me a noncoercive process from "I just don't get it!" to "I see what you mean!"

Our vocation as preachers of the Gospel is to cultivate conversion with relentless gentleness, to foster life-giving transformation with patience and persistence, to bend all of our imaginative intelligence toward evoking an adventure of spiritual insight: "The Cross of Christ, The Love of God, the Grace of Life Made New—Yes, of course, that makes *sense!*"

Well, we're out of here. And part of me wants to tie all this together in One Grand Summary. I don't have one. I did, however, hear one uttered a few nights ago in a gathering of homiletics teachers. Summing up his painstaking research over many years that is soon to be published in a monumental volume on the history of preaching, O. C. Edwards said simply: "I think there are three marks of an effective preacher: a good mind, a rhetorical reflex, and personal holiness." All of these individually and in combination are ultimately God's gift to us. But they are also gifts we offer to God, as we share them, as faithfully as we can, with God's people.

What makes the difference between preaching that is an abortive apologetic and preaching that is an authentic apologetic? I think that O. C.'s observation is the answer: a good mind, a rhetorical reflex, personal and holiness.

Apologetics is all this conference has been about—all that preaching is about. Because all that we are about, as preachers of the Gospel, is bringing agile minds, verbal skills, and humble spirits into helping others discover how bathed they truly are in the boundless wisdom of God's wondrous love.

David J. Schlafer is co-editor of this volume.